THE AGE OF WELLBEING

A NEW LEADERSHIP MODEL FOR A HAPPIER WORLD

DAVID GREEN

david@improveon.co.uk

8 Dacombe Close, Upton, Dorset BH16 5JR, England.

Printed in the United Kingdom

ISBN 979-8570322905

Printed and bound in Great Britain by KDP.

Cover art by Robin Seccombe (www.direction123.com). Interior figures designed by Robin Seccombe. Cover design by Joseph Sale.

Created with Vellum

This book is dedicated to my wife and two sons.

Mel. Thank you for your patience, love and fantastic meals you've cooked to keep up my energy throughout! You are my soulmate and I am very lucky to have you in my life.

Harry and George. I love you both and am extremely proud of the young men you have both become. Keep going. You know what I mean!

CONTENTS

FOREWORD

The following terms, concepts and ideas have all begun to permeate public consciousness to varying degrees of success:

'Business as a Force for Good'
'Purposeful Businesses'
'Conscious Capitalism'
'The Circular Economy'
The UN Sustainable Development Goals
Benefit Corporations
Gross National Happiness versus Gross Domestic Product
Triple Bottom Line Accounting
'Impact Investing'

But what do they all mean? What is good? What is purposeful? What is responsible or conscious or beneficial?

What joins all of these terms, ideas and concepts together? What is the focus of their combined efforts?

The answer, I believe, is wellbeing.

When we view the divisive politics of 'Brexit' and the most recent

USA presidential election campaign, it's clear that many parts of the West are in crisis, nobody knowing where to turn, who or what to believe in, or how to improve our lives. Wellbeing has the potential to provide us all with a unifying vision. Though already gaining traction in many fields, this book is part of my approach to influencing existing and aspiring leaders to focus on wellbeing as the driving motivational force in their work.

The book is a reflection of my own beliefs about the leadership required to take us successfully into the future, putting forward the argument that there is a better way for leadership to balance people, purpose, profit, and planet.

Defining leadership is complex. Time, circumstance, philosophy, attitudes and beliefs, amongst many other influences, all play a part in how people define leadership. With so many variables, it's no surprise there are many different definitions.

The Oxford dictionary says leadership is: 'The action of leading a group of people or an organization, or the ability to do this' whereas the Chartered Institute of Professional Development (CIPD) outlines that: 'Leadership can be defined as the capacity to influence people, by means of personal attributes and/or behaviours, to achieve a common goal.'

However, these definitions make no reference to the quality of leadership. I'm interested in leadership that helps make the world better. Therefore, in the context of this book, leadership is seen as:

- **Inspiring positive change in both people and process**. Providing people with a vision of a better place to be and then defining the best path to get there.
- **Systemic**. It doesn't happen in a vacuum. Leadership attributes, characteristics, styles, personalities and behaviours all need to **relate to and consider the system** in which they operate. This includes culture, processes, people, customers, communities and even the world at large.

- **More courageous**. We are facing unprecedented times where we will have to make some stark choices that will not always be popular. Leaders will require strong values, courage, and the skills to carry people with them.

The CANBE Wellbeing Model, introduced throughout this book, builds on this and will help inspire positive change through people at all levels. It is relevant to leaders across public and private organisations as well as business owners, politicians, educators or indeed anyone in a leadership position. Whilst the book has been written with leaders in mind, the concepts and ideas are universal. As such they can be used to improve **personal**, **team**, **organisational**, **community** and even **national** wellbeing. **Leadership, after all, operates at each of these levels**. Whether you want to 'lead' yourself to a better life or your nation to a better future this book has something for you. Depending on your motivations please choose to focus at whichever level, or combination of levels, you find most useful.

As such, this book is designed to:

- Introduce you to this new model of leadership.
- Help you review your current performance using the model.
- Help you set goals and take action in areas you'd like to improve on.

In line with the complexity in defining leadership, and the many different situations and factors that might influence how you choose to operate, this book will raise your awareness and encourage you to take responsibility. However, it won't solve all your problems or provide you with neat answers to every question. As you read through, you will have to fill in the blanks and harness your own intuition to become the fantastic leader you want to be.

Whether you are an existing or aspiring leader, I hope this book will get you thinking differently about leadership and the outcomes of your actions at personal, team, organisational, customer, community, and a world level.

Now, more than ever, we need courageous leaders who can lead us through potential apocalyptic threats to a place where we can all thrive.

ACKNOWLEDGEMENTS

Like many books a great deal of the content has been influenced by the work of some of the best people in their fields of expertise. This book really does 'stand on the shoulders of giants.' The inconclusive list of acknowledgements below includes learning from over 30 years in business. However more specifically, in respect to wellbeing, over the last eight years I have devoured videos, books, blogs, research papers, surveys, webinars, Massive Open Online Courses (MOOCs), website content and more to build as much knowledge as possible.

In the area of Leadership & Personal Development, whether their work is referenced or not, the book is influenced by Dale Carnegie, Stephen Covey, Brian Tracey, Richard Koch, Susan Jeffers, Jim Collins, Jack Canfield, Mark Victor Hansen, Les Hewitt and Robert Cialdini to name a few.

From the worlds of Wellbeing & Positive Psychology the work of Viktor Frankl, Mihaly Csikszentmihalyi, Martin Seligman, Daniel Pink, Shawn Achor, Angela Duckworth, Carol Dweck, Susan David, Arianna Huffington, Dacher Keltner and the Greater Good Science Centre have been central to informing this book. MOOCs in well-being at Yale, Berkeley and Edinburgh Universities have also been extremely informative in addition to a Mindfulness For Wellbeing MOOC at Monash University.

Over the years I have expanded my knowledge from wellbeing organisations such as Virgin, the Network of Wellbeing (NOW), Gallup, Happy Planet Index, Wellbeing Economy Alliance and their work with Wellbeing Economy Governments partnerships (WEGo), The Legatum Institute, Business In the Community and Action for Happiness.

In respect to environmental and economic wellbeing I have drawn extensively from the United Nations work on Sustainable Development Goals (SDGs), International Panel on Climate Change (IPCC), the work of Amartya Sen, New Economics Foundation, OECD, B Corp and Blueprint for Better Business.

Books and studies from neuroscience, emotional intelligence and the power of habits such as the work of Daniel Kahneman, Daniel Goleman and Charles Duhigg have also been more than influential. You may also recognise the influence of the late Sir Ken Robinson, in the section on Education particularly, but also in other elements in the book.

References to coaching draw from my experiences of being coached by Sir John Whitmore (sadly now deceased) and his book *Coaching For Performance.* I have also used my studies with The Coaching Academy and ongoing professional development with the World Business Executive Coaching Summit (WBECS) and their excellent presenters.

I am grateful to all of the above people and organisations for helping shape my thinking. What I have realised in over 30 years of immersing myself in this work is that there is one common theme. That theme is wellbeing.

GRATITUDE

I have many people to be thankful for in helping me write this book.

First and foremost, I'd like to thank Joseph Sale. Joseph is an established writer and a coach to many authors. He has helped me restructure, shape and edit this book with great empathy, perseverance and creativity. Our conversations along the journey of writing the book have been invaluable both from a motivational and inspirational perspective. Thank you Joseph.

The diagrams in the book proved a real challenge due to size restrictions. Enter Robin Seccombe, a long term friend and master graphic designer. Robin quickly and efficiently applied his considerable experience and expertise to provide an excellent solution. Thank you Robin.

I would also like to thank the following people who have all helped me in one way or another:

- Steve Bedford, for his advice on including diagrams at the start of each chapter
- Ian Davey for his general feedback on the book

- Nicky Durant-Lewis for ideas that have helped make the book more consistent and an easier read
- Chris Found for his positive support and constructive feedback
- Richard Gillingwater for words that inspired and filled me with confidence
- To all the other people who offered to review and provide feedback to make the book the best it could be.

MAKING THE MOST OUT OF THIS BOOK

Throughout this book, we will explore the concepts of wellbeing **domains** and **dimensions**. The **domains** of wellbeing: mental, emotional, physical, spiritual, social, cultural, environmental and economic should be considered as the **areas or territories** of wellbeing.

Wellbeing Domains - 'Territories' - Interconnected areas of our lives							
Mental Our thoughts	Emotional Our emotions	Physical Our actions	Spiritual Our spirit	Social Our communities	Cultural Our way	Environmental Our spaces	Economic Our trade

These are the domains that an individual, team, organisation or even the collective human race should consider as part of an assessment of the quality of wellbeing. They are as important for an individual as they are for the human race overall. For example, environmental wellbeing can be viewed from the perspective of the immediate space around a person to the impact individuals and organisations have on the planet!

We'll also look at the **dimensions** of wellbeing; **C**reating meaning, **A**chieving potential, **N**urturing relationships, **B**uilding resilience, and **E**nriching lives (The CANBE Wellbeing Model).

Wellbeing Dimensions 'Highways' Intertwined routes we use to navigate our lives	Creating meaning
	Achieving potential
	Nurturing relationships
	Building resilience
	Enriching lives

These should be considered as the **highways** to help us navigate these territories successfully. Again, each of these is as important for a group as it is for a team or an individual.

The **indicators:** suffering, struggling, surviving, striving and thriving, help us understand where we are on our journey across each of the domains.

Thriving
Striving
Surviving
Struggling
Suffering

Finally I provide the **'signposts',** which are factors to consider for improving wellbeing.

Mental Our thoughts	Emotional Our emotions	Physical Our actions	Spiritual Our spirit	Social Our communities	Cultural Our way	Environmental Our spaces	Economic Our trade
Thinking	Feelings	Behaviour	Identity	Friendship	Way of life	Affinity	Needs
Focus	Control	Mastery	Motivation	Teamwork	Governance	Cultivation	Impact
Regard	Empathy	Interaction	Stories	Trust	Belonging	Cohesion	Fairness
Flexibility	Agility	Health	Growth	Support	Diversity	Adaptation	Integrity
Imagination	Wisdom	Energy	Purpose	Empowerment	Integration	Renewal	Freedom
Wellbeing Factors - 'Signposts' - Interconnected things that can help us improve wellbeing							

The best way of using this book is to be flexible. The framework is not supposed to 'box you in'. With 8 domains, 5 dimensions and forty 'signposts', each with their own numerous elements, the combinations are far greater than securing a win on your national lottery. In fact I'd go so far as to say that there are more combinations than there are people on the planet!

Reading across, down, jumping from point to point, the domains, dimensions, indicators and signposts will help you build a fantastic picture of your individual, organisational, community or even national wellbeing. Use it to develop your own story so far and plan the next stages of your journey towards greater wellbeing.

Whilst the book doesn't include detailed descriptions of exactly how to approach every level, it does include content, questions, and prompts that you can use flexibly for each, depending on your goals.

This is intentional. Leadership is only really effective when it is understood in the context of the system in which it operates. When we develop new leadership knowledge, skills, attitudes, and habits, we need to understand how this will impact on our team, community and the world at large.

Throughout the book there are **questions** to help you reflect and **charts of behaviours** for you to self-score against and identify any you would like to work on.

As you will have gathered, this book is about more than providing **knowledge**. It will also challenge you to explore your values, beliefs and **attitudes** (certainly writing it challenged me to explore mine!).

New knowledge is limited in value if we fail to use it to change **behaviour** and **habits**. With this in mind, the book includes some of the latest research on habits.

Science tells us that we should focus on changing key habits rather than trying to change too many things at once. Charles Duhigg[1] refers to these as keystone habits. For example, on a personal level, exercise has been found to be a keystone habit that impacts on many other habits. People who improve their exercise are more likely to sleep better, be less stressed, and feel more energetic. So the one habit of exercise can have a massive impact on many areas of a person's life. When you've read through the book, choose the key habit you would like to change and will have the biggest impact for you. Focus on this first. When you've made progress and feel comfortable, move on to the next thing you'd like to improve.

I have received positive feedback, from people who reviewed this book, that the thorough approach, whilst clearly a strength, may also be a source of weakness for some. I make no apologies for this, as I believe it is important to see the 'big picture' before making decisions about the interconnected component parts. This enables us to understand links and patterns so that we can make wiser decisions.

However, I do want to prepare you for the amount of ideas and content there is. You might think: 'How the hell am I supposed to be good at everything here?' That's not the point. None of us can be good at every single element of what makes a great leader. This book will help you identify what you're already good at and where you might like to improve. You can also use it to highlight areas where you need support. No one has all the knowledge, skills, attitudes, and habits to be the ultimate leader. That person just doesn't exist. However, by collecting a great team around us, with complementary and diverse skills, we might get somewhere close.

We can also all benefit from working with a coach. A good coach can help us and our teams develop goals, generate motivation, overcome limiting beliefs, and remain resilient along the way. Leadership can be lonely and a good external coach can provide an objective perspective to our challenges and successes.

Finally, this book is designed to support your journey. Re-visit it regularly. The charts for scoring your personal, team, and organisational wellbeing can be reviewed so that you can see the visible growth and success you are achieving in each area over time. Why not review it every 6 months?

Ultimately, you can read this book in whatever way you wish: dipping into chapters that take your fancy, reading it cover to cover, or focusing on one particular section that you think can help you most right now. This book is written for your benefit, for your wellbeing, so please use it in a way that best suits you and your style.

CHAPTER ONE

COURSE CORRECTION

"The world as we have created it is a process of our thinking. It cannot be changed without changing our thinking."

ALBERT EINSTEIN

A simplified journey through human history sees us develop from three species scattered across the globe to one species living worldwide. Our brains have developed from simple 'fight or flight' reptilian mode to emotional (limbic system) and cognitive (neo cortex) feeling and thinking ones.

Whilst once dependent on day-to-day hunting we have become gatherers, storing and cultivating food so we can consume it as and when we need it. The basic tools on which we were once reliant have been turned into sophisticated technology.

Around the 1800s, we entered the modern era, with the introduction of the Industrial Revolution. This saw the shift from a largely agricultural economy to mass industrial production resulting in global trade and increased cultural exchange. The most notable recent development, from around the 1970s, was our transition to the 'Information Age' which has largely shifted traditional industry to an economy based on information technology.

Throughout our journey it is clear that, as a race, we have made fantastic progress. There's less poverty, less war, and we generally have more freedom and security. For many, life is easier and more comfortable now. However, we have also taken actions that, whilst well-intentioned, have led us to a cliff edge. If we keep progressing in the same direction, the consequences could be dire or even apocalyptic.

We're now at a key point in our journey and the decisions we make will either have catastrophic or transcendent effects on existing and future generations. As you read on, you'll notice that these are global issues requiring an international co-operative approach. Leaders can no longer afford to operate merely in the interests of 'their own'. The 'Human Race' needs humane leaders.

Let's look at some of the key challenges, opportunities and decisions we'll need to make.

NEW OPPORTUNITIES TO LEARN AND GROW

It is estimated that 90% of the world's data has been generated in the last few years. Scientifically backed developments are informing new approaches to the way we think and understand across all areas of life. This provides leaders with new opportunities to learn and grow and achieve even greater impact.

The growing empowerment of women and recognition of what were often categorised as 'female traits' are increasingly seen as positive skills. Emotional Intelligence, thanks largely to Daniel Goleman[1], has taken its place alongside IQ and even surpassed it as a recognised driver of success. A mastery of softer skills is now understood to be a key part of what it takes to make a good leader. These skills will also be increasingly relevant for the era of automation and artificial intelligence.

A win at all costs competitive approach, with the leader as 'hero' telling everyone else what to do, is being tempered and adjusted to a more collaborative approach, with the leader as facilitator, enabling and empowering the team.

ADAPTING TO THE INCREASING PACE OF CHANGE

We are living in an increasingly volatile, uncertain, complex and ambiguous (VUCA) world. With increased volatility, leaders need to build slack into plans and mitigate risk. Increased uncertainty means leaders need better knowledge to help them make more informed decisions. With complexity, leaders need focus and support to help them simplify. Lastly, with ambiguity, leaders must be more flexible and experimental in their approach.

Technological innovations such as the internet, algorithms, mobile, automation, robotics, augmented reality, artificial intelligence, and most recently the introduction of block-chain technology, are leading to massive disruption. A successful business model can now be quickly replaced by new advances. The transport and hospitality sectors are just two examples of age-old business models radically disrupted by new models introduced by Uber and Airbnb. This requires leadership to be more adaptable, creative, resilient, and proactive.

Massive transformation of work through automation will lead to new skill requirements and demands on education, regional shifts in employment, and burdens on welfare, social, and political systems.

MANAGING STRESS, ANXIETY & DEPRESSION

Mental health is a global problem and common mental disorders such as stress, anxiety, and depression are increasing to become amongst the leading causes of ill-health and disability worldwide.

Between 1990 and 2013, the number of people suffering from depression and/or anxiety increased by nearly 50%, from 416 million to 615 million[2]. Close to 10% of the world's population is affected, and mental disorders account for 30% of the global non-fatal disease burden.

It is perhaps no surprise then that the promotion of good health and wellbeing have been explicitly included in the United Nations Sustainable Development Goals as an area of focus from 2015 -2030[3].

In the area of mental health it is clear leaders have a role to play in creating environments where there is greater understanding, acceptance, and support.

RIDDING OURSELVES OF HUNGER & OBESITY

The Food & Agriculture Organisation of the United Nations reports in 2017 the share of undernourished people in the world was approximately 10.9 percent[4]. In its 2018 report "The State of Food Security and Nutrition in The World" it states that, for the third year in a row, there has been a rise in world hunger driven largely by conflict, adverse climate and economic slowdowns.

On the other side of the coin, reflecting the growing divide between the 'haves' and 'have-nots', world adult obesity has been increasing steadily between 1975 and 2016. **It is a staggering fact that, across the world, more people are now obese than underweight.** The irony here is that both groups suffer lack of access to nutrient rich food.

Whichever way you look at this, we are facing a crisis. Food insecurity and associated hunger lead to greater loss of life through starvation. Irresponsible production and consumption of food leads to diabetes, high blood pressure, and the increased likelihood of stroke linked with obesity. The increased strain this places on health services must be avoided.

Leaders have an opportunity to play a role in raising awareness, education, promotion, and support for all people wherever they are on this spectrum.

REFOCUSING AWAY FROM MATERIALISM & CONSUMERISM

Perhaps two of the most obvious signs we're losing our way, spiritually at least, are our growing focus on 'materialism', valuing things over experiences, and 'consumerism', the unbalanced promotion of consumer interests.

Two notable events which reflect these trends are 'Earth Overshoot Day'[5], the day each year when we pass the point of consuming more resources than the planet can replenish, and the advent of 'Black Friday', a day when we spend limitless amounts on our credit cards to purchase items with a fervour more typically associated with a hungry pack of wolves. It's interesting that the majority of people have probably not heard of Earth Overshoot Day, which shows a lack of concern or perhaps awareness of the 'collision course' we're on.

It is clear that leaders must encourage more responsible production and consumption of both goods and services.

BALANCING RIGHTS AND RESPONSIBILITIES

The Universal Declaration of Human Rights[6] is the most important foundation to help achieve freedom, peace, and justice for people in the world who are deprived of those things. Of course we should continue to support and uphold these rights wherever we find them to be lacking.

However, we also need to be very careful about the potential imbalance between the rights of people and the responsibilities that go along with these rights. If we have the right to health then we also have the responsibility to live healthily. The problem is that the consequences of not living healthily, and any associated illnesses resulting from this, are borne by the whole community through the provision of health services. We must encourage responsibility for more healthy living, whilst also recognising that health is a complex issue that can be influenced by social, cultural, environmental and economic factors beyond the control of an individual.

We have a right to freedom of speech, but with this right there should be a responsibility to listen to the views of others and to treat people with respect. Outpourings on social media and some of the divisive behaviour we have seen amongst our politicians highlight this as another area where rights and responsibilities may have become a little imbalanced.

It is also a fact that some cultures view the concept of 'rights' very differently. In the East, collectivism, where the group is prioritised over self, is predominant. In the West we are widely recognised for having more individualistic cultures based on the rights of the individual. This was reflected at the highest level through the adoption of the Universal Declaration of Human Rights in 1948. This 'non-binding' declaration includes civil, political, economic, social and cultural rights. However, different countries have embraced certain elements of these rights with greater or lesser enthusiasm.

From this perspective, I urge leaders to think more about the balance between rights and responsibilities. Too many rights with not enough responsibility, and people can become entitled or spoilt. Too many responsibilities with not enough rights, and people feel oppressed. Rights go with responsibilities. When individuals recognise this and act responsibly towards others and the world around them, our systems will work more effectively.

I have taken the liberty of paraphrasing the UN Declaration of Human Rights in the table below. To demonstrate congruence of rights and responsibilities with wellbeing the table has been organised by categorising them in relation to the eight domains of wellbeing which we'll come onto in greater detail later in the book. The only responsibilities mentioned or implied in the Declaration include the following:

- to act in a spirit of brotherhood

- duties to community
- to recognise and respect the rights and freedoms of others
- to abide by the law

It was also quite apparent from this review that there were no expressed rights or responsibilities relating specifically to the environment. I wonder whether it might be time for the UN and mankind to revise and review our rights and responsibilities for the modern world? Here's my starter for 10. Whilst many of the responsibilities mirror the rights, I think it is an important point to emphasise them.

	Right to...	Responsibility to...
Mental	• Freedom of thoughts • Education for full development of human character	• Respect the thoughts of others • Develop self and those in your care throughout life
Emotional	• Dignity	• Respect how others feel
Physical	• Life • Freedom of opinion and expression	• Protect life • Be healthy • Listen to others opinions and expressions with an open mind
Spiritual	• Be recognised as an individual • Freedom of beliefs	• Respect the beliefs, identities and personalities of others
Social	• Privacy and protection of reputation • Freedom of peaceful assembly and association	• Respect the privacy and reputation of others • Be peaceful • Promote humanity
Cultural	• Diversity • Liberty • Equal protection from the law and a fair trial • Presumed innocent until proven guilty • Nationality and to change nationality • Marriage and to found a family • Take part in governance directly or through freely elected representatives • Equal access to public service • Rest, leisure and holidays • Participate in cultural life	• Respect diversity • Protect the freedom of others • Abide by the law • Be fair • Not judge others • Participate in governance either directly or through freely elected representatives • Vote • Rest and relax
Environmental	• Security • Freedom of movement and residence • Asylum	• Be brave and tackle fears • Respect the places and spaces of others • Protect the environment
Economic	• Own property • Social security that protects dignity and develops personality • Free choice of work • Equal pay for equal work • Join trade unions • A standard of living adequate for health and wellbeing • Protection of authorship and invention	• Respect the property, ideas and inventions of others • Take a fair share based on needs and merits • Contribute to the health and wellbeing of others to the fullest of ability

This leads us to the next point.

'ME, WE, WORLD' NOT 'ME, ME, ME' OR 'WE, WE, WE'

With globalisation and the merging of cultures over time, the polar concepts of individualism and collectivism will be challenged and evolved. There is a balance to be found here, and leaders will be required to foster greater understanding between cultures and of our responsibility towards the planet. Perhaps the best description of this is the concept of 'interdependence'. This is the view that as individuals we are connected to, and are also dependent on others and the world around us. In essence we need to start thinking more 'Me, We, World' and less 'me, me, me' or 'we, we, we', depending on your particular worldview.

REBUILDING DECLINING LEVELS OF TRUST

Levels of trust in leadership across business, politics, and other areas of society are falling in many countries. And yet trust is pivotal to healthy relationships, whether with a person, group, or institution.

This has been influenced by numerous factors, such as the 2008 financial crash, increased immigration, corruption, fake news, high profile hacking, data breaches, and fears about the impact of automation on jobs. At the heart of many of these issues is the concept of being treated fairly.

The world is much more open and transparent now. The internet provides a resource to find out pretty much anything almost instantly. The drawback is that not all of the information we find there is accurate! Social media has put the power back into our hands with the ability to self-teach and find like-minded people like never before, but also the ability to set up damaging campaigns and reviews in a matter of minutes. More recently the introduction of Distributed Ledger Technologies (DLTs), with Blockchain being the most high profile representation of these, provides us with the potential to circumnavigate centralised institutions that we previously put our trust in.

With this greater openness and transparency, there is a requirement for leaders to act with increasing responsibility and awareness about the impact of their actions on the people and communities they serve. But leaders will also need to embrace these new technologies to put trust back in the hands of people.

As the renowned Edelman Trust Barometer reveals in 2019, trust is becoming more local[7]. People are shifting their trust to the relationships within their control. This is a great opportunity for employers. The report states that "Globally, 75 percent of people trust "my employer" to do what is right, significantly more than NGOs (57%), business (56%) and media (47%)."

The report goes on to comment that 'the world is united on one front—all share an urgent desire for change.' With only one in five people now believing the system is working for them, there is a great opportunity for leaders to stand up and do what is right. More than 'three-quarters (76%) of the general population say they want CEOs to take the lead on change instead of waiting for the Government to impose it.'

MANAGING DIVERSITY

'Globalisation' combined with improving technology and infrastructure has made it easier to cross boundaries and means organisations are more multicultural than ever before. Mass migration, driven largely by war and economics, has also added to this increased diversity.

Our reality is people are moving closer together. The world is becoming less rural and more urban. Our neighbourhoods, communities, workplaces, and countries are becoming more diverse whether we like it or not. Of course, our virtual world also provides opportunities for different people to be closer together.

And diversity can have both positive and negative consequences. As different people come together, there can be clashes between ideals, personality, and just about anything else you can think of. In a work environment this can lead to conflict, negative emotions, and even hinder performance. Language barriers are an obvious problem, and cliques can form if people aren't encouraged to step outside of their typical groups.

But there are also many positive advantages to diversity. Benefiting from increased knowledge and varied experiences is an obvious place to start. Local knowledge can help companies expand into new territories more smoothly and varied experiences can help with new ideas, marketing, product development, and strategy. Exposure to new foods, customs, religions, and traditions can make neighbourhoods and communities so much richer.

Building on a point made earlier, the starting place for diversity is recognising the interdependence of humanity, cultures and the natural environment. Diversity requires an approach that will mitigate these negative consequences and recognise and respect the rights of each individual group whilst ensuring the most beneficial interactions between them.

CLIMATE CHANGE

The Intergovernmental Panel on Climate Change (IPCC) is the United Nations body for assessing the science related to climate change. As such, it is probably the most trusted body in respect to reporting on science in an unbiased and neutral manner.

Its special 2016 report 'Global Warming of 1.5°C'[8] predicted, with high levels of confidence, that 'Global warming is likely to reach 1.5°C between 2030 and 2052 if it continues to increase at the current rate'. It goes on to headline that 'Climate-related **risks to health, livelihoods, food security, water supply, human security, and economic growth are projected to increase** with global warming of 1.5°C'.

In the models used to predict likely outcomes, it anticipated CO_2 emissions would need to decline by about 45% on 2000 levels by 2030 to achieve no or limited overshoot of a 1.5°C temperature rise. It also said that 'rapid and far-reaching transitions' would be required to achieve this.

However the reality, as outlined in the report, is that current actions being taken across the world "will not limit global warming to 1.5°C, even if supplemented by very challenging increases in the scale and ambition of emissions reductions after 2030."

Time is running out. Whether operating at individual, organisational, community, or national level, we all have a role to play in reducing the effects of climate change. The time to act is now.

BIODIVERSITY

The Intergovernmental Science-Policy Platform on Biodiversity and Ecosystem Services (IPBES) Report 'Nature's Dangerous Decline Unprecedented; Species Extinction Rates Accelerating'[9] in May 2019 explains that 'nature is declining globally at rates unprecedented in human history'. The chair of this report, Sir Robert Watson, is quoted as saying 'We are eroding the very foundations of our economies, livelihoods, food security, health and quality of life worldwide'.

It isn't too late to get out of the hole we're digging for ourselves but this will require 'transformative change across technological, economic and social factors, including paradigms, goals and values.'

This reference to paradigms, goals, and values is perhaps what sits at the heart of all the issues and opportunities outlined in this section. In other words, we need to change our mindsets, what we are striving for, and what we value.

- Paradigm - If we keep thinking the same way and doing the same things, we'll get the same or worse results. If we keep thinking 'me, me, me' and not 'me, we, world'. If we keep thinking that it is ok to consume more than we need. If we keep placing the ownership of materials over and above experiences. If we keep thinking about national interests over and above international ones. All of this thinking needs to change.
- Goal - If we keep a relentless emphasis on economic growth as our goal, we will be going in the wrong direction. The sustainable development goals take us in the right direction but, as we'll see a little later, to thrive

we really need to focus on wellbeing, not just sustainable development.

- Values - If we continue valuing unchecked consumption, money, and wealth over wellbeing, the consequences could, quite literally, be fatal.

RE-DISTRIBUTING WEALTH AND WELLBEING

Most research in this area has previously studied the impact of differences in income at the national and individual level. However there is a growing understanding that other elements of wellbeing such as health, for example, can have a far greater impact on people's assessment of their lives than income.

What is clear is that there remains an unfair distribution of wealth and wellbeing between countries, within countries, and between people. Why is this important?

When people feel they are being treated unfairly this leads to mistrust and in the worst cases social unrest. Unfortunately, due to many of the issues discussed in this section, the gaps in distribution of wealth and wellbeing are growing.

At a national level we are seeing mass migration, predominantly from developing and/or war torn nations to richer developed nations. When people perceive their leaders as corrupt it leads to civil unrest and in some cases revolution.

At the local level, in the workplace, unfair treatment can lead to lower motivation and performance. It can also result in increased absence, higher levels of stress and sickness that all impact poorly on business outcomes. Of course, treating people unfairly can also be seen as discrimination and lead to lawsuits.

INTERNATIONALISM VERSUS NATIONALISM. CONSIDERATION VERSUS COMPETITION

Just as with the argument about how we need to change our thinking as individuals, we also need to change the way we think as nations and organisations. Most of the problems we've discussed here are global in nature. Technology developments, the increasing pace of change, stress and anxiety, hunger and obesity, levels of trust, rights and responsibilities, climate change, biodiversity, distribution of wealth and wellbeing are all global issues. To tackle them we need a global, united approach, not a nationalist, protectionist view.

Perhaps the best example of this is the current approach to climate change facilitated by the United Nations. Whilst research has been conducted and targets have been set, the overwhelming rhetoric from developed countries is effectively: 'We'll reduce our carbon emissions by a higher % if other countries reduce their emissions by a higher % too. Until such time we're going to reduce our emissions by a lower %'.

The consequences of this attitude are potentially devastating. Where is the strong leadership? We need nations, perhaps led by one courageous country, to put aside self interest and deliver the ambitious targets set.

Just as we outlined with the 'me, we, world' perspective, this doesn't mean we need to give up on our national identities or pride. In fact, taking a lead in this area could actually help build a national identity. But it does mean we need to think more interdependently. Each country in the world has its own unique resources, talents, traditions, and character. These should be celebrated. But it is only by working together we can tackle the challenges faced.

This is just as true for leadership in organisations. Leaders must rethink the balance between competition and consideration, between what is good for the organisation and how that balances with the needs and wellbeing of other stakeholders.

BALANCING PEOPLE, PURPOSE, PROFIT AND PLANET.

People are increasingly questioning capitalism as an economic model, with the introduction of 'conscious capitalism' as one example of how this is being re-focused. Recognition, amongst a growing number of countries, that Gross Domestic Product is a very narrow measure of success has led to the development of broader measures focused on wellbeing.

Leadership will increasingly be required to think about the impact of business decisions on all stakeholders and not just on shareholders and the bottom line. Balancing people, purpose, profit, and planet whilst not yet mainstream, is certainly gathering momentum. Leadership across the world is constantly challenged to do more with less.

At a macro level, the UN Sustainable Development Goals will increasingly filter down into organisations, with the resulting impact that this will rise higher up the leadership agenda. This will impact on areas as diverse as resource efficiency, equal pay for equal roles, employment of youth and minority groups, innovation and research, technology adoption, and use of sustainable energy. In essence, a leader will need to think more responsibly about sustainability as it becomes 'business as usual' rather than an additional project.

FINITE AND SCARCE RESOURCES

We have limited resources and unequal access to them. Let's take water, for example. Other than the air we breathe, this is probably our most precious resource. Whilst water covers approximately 70% of our planet, only about 3% is freshwater, the stuff we can actually drink, use for irrigation, or bathe in.

Of this 3%, much is actually contained in frozen glaciers or is unavailable for use. As a result, about 1 in 7 of the world population lack access to water and over one third suffer from water scarcity for at least one month each year. I want to emphasise this point again:

- 1 in 7 of the world population lack access to water
- Over one third suffer from water scarcity for at least one month each year

Of course climate change is adding to the problem, with erratic weather conditions causing even further shortages in some areas and flooding in others.

The problem is not going away and it is estimated that almost half the world's population will be living in areas of high water stress by 2030.

Other non-renewable resources such as fossil fuels and minerals are also under stress due to increasing use, the focus on economic growth, and climate change.

POPULATION GROWTH AND AGEING

Compounding our limited and scarce resources is the growth and ageing of the world population. There has been a 105% increase in the global human population (from 3.7 to 7.6 billion) since 1970[10] and this has been spread unevenly across countries and regions. Following this trend, it is expected that the world population will grow by another 2.2 billion by 2050, with more than half of that growth predicted to come in sub-Saharan Africa due to limited access to healthcare, education, and continuing gender discrimination.

The increasing age of the population, particularly in well-established economies, will put pressure on pensions and healthcare. Consumption patterns will change and there will be an increasing demand on limited resources. Leadership will increasingly be about doing more with less. Thinking about what not to do, or what to stop doing, will become as important as thinking about what we will do.

SUMMARY

The human race has made great progress in improving the quality of life but since the dawning of the industrial revolution we have started to go off course. In fact, we are in danger of going so far off course that, unless immediate action is taken, the future existence of our race, other species, and the planet itself, will come under threat.

However, on the up side, these problems also present us with great opportunities to take our existence to another level. By solving them, we can create a new better life for everyone, with wellbeing at the heart of it.

When you look at the issues we face there are some key principles we should apply in meeting them:

1. **We need a vision for a better world.** Unless we know where we're going, how will we know when we've got there? This vision is severely lacking at present. Type 'vision for the world' into Google and you'll most probably see results from individuals, smaller organisations, and some examples of how to write good vision statements! Type 'United Nations vision for the world' and you start to get links to the UN Sustainable Development Goals but no real vision. Where is it we all really want to go? Think about it for a moment. What is *your* vision for a better world?
2. **We need strategies for our mental, emotional, physical, spiritual, social, cultural, environmental and economic wellbeing.** These problems aren't just social, environmental or economic. They go much deeper than that into what we really value as a human race and how we see our future.
3. **We need a big picture approach that reflects the relationships between issues and addresses them as a whole as well as the parts**

themselves. You may have noticed that the problems themselves are connected. Mental health issues can be related to our busy lifestyles and focus on acquiring things which in turn is linked to the relentless focus on economic growth. Our increasing consumption can be linked to the threats of climate change. Trust is impacted by how we manage diversity and the growing polarisation between the 'haves and have nots'. Of course, the issues are much more complex than I've highlighted here and there are many different drivers for each. However, they are connected and need approaching as such.

4. **These problems require co-ordinated action at all levels** by individuals, organisations, towns, governments, and the international community. This means we must describe the problems and the solutions in a way that means something to everyone and is clearly understood by all of these groups.

So where do we go from here and which approaches will be the most successful in overcoming the challenges and seizing the opportunities we face?

CHAPTER TWO

SUFFER, SURVIVE, OR THRIVE?

"This is the way the world ends. Not with a bang but a whimper."

T.S. ELIOT

In respect to the future of the human race, it seems we all face a choice: greater suffering, merely surviving, or thriving. Whilst this might seem a little dramatic, and there are questions over exactly how long it might take, our current direction of travel is taking us towards the wrong end of this spectrum.

Our world is changing rapidly. We can choose to 'die on the hill' of old methodologies and ways of thinking, scrape by with the bare minimum change necessary for survival, or we can take the bull by the horns and thrive in this period of change and opportunity.

Thinking about this challenge in respect to our families and friends, the answer is obvious. We'd all like to thrive. However,

knowing what we'd like and actually **doing** what is required to get there are two totally separate things.

Unfortunately, many of us are acting in ways which won't help ourselves, our families, friends or future generations to thrive.

But what is it to 'thrive' and what frameworks do we have for dealing with these immense challenges?

The best attempt I've seen at answering this question, and dealing with the challenges posed, has been provided by the United Nations. The United Nations Sustainable Development Goals **(SDGs)** are put forward as the 'blueprint to achieve a better and more sustainable future for all'. Let's take a closer look at these goals.

THE UN SUSTAINABLE DEVELOPMENT GOALS

There are 17 interconnected goals designed to address the global challenges we face by 2030. They are as follows:

1. No poverty
2. Zero hunger
3. Good health & wellbeing
4. Quality education
5. Gender equality
6. Clean water and sanitation
7. Affordable and clean energy
8. Decent work and economic growth
9. Industry, innovation and infrastructure
10. Reduced inequalities
11. Sustainable cities and communities
12. Responsible production and consumption
13. Climate action
14. Life below water
15. Life on land
16. Peace, justice and strong institutions
17. Partnerships for the goals

I largely support these goals. Some are great stepping stones, whereas others take us further along the road to where we want to be. However, whilst 'no poverty' is a gallant goal, it doesn't tell the whole story. It is well known that the vast majority of wealth and resources in the world are held by the minority. A more compelling vision and goal would be *prosperity for all*. This should involve raising people up past poverty to prosperity and also finding ways to redistribute wealth and wellbeing from those who have gained through ill means, loopholes, or other unfair mechanisms.

In respect to 'zero hunger', this is another great step forward, but what we really should be aiming for is *nutritious diets for all*. We have a problem with obesity in many countries, so this isn't just about hunger. It is about ensuring all people have access to nutritious, healthy food. Part of the reason for the strain on our health services is excessive and irresponsible consumption of food and alcohol so we need to work at this level too.

In a similar vein, the UN SDG on 'Health & Wellbeing' is largely focused on reduction of death, disease, accidents, and greater access to health-care and medicines. There is little to no recognition of positive mental health such as creativity and imagination. We need to think differently about health and create lifestyles where people can be mentally creative, physically fit, and spiritually awakened.

The 'Quality Education' goal makes no mention about the potential impacts of automation and artificial intelligence. These two challenges and opportunities could have a profound impact on jobs and the future skills we need. Achieving greater participation and proficiency in basic education, such as reading and mathematics, is great but we need to refocus education on technology, interpersonal, and creative skills.

Following from this is the 'Decent Work and Economic Growth' goal. The continued focus on economic growth and increasing productivity is one of the biggest challenges we face. No one wants to see the quality of their life eroded and I think this is one of the main fears people maintain in developed nations when talking about sustainability.

However, there is clearly an imbalance that needs to be addressed. The world's population is growing and many of the resources we have are finite. We need to view growth and progress differently. We need to link them with wellbeing and not just economic measures.

The UN has begun this journey with the introduction of the System of Environmental-Economic Accounting (SEEA) which was adopted in 2012 by the UN Statistical Commission. This seeks to measure the impact on Land, Forest, Water & Mineral resources in relation to economic activity. The focus is on decoupling economic growth from environmental degradation. However it largely fails to recognise the impact of economic activity, both positive and negative, on mental, physical, spiritual, social or cultural wellbeing.

What if we could improve the quality of our lives by working less and doing more of what we want? What if we could consume less of what is bad for our wellbeing and more of what is good?

Finally, 'equality' is a fallacy. There is no such thing. We are all unique. What we should be aiming for is fairness, diversity, unity and harmony. In arguing against a focus on equality I in no way diminish the need to eradicate discrimination across the world. It is clear that there are many ways in which people are still treated unfairly and even abhorrently. However, we should focus on creating a fairer, more diverse, unified and harmonious world for all whether women, men, black, white, gay, straight or another.

I must say, at this point, that I am not putting myself above the thousands of experts who have contributed to the UN SDGs or the UN itself. They are much more intelligent and expert than I in each of their particular fields and the UN is a fantastic organisation focused on bringing humanity together, which is exactly what we need. I have read many of their papers and have used much of their research and the SDGs to shape my own thinking.

However I do think that, whilst the work is steeped in technical expertise, it lacks real vision and imagination. The goals take us in the right direction but we need to go further. In relation to this, the UN describes these goals as interconnected but doesn't actually say what connects them. I assume they believe it is 'sustainable development' but is that what we really aspire to?

I put forward that what connects them is a focus on improving wellbeing and that a 'world where we can all thrive' is a vision that builds on the SDGs but takes us further.

HOW WELLBEING COMPLEMENTS THE UN SDGS

As you can see from the diagram below the UN SDGs support a focus on wellbeing. To use an example the UN Goal of 'No Poverty' has the following targets:

1. By 2030, eradicate extreme poverty for all people everywhere, currently measured as people living on less than $1.25 a day
2. By 2030, reduce at least by half the proportion of men, women and children of all ages living in poverty in all its dimensions according to national definitions
3. Implement nationally appropriate social protection systems and measures for all, including floors, and by 2030 achieve substantial coverage of the poor and the vulnerable
4. By 2030, ensure that all men and women, in particular the poor and the vulnerable, have equal rights to economic resources, as well as access to basic services, ownership and control over land and other forms of property, inheritance, natural resources, appropriate new technology and financial services, including microfinance
5. By 2030, build the resilience of the poor and those in vulnerable situations and reduce their exposure and

vulnerability to climate-related extreme events and other economic, social and environmental shocks and disasters

6. Ensure significant mobilisation of resources from a variety of sources, including through enhanced development cooperation, in order to provide adequate and predictable means for developing countries, in particular least developed countries, to implement programmes and policies to end poverty in all its dimensions
7. Create sound policy frameworks at the national, regional and international levels, based on pro-poor and gender-sensitive development strategies, to support accelerated investment in poverty eradication actions

These targets can be mapped to the Social, Cultural, Environmental and Economic dimensions of the CANBE Model. Achieving these targets will take us towards greater wellbeing but they will not help us all thrive. I have done exactly the same with the other UN SDGs and targets. As outlined earlier in the book there are gaps and holes but they largely take us in the right direction.

UN SDGs								
	Mental	Emotional	Physical	Spiritual	Social	Cultural	Environmental	Economic
1					No poverty	No poverty	No poverty	No poverty
2			Zero hunger		Zero hunger	Zero hunger	Zero hunger	Zero hunger
3	Good health and wellbeing		Good health and wellbeing		Good health and wellbeing	Good health and wellbeing	Good health and wellbeing	Good health and wellbeing
4	Quality education					Quality education	Quality education	Quality education
5			Gender equality		Gender equality	Gender equality	Gender equality	Gender equality
6			Clean water and sanitation		Clean water and sanitation	Clean water and sanitation	Clean water and sanitation	Clean water and sanitation
7						Affordable and clean energy	Affordable and clean energy	Affordable and clean energy
8			Decent work and economic growth		Decent work and economic growth	Decent work and economic growth	Decent work and economic growth	Decent work and economic growth
9	Industry, innovation and infrastructure				Industry, innovation and infrastructure	Industry, innovation and infrastructure	Industry, innovation and infrastructure	Industry, innovation and infrastructure
10					Reduced inequalities	Reduced inequalities	Reduced inequalities	Reduced inequalities
11			Sustainable cities and communities		Sustainable cities and communities	Sustainable cities and communities	Sustainable cities and communities	Sustainable cities and communities
12			Responsible production and consumption		Responsible production and consumption	Responsible production and consumption	Responsible production and consumption	Responsible production and consumption
13	Climate action				Climate action	Climate action	Climate action	Climate action
14	Life below water					Life below water	Life below water	Life below water
15			Life on land		Life on land	Life on land	Life on land	Life on land
16			Peace justice and strong institutions		Peace justice and strong institutions	Peace justice and strong institutions		Peace justice and strong institutions
17					Partnerships for the goals	Life on land	Life on land	Life on land

As you can see the UN SDGs are weighted more to social, cultural, environmental, and economic factors and have less emphasis on the mental, emotional, physical, and spiritual domains. This is to be expected as the goals are more focused on 'sustainable development', inspiring action amongst nations and organisations, rather than individuals.

However, it fails to acknowledge that to change, as a human race, we need to understand where we are heading and have stronger motivation to get there. We need to have renewed spiritual purpose and character amongst our leaders. We have to reach people as individuals in order to inspire them and create change.

In the words of Peter Drucker: 'Whenever anything is being accomplished, it is being done by a monomaniac with a mission.' Often small groups of people with drive, focus, and purpose can do more than large, unwieldy mobs.

So, my call is for leaders to focus on wellbeing. The UN SDGs can play a role in taking us in the right direction but they are not the complete solution; wellbeing is. To do this effectively, we need a *model* for wellbeing and more accurate metrics of how to measure it. This will allow us to:

1. Find solutions by breaking down wellbeing into component domains and dimensions, which leads to insight
2. See the big picture of organisational, communal, national and global wellbeing
3. Utilise a shared language that can be understood by individuals, teams, communities, nations and the whole international community.
4. Move past survival, problem-solving goals, to thriving opportunity-focused goals.

For these reasons I believe leadership should focus on wellbeing as a progressive approach to complement and surpass the UN Sustainable Development Goals.

It is now up to leaders across the world to take positive action and lead us into the 'Age of Wellbeing'.

THRIVING AND THE 'AGE OF WELLBEING'

But why should leadership focus on wellbeing? The reasons for this are simple:

It will help you meet the new requirements of leader-

ship. As outlined in the Chapter 'Course Correction', many of the new opportunities to learn and grow are coming from wellbeing research or are supported by it. Wellbeing itself encourages a creative, flexible, resilient, growth mind-set which will also help leaders navigate better in this volatile, uncertain, complex and ambiguous world. It can help us to do more with less whilst ensuring we keep a watchful eye on the impact we're having on the planet.

It's visionary. Who wouldn't want to be in a world that offers more mental creativity, emotional wisdom, physical vitality, spiritual awakeness, social empowerment, cultural harmony, a flourishing environment and real economic innovation?

It's the right thing to do. When it comes down to it, how will you measure your success as a leader? Will it just be about how much money you've made? Or how much revenue you have generated for your organisation? My belief is that most leaders view their success, and are judged, using broader measures of success. These include: how you made the world a better place through improving the lives of customers and people, your achievements, the relationships you've built, the obstacles you've had to overcome, and the way you made others feel.

If we accept that happiness is a key element of wellbeing then ***evidence shows that focusing on improving happiness will lead to more successful outcomes***[1]. This includes helping us to do better in domains such as work life, relationships, health, positive perceptions of self and others, sociability, creativity, problem solving, physical wellbeing, and coping. So, there are benefits arising from this focus in all aspects of our lives.

The studies in the meta-analysis referred to above have also correlated happiness with increased productivity, profitability, sales, performance, and return on investment so ***it's good for the bottom line*** too.

It is a universal concept that can bring people together and is based on the strength of a growing convergence between:

- Eastern philosophy which triumphs collectivism, finding the true self, the interconnection of all things in the universe, a cyclical approach to evolution, a more spiritual approach and searching inside yourself and,
- Western philosophy characterised by individualism, individual events, a linear approach, success and achievement, searching outside yourself and materialism.

Wellbeing is increasingly being recognised and adopted on the world stage. Examples of this include the UN Sustainable Development Goals[2] as previously mentioned, UK's Measuring What Matters[3], Organisation for Economic Co-operation and Development (OECD) Guidelines on Measuring Subjective Well-being[4], to name just a few. Most recently New Zealand has focused its budget planning on delivering improved wellbeing outcomes. Over the next few years, this focus at the top will increasingly influence other countries, organisations, towns, cities, communities and individuals. Why not get ahead of the game now?

So, now we've outlined how wellbeing can help us thrive and why leaders should focus on it, let's explore what it is, as well as the domains and dimensions, in more detail.

CHAPTER THREE

THE AGE OF WELLBEING

"There are grounds for cautious optimism that we may now be near the end of the search for the ultimate laws of nature."

STEPHEN HAWKING

"If more of us valued food and cheer and song above hoarded gold, it would be a merrier world."

J. R. R. TOLKIEN

So far in this book we have alluded to the domains and dimensions of wellbeing, which in turn have provided some clues as to what wellbeing actually is. However, before going any further we really must take a closer look at this definition.

WHAT IS WELLBEING?

Wellbeing has often been defined, particularly by the media, in respect to associations with health and wellness. More recently there has been greater recognition of mental health and its links to wellbeing.

However these are very narrow definitions and it is clear, backed by increasing research in the area, that wellbeing is much broader than this. What isn't quite so clear is the actual definition. In the Oxford English dictionary it is defined as: 'the state of being comfortable, healthy or happy'. 'Psychology Today' describes: 'the experience of health, happiness, and prosperity' whereas the International Journal of Wellbeing proposes a new definition as: 'the balance point between an individual's resource pool and the challenges faced'.

For me, these approaches tend towards the individualistic and western, focusing largely on wellbeing of 'self' and with a bias towards happiness. At least the International Journal of Wellbeing recognises the 'challenges' we face in life and that wellbeing is just as much about dealing with 'lows' we experience as well as 'highs', and everything in between.

Another way of considering wellbeing is through how we experience it.

EMBODIMENT

Embodiment is a concept applied to learning and wellbeing. In embodied wellbeing and learning the mind, body and brain are viewed as inseparable. For example, if you are sad or depressed your body reflects this through your facial expressions and posture. However the reverse is equally true. If you want to feel happy, then smile. If you want to feel invigorated get up and walk about. Want to feel more confident? Stand up with your head raised, chest out and make yourself look big. In short emotions regulate our body but our physical movement can also regulate our emotions.

The implications of this for our model are that whilst we have split out mental, emotional and physical wellbeing, to simplify understanding, it is clear that each influences the other. Therefore when reading through the following chapters think about the connections between your mental, emotional and physical states. Once you've done this, experiment by changing your thoughts, feelings and actions to see how they impact on your wellbeing. It is the experience and embodiment of wellbeing that will help you improve it, not just reading about it!

HAPPINESS AND WELLBEING

At this point it is worth discussing the hazy distinction between happiness and wellbeing. The two are often used interchangeably but in my mind this can be confusing. Happiness is an emotion. Wellbeing is not. Whilst happiness can be used to describe a longer term state, as in: 'Are you happy with your life?' it is probably better associated with shorter term positive emotions linked to pleasurable activities.

Wellbeing takes a more rounded view and recognises that life is both pleasurable and challenging with an emphasis on meaning, giving, investing, a focus on others, and responsibility to something greater than the self.

Happiness tends to be about *you* as an individual and can be linked more easily to consumption, fulfilling needs, desires, and taking. Don't get me wrong, happiness is an important element of wellbeing and can contribute greatly to our success in life. Feeling good helps us in many areas but we won't always feel good and nor should we expect to.

Wellbeing then is much broader than happiness and requires the consideration and balancing of interconnected domains. In this respect the mental, emotional, physical, and social domains are fairly well recognised but let's take a deeper look at this.

PSYCHOLOGICAL WELLBEING

Scientists often refer to psychological wellbeing (PWB) to describe how we think and feel about life and the meaning and purpose we derive from it. Perhaps the most well known of these PWB models is that of Carol Ryff[1]. The six factors she determined that contribute to a person's PWB include:

1. **Self acceptance** - the degree of positive attitudes you have towards yourself, your past behaviours and choices.
2. **Personal growth** - the degree to which a person feels they are realising their potential through positive change, increasing maturity, gaining knowledge and learning new skills.
3. **Purpose in life** - the degree to which a person feels they have meaning in life and is able to make a difference by being part of something bigger than themselves.
4. **Environmental mastery** - the degree of competence a person feels in being able to meet the demands of their particular situation.
5. **Autonomy** - the degree to which a person feels able to think for themselves and do things the way they want without strong pressures to conform.
6. **Relationships with others** - the degree to which a person feels connected, supported, respected and loved.

This model also reflects the understanding, drawing from the work of Aristotle's Nichomachean Ethics, that wellbeing includes elements of:

- **Eudaimonia** - meaningful activities and thoughts linked more to how we see our lives over time and what holds the greatest value for living a good life.

- **Hedonic** - pleasurable activities and thoughts linked more to our emotions and subjective wellbeing at a specific point in time.

A life full of pleasure but with no meaning would become tiresome and meaningless. We can have too much of a good thing! However a life full of meaning but with no pleasure would be dull and over-bearing. Variety is, after all, the spice of life!

Whilst this helps us understand psychological wellbeing a little better, for the purpose of this book I prefer to break it down into component domains as it can be a very subjective term and is also not particularly helpful when describing wellbeing. For one, psychological wellbeing can often be confused with **mental** or **emotional** wellbeing. It also makes little specific reference to economic, cultural, or environmental wellbeing and is a little too focused on 'self' as opposed to collective wellbeing.

A BROADER DEFINITION

So, psychological wellbeing doesn't provide us with the whole story. If you think about your own life you'll have a good understanding that your **physical** health (diet, exercise, sleep, relaxation) has a big impact on your life. But there are other domains to consider too. Think about your workplace, an organisation to which you belong or even the country in which you live. The **culture** of the institutions to which we belong have an impact on our wellbeing. Laws, policies, procedures, leadership and how we are expected to behave will all play their part.

There are two further domains. Firstly, our **environmental** wellbeing. If our personal environment is too chaotic, noisy, hot or cold, these can all impact on our wellbeing. On a larger scale, if we continue to damage the wider environment, the impact on our wellbeing will be significant.

Finally, our **economic** wellbeing, which includes not only our personal financial health but also the wider economy to which this is linked. Research tells us that more and more money does not create more and more wellbeing but to a certain degree money does bring increased levels of comfort and satisfaction with life.

It is important to take this broader view of wellbeing because any one of the domains can impact on the others. They each have a role to play in our overall wellbeing and to really thrive we need to keep a balanced view on each. Indeed people can compensate for lower wellbeing in one domain through strengths in another. However the highest level of thriving occurs when we improve across all domains in tandem.

Again, this will be perfectly apparent if you think about your own life. If you've experienced stress or depression, or know someone who has, you'll understand how this can have a significant impact on virtually every other area of your life. Or perhaps you've focused on one particular area, such as financial wellbeing and been successful at earning money. However due to the hours sacrificed this may have been to the detriment of your relationships, physical or mental health.

Based on this reasoning and for the purposes of this book I put forward the following definition of wellbeing:

Wellbeing is the quality of our lives in balance with other people, species and the planet

Put another way wellbeing is our ability to:

- Suffer WELL
- Struggle WELL
- Survive WELL
- Strive WELL
- Thrive WELL

Wellbeing doesn't mean that we will never suffer but it does mean that when we do we have the capabilities to overcome suffering and move back towards thriving.

This capability to thrive is based on a complex combination of internal and external factors which brings us to the CANBE Wellbeing Model including both *domains* and *dimensions*.

CHAPTER FOUR

THE CANBE WELLBEING MODEL

		Wellbeing Domains - 'Territories' - Interconnected areas of our lives							
		Mental Our thoughts	Emotional Our emotions	Physical Our actions	Spiritual Our spirit	Social Our communities	Cultural Our way	Environmental Our spaces	Economic Our trade
Wellbeing States 'Indicators' States of wellbeing we move through	Thriving	Creative	Composed	Vital	Fulfilled	Engaged	Harmonious	Flourishing	Prosperous
	Striving	↑	↑	↑	↑	↑	↑	↑	↑
	Surviving	Alert	Impulsive	Weary	Satisfied	Connected	Tolerant	Desolate	Poor
	Struggling	↑	↑	↑	↑	↑	↑	↑	↑
	Suffering	Distressed	Disturbed	Drained	Unfulfilled	Isolated	Conflicted	Degrading	Destitute
		↑	↑	↑	↑	↑	↑	↑	↑
Wellbeing Dimensions 'Highways' Intertwined routes we use to navigate our lives	Creating meaning	Thinking	Feelings	Behaviour	Identity	Friendship	Way of life	Affinity	Needs
	Achieving potential	Focus	Control	Mastery	Motivation	Teamwork	Governance	Cultivation	Impact
	Nurturing relationships	Regard	Empathy	Interaction	Stories	Trust	Belonging	Cohesion	Fairness
	Building resilience	Flexibility	Agility	Health	Growth	Support	Diversity	Adaptation	Integrity
	Enriching lives	Imagination	Wisdom	Energy	Purpose	Empowerment	Integration	Renewal	Freedom
		Wellbeing Factors - 'Signposts' - Interconnected things that can help us improve wellbeing							

So now we understand what wellbeing is, what can we do to improve it? There's an old saying that a craftsman is 'Only as good as their tools' and there is some degree of truth in this. In the realm of wellbeing, the CANBE Model is an ideal tool and framework to help you and those around you get to where you want to be. Taking a systemic approach, it looks not only at individuals, but teams and organisations, and even beyond that: the societies, cultures, and nations in which our organisations survive or thrive. CANBE looks at the whole picture, as well as each component within that picture, and, finally, the relationships between these components.

Leadership development can often fall into the trap of just focusing on *personal* development of the leader. Helping a leader to improve how they manage stress, for example, will undoubtedly be personally beneficial. However the leader also has a role in helping their *people* manage stress and working at the *organisational* level to create the right environment for that to happen.

My leadership model, CANBE, challenges a leader to think and take action at *personal*, *team* and *organisational* levels. Continuing the stress example, this model encourages leaders to think about all of the things that might be contributing to stress and the relationships between them. This would include everything from an unclear business strategy and vision, through to personal relationships and organisational policy.

More than this it challenges leaders to think of the external impact of their actions on the wider *community* and the *world*. Organisations and leaders will be judged more in all of these areas so a systemic approach is increasingly important.

This model has been derived from a review of many disciplines including personal development, positive psychology, neuroscience, emotional intelligence, wellbeing, branding, employee engagement, business management, other leadership models and performance coaching. The strength of the model is that all of the best guiding principles from each of these disciplines are covered. What I have found during the process of creating CANBE and this book is that the model is an umbrella that is able to encompass ancient wisdom as well as modern personal development and research on wellbeing.

Let's take a look at the model in greater detail.

DOMAINS

Wellbeing Domains - 'Territories' - Interconnected areas of our lives							
Mental Our thoughts	Emotional Our emotions	Physical Our actions	Spiritual Our spirit	Social Our communities	Cultural Our way	Environmental Our spaces	Economic Our trade

The CANBE Model divides wellbeing into eight *domains*. We discussed the eight domains earlier. To recap, these are:

- mental
- emotional
- physical
- spiritual
- social
- cultural
- environmental
- economic

For now, try to view the *domains* as the '**territories'** on the map of our lives. Imagine them spread out before you, like countries on a globe. The domains are interconnected, just as countries or neighbouring territories are, and, in fact, interdependent. For example, our mental state is impacted by our physical, spiritual, social, cultural, environmental and economic wellbeing. However, one can also say the reverse is true too: our mental state impacts our emotional, physical, spiritual, social, cultural, environmental and economic wellbeing! One part, or domain, cannot exist without the other seven, and equally the other seven cannot exist without the missing one. That is the holistic nature of this approach.

INDICATORS

<table>
<tr><td rowspan="5">Wellbeing States

'Indicators'

States of wellbeing we move through</td><td>Thriving</td></tr>
<tr><td>Striving</td></tr>
<tr><td>Surviving</td></tr>
<tr><td>Struggling</td></tr>
<tr><td>Suffering</td></tr>
</table>

For each of the domains we can determine whether we are suffering, struggling, surviving, striving or thriving.

- Thriving means to prosper and grow, to flourish. It implies ease and comfort.
- Striving comes from the word strife and means to make great efforts towards accomplishing something.
- Surviving means to remain or continue in existence.
- Struggling means difficulty in coping and resisting
- Suffering means a state of pain, distress or hardship

Think of these as representative of the **journey**. The journey can take many twists and turns. Of course our aim is to thrive but sometimes we might get knocked off course or get a setback or obstacle in our path. Wellbeing is dynamic. It isn't about not suffering but it is about how we deal with suffering to get ourselves back on track.

Taken together the domains and indicators can be used as a simple 'dashboard' to assess the state of our wellbeing at any point in time. Of course once we understand where we are on our journey we need a route and some guidance to help us get to where we want to be. This is the role of the dimensions and 'signposts' in the model.

DIMENSIONS

Wellbeing Dimensions 'Highways' Intertwined routes we use to navigate our lives	Creating meaning
	Achieving potential
	Nurturing relationships
	Building resilience
	Enriching lives

The five *dimensions* of wellbeing, are the **'highways'** you will use to cross these territories successfully. They form the acronym CANBE:

- **C**reating meaning
- **A**chieving potential
- **N**urturing relationships
- **B**uilding resilience
- **E**nriching lives

As you'll see throughout the book they are based on scientifically backed principles of what helps us to create a great life for ourselves and others.

SIGNPOSTS

Mental Our thoughts	**Emotional** Our emotions	**Physical** Our actions	**Spiritual** Our spirit	**Social** Our communities	**Cultural** Our way	**Environmental** Our spaces	**Economic** Our trade
Thinking	Feelings	Behaviour	Identity	Friendship	Way of life	Affinity	Needs
Focus	Control	Mastery	Motivation	Teamwork	Governance	Cultivation	Impact
Regard	Empathy	Interaction	Stories	Trust	Belonging	Cohesion	Fairness
Flexibility	Agility	Health	Growth	Support	Diversity	Adaptation	Integrity
Imagination	Wisdom	Energy	Purpose	Empowerment	Integration	Renewal	Freedom
Wellbeing Factors - 'Signposts' - Interconnected things that can help us improve wellbeing							

The words used at each of the intersections of these domains and dimensions are like the **'signposts'** or **'navigational system'** to check we're on course and going in the right direction. They are not absolutes but they do provide us with known factors that contribute to wellbeing and practical guidance on what to do. For example, by changing the way we *think* and with greater *focus* we can improve our wellbeing.

It is worth bearing in mind that this is just a framework! Whilst it is generally accepted that creating greater meaning in life will help improve wellbeing, people will create meaning in many different ways. We each have to discover the best way for us.

But first, why use this model?

It provides the big picture and breaks down individual components. As we've discussed wellbeing requires balancing all of these domains and dimensions across all areas of our lives. To focus on one at the expense of another can leave us no better, or even worse off. The breadth of the wellbeing concept fosters a 'wiser' approach to improvement. Too often we can focus on improving one thing to the detriment of another. Improve sales at the cost of reduced customer service. Improve profitability to the detriment of fewer jobs. Improve the amount of money we earn to the detriment of the time we spend on our most valued relationships. A focus on wellbeing challenges us to improve with a balanced perspective by understanding the big picture first and then focusing on the individual elements.

It complements and goes beyond the UN Sustainable Development Goals, challenging us to thrive, not just survive. So, if you are already using the UN SDGs in your organisation, the model will help you align that work with your wellbeing strategy.

The focus on wellbeing. If we take wellbeing as a concept and can agree that, generally speaking, most people are aiming to improve their wellbeing and that businesses, organisations and even governments are created to help improve people's lives then why wouldn't it make sense to focus on improving wellbeing.

It is both problem and opportunity focused. Too often we focus only when a problem arises. This encourages a culture of complacency and doing just enough. To thrive and really progress we need to become more opportunity focused.

It provides us with an easily understood, common language. This will help co-ordinate and focus activity at all levels, whether at an individual, team, community or country level..

It is both 'self' and 'group' focused. Too many models are overly biased towards 'self'. Wellbeing is both an individual and collective affair and the CANBE Model recognises our responsibility to create wellbeing for ourselves and others.

It is inclusive and designed to bridge divides. It is driven from what is good for our wellbeing not from any particular political or religious perspective.

It recognises our reliance on the planet that supports the wellbeing of the human race.

A flexible framework

Wellbeing is personal but it is also universal. Your definition may well vary from someone else's but there are characteristics and elements that apply to everyone. The CANBE Model provides these characteristics and elements to create a framework with the flexibility for you to adapt it to your specific circumstances.

As an example, you'll benefit from having a sense of meaning and purpose in your life and understanding your values will contribute to this. However, it's up to you to determine what your values are. You'll also want to achieve things in your life and setting goals will help. The goals you set, however, will be unique to you.

Just like any framework if you remove one of the elements or pieces it becomes weaker. Achieving goals in your life can seem empty if they don't have real meaning or are out of line with your values. Conversely, having a purpose in your life without achieving anything wouldn't have much purpose!

Hopefully it has become clear that the strength of the model and your wellbeing will be leveraged when all of the elements and pieces are brought together. Getting a big picture view and then focusing on the things that are most relevant. Using the CANBE Model in this way will provide you with the greatest personal, team and organisational success.

Let's look at each of the dimensions of the CANBE Model in turn.

CREATING MEANING

Wellbeing Domains - 'Territories' - Interconnected areas of our lives

Wellbeing Dimensions 'Highways' Intertwined routes we use to navigate our lives	**Mental** Our thoughts	**Emotional** Our emotions	**Physical** Our actions	**Spiritual** Our spirit	**Social** Our communities	**Cultural** Our way	**Environmental** Our spaces	**Economic** Our trade
Creating meaning	Thinking	Feelings	Behaviour	Identity	Friendship	Way of life	Affinity	Needs
Achieving potential	Focus	Control	Mastery	Motivation	Teamwork	Governance	Cultivation	Impact
Nurturing relationships	Regard	Empathy	Interaction	Stories	Trust	Belonging	Cohesion	Fairness
Building resilience	Flexibility	Agility	Health	Growth	Support	Diversity	Adaptation	Integrity
Enriching lives	Imagination	Wisdom	Energy	Purpose	Empowerment	Integration	Renewal	Freedom

Wellbeing Factors - 'Signposts' - Interconnected things that can help us improve wellbeing

"I want to work for a company that contributes to and is part of the community. I want something not just to invest in. I want something to believe in."

ANITA RODDICK

An elderly architect was fast approaching retirement. He told his employer of his plans to leave the business to live a more leisurely life with his wife and family. The employer was sorry to see his good worker go and asked if he could design just one more house as a personal favour. The architect said yes, but it was easy to see that his heart was not in his work.

His designs were 'run of the mill' and 'off the shelf'. Nothing was bespoke or tailored. There was little creativity in his work and he had resorted to using inferior materials. It was an unfortunate way to end a dedicated career.

When the architect finished his work the employer came to inspect the designs. It was then he delivered some unexpected news: 'This is your house... my gift to you.' The architect was shocked!

What a shame! If only he had known he was designing his own house, he would have done it all so differently.

So it is with us. We create our lives, one day at a time, sometimes putting less than our best into the design. Then, with shock, we realise we have to live in the house we have built. If we could do it over, we would do it very differently.

But, you cannot go back. Every day you design the life that you live. The more effort, pride, and creativity you put into that design, the more meaning it will hold for you. With work and determination you will come to love and cherish it.

As a leader, you are clearly the architect of your own life, but you also influence the design and experience of the lives of others. With this influence comes great responsibility, so please design carefully.

As humans we are built to give meaning to our experiences and there are many ways to create meaning and construct a life experience you want for yourself and others. In summary 'creating meaning' is largely about knowing who we are as unique individuals through exploring personal values, beliefs, purpose, character and personality and applying that throughout our lives. Looking across the domains of wellbeing this can include:

- Mental wellbeing - improving our understanding and *thinking*

- Emotional wellbeing - being able to name emotions and *feelings*, gaining awareness of ourselves and others
- Physical wellbeing - expressing ourselves freely through our *behaviours*
- Spiritual wellbeing - living in alignment with who we are, our *identity*
- Social wellbeing - developing *friendships*
- Cultural wellbeing - having a *way of life* that fits with who we are
- Environmental wellbeing - having an *affinity* for the places in which we live, work and play
- Economic wellbeing - through the *needs* we have.

However, creating a meaningful life without achieving our potential as an individual or group can also be a shallow experience. Let's take a closer look at achieving our potential.

ACHIEVING POTENTIAL

		Wellbeing Domains - 'Territories' - Interconnected areas of our lives							
		Mental Our thoughts	Emotional Our emotions	Physical Our actions	Spiritual Our spirit	Social Our communities	Cultural Our way	Environmental Our spaces	Economic Our trade
Wellbeing Dimensions 'Highways' Intertwined routes we use to navigate our lives	Creating meaning	Thinking	Feelings	Behaviour	Identity	Friendship	Way of life	Affinity	Needs
	Achieving potential	Focus	Control	Mastery	Motivation	Teamwork	Governance	Cultivation	Impact
	Nurturing relationships	Regard	Empathy	Interaction	Stories	Trust	Belonging	Cohesion	Fairness
	Building resilience	Flexibility	Agility	Health	Growth	Support	Diversity	Adaptation	Integrity
	Enriching lives	Imagination	Wisdom	Energy	Purpose	Empowerment	Integration	Renewal	Freedom
		Wellbeing Factors - 'Signposts' - Interconnected things that can help us improve wellbeing							

"Good business leaders create a vision, articulate the vision, passionately own the vision, and relentlessly drive it to completion."

JACK WELCH

Achievement, especially when congruent with our values and intrinsic motivations, makes us feel good and helps build confidence.

Human nature throughout time has demonstrated a need for continued progress, and as Maslow determined, we're motivated to meet our needs to survive and eventually thrive.

However, a focus on achievement alone can, ironically, leave people feeling empty and unfulfilled. You achieve your targets and then new ones are set. You achieve those and then the bar is raised again.

The argument put forward in this book is that, you, your people and your organisation will achieve more if you focus on creating well-being through the CANBE Model rather than an unbalanced focus on hitting targets and just 'getting the job done'. Some of the ways leaders can facilitate this across the domains of wellbeing include:

- Mental wellbeing - Increasing *focus* through vision, strategy, objectives, mindfulness and removing distractions
- Emotional wellbeing - *controlling* our response to emotions, or in other words, the difference between what happens to us and how we respond to what happens to us
- *Physical wellbeing* - helping people *master* the skills they need
- Spiritual wellbeing - understanding what *motivates* people based on who they are and finding a good balance between intrinsic and extrinsic rewards
- Social wellbeing - developing strong *teamwork*
- Cultural wellbeing - providing good *governance* through strong leadership, policies, traditions and infrastructure
- Environmental wellbeing - *cultivating* environments which enhance performance
- Economic wellbeing - measuring and demonstrating the *impact* of performance

But none of this can be achieved without strong relationships between people.

NURTURING RELATIONSHIPS

		Wellbeing Domains - 'Territories' - Interconnected areas of our lives							
		Mental Our thoughts	Emotional Our emotions	Physical Our actions	Spiritual Our spirit	Social Our communities	Cultural Our way	Environmental Our spaces	Economic Our trade
		↑	↑	↑	↑	↑	↑	↑	↑
Wellbeing Dimensions 'Highways' Intertwined routes we use to navigate our lives	Creating meaning	Thinking	Feelings	Behaviour	Identity	Friendship	Way of life	Affinity	Needs
	Achieving potential	Focus	Control	Mastery	Motivation	Teamwork	Governance	Cultivation	Impact
	Nurturing relationships	Regard	Empathy	Interaction	Stories	Trust	Belonging	Cohesion	Fairness
	Building resilience	Flexibility	Agility	Health	Growth	Support	Diversity	Adaptation	Integrity
	Enriching lives	Imagination	Wisdom	Energy	Purpose	Empowerment	Integration	Renewal	Freedom
		Wellbeing Factors - 'Signposts' - Interconnected things that can help us improve wellbeing							

"The key to successful leadership is influence, not authority."

KENNETH H. BLANCHARD

We all know the truth: relationships can be heaven or they can be hell. To be an effective leader, then, requires an excellent understanding of yourself and other people. How you, and they, think, feel and act under different circumstances.

The CANBE Model will help you build stronger relationships in the following ways:

- Mental wellbeing - If we can hold ourselves and others in high *regard* this is a great starting place for strong relationships
- *Emotional wellbeing - Empathy,* the ability to feel what others are feeling will help us build stronger connections
- *Physical wellbeing - Interacting* effectively is a core leadership skill. How we affect others and they affect us is core to wellbeing
- Spiritual wellbeing - Shared *stories* help people come together in understanding
- Social wellbeing - building *trust* is the foundation of all relationships
- Cultural wellbeing - helping people feel like they *belong*
- Environmental wellbeing - developing *cohesive* environments where people can collaborate
- Economic wellbeing - ensuring people receive *fair* access to resources and reward for their contribution

However, things don't always go according to plan and people don't always react the way we expect them to. Life is full of highs and lows. For these times, we need resilience.

BUILDING RESILIENCE

Wellbeing Domains - 'Territories' - Interconnected areas of our lives

		Mental Our thoughts	**Emotional** Our emotions	**Physical** Our actions	**Spiritual** Our spirit	**Social** Our communities	**Cultural** Our way	**Environmental** Our spaces	**Economic** Our trade
Wellbeing Dimensions 'Highways' Intertwined routes we use to navigate our lives	Creating meaning	Thinking	Feelings	Behaviour	Identity	Friendship	Way of life	Affinity	Needs
	Achieving potential	Focus	Control	Mastery	Motivation	Teamwork	Governance	Cultivation	Impact
	Nurturing relationships	Regard	Empathy	Interaction	Stories	Trust	Belonging	Cohesion	Fairness
	Building resilience	Flexibility	Agility	Health	Growth	Support	Diversity	Adaptation	Integrity
	Enriching lives	Imagination	Wisdom	Energy	Purpose	Empowerment	Integration	Renewal	Freedom

Wellbeing Factors - 'Signposts' - Interconnected things that can help us improve wellbeing

"Failure is an option here. If you're not failing you're not innovating enough."

ELON MUSK

POTATOES, EGGS AND COFFEE

A daughter once complained to her father that her life was miserable and that she was tired of fighting and struggling all the time. Just as one problem was solved, another seemed to follow.

Her father, a chef, took her to the kitchen and filled three pots with water. He placed each on a fire and once they began to boil he put potatoes in one pot, eggs in the second and ground coffee beans in the third. He then let them sit and boil, without saying a word. The daughter, moaned and waited impatiently, wondering what he was doing.

After twenty minutes he took the potatoes and eggs out of the pot and placed them in a bowl. He then ladled the coffee into a cup. Turning to her he asked. "Daughter, what do you see?" "Potatoes, eggs, and coffee," she hastily replied. "Look closer," he said, "and touch the potatoes." She did and noted that they were soft. He then asked her to take an egg and break it. After pulling off the shell, she observed the hard-boiled egg. Finally, he asked her to sip the coffee. Its rich aroma brought a smile to her face. "Father, what does this mean?" she asked.

He then explained that the potatoes, eggs and coffee beans had each faced the same adversity– the boiling water. However, each one reacted differently. The potato went in strong, hard, and unrelenting, but in boiling water, it became soft and weak. The egg was fragile, with the thin outer shell protecting its liquid interior until it was put in the boiling water when it became hard.

However, the ground coffee beans were unique. They changed the water and created something new. "Which are you," he asked his daughter. "When adversity knocks on your door, how do you respond? Are you a potato, an egg, or a coffee bean? "

In life, things happen around us and to us, but the only thing that truly matters is what happens within us. Which are you? A potato, an egg or a coffee bean.

With greater resilience, we are better at overcoming challenges, bouncing back and even growing stronger when things don't go the way we planned. But resilience isn't just about recovery. As outlined earlier, it is also about having the capacity to adapt and navigate change effectively.

Wellbeing, resilience, and change are inherently linked. If you don't have the tools or mind-set to adapt to change you may become anxious and frustrated with obvious impacts on wellbeing. If you are emotionally, physically, socially, and spiritually resilient, and have higher levels of wellbeing, you will adapt more effectively. As the saying goes: "What doesn't kill you makes you stronger".

Using the CANBE approach helps us in the following ways:

- Mental wellbeing - Building a *flexible*, growth mind-set will help us adapt more quickly and plan for change rather than 'have change happen to us'.
- Emotional wellbeing - *emotional agility*: using the right emotions, at the right time, with the right person, in the right place. It's about learning from our emotions and understanding how to use them to our advantage.
- *Physical wellbeing* - Physical *health* enables us to deal with daily challenges and overcome obstacles in our path.
- Spiritual wellbeing - Learning, *growth* from our experiences, helps us deal with repeat or similar events as they arise.
- Social wellbeing - Having, and belonging to, a strong, compassionate *support* network is one of the greatest aids to resilience
- Cultural wellbeing - *Diversity* brings new perspectives and ideas to approach problems and opportunities. It also helps to spread risk so that we can be more resilient.
- Environmental wellbeing - Being able to *adapt* to our changing environment is a key part of resilience
- Economic wellbeing - *integrity* in our economic systems

from both a moral and systemic perspective helps us weather the ups and downs of markets

THE COSTS OF POOR RESILIENCE

It makes sense that someone who is physically, mentally, socially and financially 'fitter' will be less likely to take sick days, stronger in the face of difficult challenges at work, perform better and be more creative.

Amazingly, according to the latest absence survey from the Chartered Institute of Professional Development (CIPD), just one third of employers say they monitor the costs of absence[1]. If the major cost for most organisations is employees, and your organisation is not measuring how much it costs when people aren't at work, then something isn't right!

To put this into context, the same survey outlines the overall median cost of absence per employee at £522. So, even in a company of 200 people the costs amount to over £100,000 per annum. Now the costs do vary by industry and private, public, and voluntary sector - but surely the message is clear? As a responsible leader, we need to get an understanding of the key causes of absence and what it is costing our teams and organisations. Once we understand this, we will be in a better position to put in place support and activities to improve the situation. Not only can we deliver a good return on investment, it's an empathetic and more human approach!

THE BENEFITS OF RESILIENCE

Resilience is a key building block of growth. Without it, we are more likely to give up in the face of an obstacle. Building resilience isn't about a one off programme or training event, it is part of the culture, and this book covers key areas where you can develop personally and introduce initiatives that will benefit those around you and your organisation.

To build resilience effectively, we need to develop a 'growth mind-set' where we learn from adversity in our past and can adapt to obstacles in the future. Please keep these past and future perspectives in mind as we review the different types of resilience. Here are a couple of questions to think about as we go through each:

- What knowledge, skills, attitudes or habits have you acquired from past experiences that could help you be more resilient in the future?
- What new knowledge, skills, attitudes or habits do you need to help you adapt better in the future?

As we grow and develop through our experiences, both good and bad, we are better placed to be able to enrich our own lives and the lives of others.

ENRICHING LIVES

		Wellbeing Domains - 'Territories' - Interconnected areas of our lives							
		Mental Our thoughts	**Emotional** Our emotions	**Physical** Our actions	**Spiritual** Our spirit	**Social** Our communities	**Cultural** Our way	**Environmental** Our spaces	**Economic** Our trade
		↑	↑	↑	↑	↑	↑	↑	↑
Wellbeing Dimensions	Creating meaning	Thinking	Feelings	Behaviour	Identity	Friendship	Way of life	Affinity	Needs
'Highways'	Achieving potential	Focus	Control	Mastery	Motivation	Teamwork	Governance	Cultivation	Impact
Intertwined routes	Nurturing relationships	Regard	Empathy	Interaction	Stories	Trust	Belonging	Cohesion	Fairness
we use to navigate	Building resilience	Flexibility	Agility	Health	Growth	Support	Diversity	Adaptation	Integrity
our lives	Enriching lives	Imagination	Wisdom	Energy	Purpose	Empowerment	Integration	Renewal	Freedom
		Wellbeing Factors - 'Signposts' - Interconnected things that can help us improve wellbeing							

"You are not here merely to make a living. You are here in order to enable the world to live more amply, with greater vision, with a finer spirit of hope and achievement. You are here to enrich the world, and you impoverish yourself if you forget the errand."

WOODROW WILSON

> "That has always been the objective of Apple: to do things that really enrich people's lives. That you look back on and you wonder, 'How did I live without this?'"
>
> TIM COOK

As will hopefully have become apparent wellbeing is not just an individual thing. If we have high levels of wellbeing we are able to pass this to others. In fact, by helping others voluntarily, we find our own wellbeing also benefits.

We do this through the CANBE Model in the following ways:

- Mental wellbeing - Using our *imagination* to help us move to new and better places
- Emotional wellbeing - *wisdom* through how we manage our emotions for the positive benefit of ourselves and others
- Physical wellbeing - Helping us and others feel good by creating positive *energy*
- Spiritual wellbeing - Living according to our *purpose* gives us direction and greater motivation
- Social wellbeing - By *empowering* others we too can benefit from their collective growth
- Cultural wellbeing - True *integration* requires less energy and resources than if we live with tension and conflict. We benefit from the collective strength of diverse individuals and groups
- Environmental wellbeing - *Renewing* our environments and ourselves so we and future generations can all benefit
- Economic wellbeing - Real *freedom* is when we use our scarce and finite resources most effectively for the benefit of all

Now we've taken a look at the CANBE Model it's time to explore the 'signposts' at the intersections of the domains and dimensions to see how they can help us navigate our journey to higher levels of wellbeing.

CHAPTER FIVE

IMPROVING MENTAL WELLBEING

		Wellbeing Domains - 'Territories' - Interconnected areas of our lives							
		Mental Our thoughts	**Emotional** Our emotions	**Physical** Our actions	**Spiritual** Our spirit	**Social** Our communities	**Cultural** Our way	**Environmental** Our spaces	**Economic** Our trade
Wellbeing Dimensions **'Highways'** **Intertwined routes we use to navigate our lives**	Creating meaning	Thinking	Feelings	Behaviour	Identity	Friendship	Way of life	Affinity	Needs
	Achieving potential	Focus	Control	Mastery	Motivation	Teamwork	Governance	Cultivation	Impact
	Nurturing relationships	Regard	Empathy	Interaction	Stories	Trust	Belonging	Cohesion	Fairness
	Building resilience	Flexibility	Agility	Health	Growth	Support	Diversity	Adaptation	Integrity
	Enriching lives	Imagination	Wisdom	Energy	Purpose	Empowerment	Integration	Renewal	Freedom
		Wellbeing Factors - 'Signposts' - Interconnected things that can help us improve wellbeing							

"The cheerful mind perseveres, and the strong mind hews its way through a thousand difficulties."

SWAMI VIVEKANANDA

> "Experience is not what happens to you — it's how you interpret what happens to you."
>
> ALDOUS HUXLEY

In the modern world of fitbits, Instagram body-image, and more and more data on food and how it affects us, we are very aware of our physical health. We are often less aware, however, of our mental health. Partly, perhaps, because it is more subtle and nuanced.

Just like physical health, we all have mental health and it too can be good, bad, or anywhere in between. What I'm promoting in this book is the spectrum of mental health. Some people might require support through times of poor mental health but we should also work on positive mental health too. And yet there is more 'stigma' attached to 'mental health'. We tend to see it only as the negative. Perhaps it's the word 'mental' or its strong connection with emotions and how we feel.

Whilst significant progress has been made in the UK, it's clear that there is still a real disconnect between how well business owners, CEOs, Board members and Directors believe their organisation supports mental wellbeing and the experience of people in the workplace.

Business in the Community, Mental Health at Work Study 2016[1], reports that 63% of line managers believe they have to put the interests of the organisation before employee wellbeing and that just 22% of line managers have undertaken mental health training. The report goes on to outline the 'culture of silence' that pervades many organisations and the important role of line managers in supporting colleagues. I am sure the UK is at least somewhat reflective of other countries across the world.

As a leader, you can influence the levels of mental health support in your organisation by understanding any gaps in provision, assessing risks, setting a positive tone to conversations, ensuring you and your managers have the right training to support colleagues, and tackling the 'culture of silence'.

But we can also help by understanding the things we can support and others where external support may be more beneficial. For example, stress is something that can potentially be managed 'in house' or with the support of experienced coaches. Normally with stress, a person can identify 'stressors'.

With half a million people in the UK believing that they have work-related stress at a level that is making them ill, and the cost to UK employers of 10.4 million work days lost[2], how can we build greater resilience to stress as individuals, teams, and organisations?

The top causes of stress ('stressors') are:

1. workloads
2. management styles
3. organisational change

This would indicate a focus on balancing priorities and managing workloads effectively, training for managers, and effective support for staff to deal with change, as good starting points. In this situation, management and leadership can work to put in place activities that may help to mitigate or avoid these 'stressors' so that colleagues feel more 'at ease'.

Where can we give people more control over what they do and more autonomy to do it in the way they want to? Freeing people up, empathising, listening, asking great questions, and communicating effectively all help reduce stress. Other options include: making adjustments to the job itself (including responsibilities, tasks, working hours, people that may be causing conflict), location of work, and the work environment. When the job can't be altered, then looking at things including prioritisation of tasks, support, training, counselling, and even compassionate leave are other effective measures.

On a personal level, good exercise, diet and sleep also help with managing stress, as we'll come onto in the chapter on Physical Wellbeing. Personal efficacy and use of time, which we'll review later in this chapter, can also help.

Tackling these 'stressors' is important as longer term stress, left unaddressed, can lead to anxiety and depression.

However we won't always have resources available to support the people around us effectively. Anxiety and depression are often longer term and characterised by people not being able to identify 'stressors'. They can also be linked to chemical changes in our brain. These are times when a medical diagnosis and external support are far more appropriate. It is important for leaders to recognise this and develop knowledge of the best pathways to put people on when internal support won't suffice.

Just for the moment, and before we move onto other areas of mental health, I'd like to continue on the theme of stress. I share the next piece of research, not because I'm dismissive of stress, anxiety, depression or any other mental illness but because I am concerned about our focus. I believe there is a danger that we could be drawn into 'thinking ourselves down'. If we become overly focused on what can hurt us, without remembering what can help us, we may induce our own neurosis. We must keep a balance, which is why I argue for a balanced approach to mental health.

The research I refer to shows that a growth mind-set, which we'll explore later in this chapter, has been shown to have positive effects on stress. This research suggests that our 'stress mind-set' is a key variable in determining our response to stress. In "Rethinking Stress: The Role of Mind-sets in Determining the Stress Response"[3], Crum, Salovey and Achor challenge the long held notion that whether stress is debilitating or not depends purely on its frequency, intensity, and duration. They put forward the view that: "the mind-set one adopts when approaching stress is a critical factor in determining whether stress will have debilitating or enhancing effects for individuals."

In essence, the way we think about stress will also impact on how we deal with it. Think about a last minute deadline. We could approach that with added excitement as a result of the satisfaction achieved on getting the task done in such tight timescales. On the other hand, we could also approach it with a sense of futility or feel overwhelmed that we can't possibly get it done in time.

It is important to note that this research does not dismiss the debilitating effects of long term stress, nor does it suggest that just by changing our mind-set all problems will disappear. What it does suggest is that by thinking differently about stress, along with other interventions and approaches outlined in this book, we might be able to change our relationship with it. Stress has had so much bad coverage in the media that our general reaction has become negative. When you see the word stress, what is your first reaction? What words do you associate with it?

The point here is to remember there is both good and bad stress. On the positive side, it improves both our physical and mental functioning to meet the imminent demands we face. In the workplace, when channelled correctly, this can lead to greater initiative taking, focus on the task at hand, speed of thinking, and improved motivation to solve problems. It can also boost memory and overall performance.

So mental wellbeing is so much more than managing stress, anxiety, depression or others disorders. Whilst it is key that mental health is protected we should remember that most people in the workplace won't suffer from poor mental health issues. If we only focus on managing **'distress'** we will remain in suffering mode. To thrive, we also need to focus on developing better **thinking**, **focus**, **regard**, **flexibility** and **imagination.**

THINKING

		Wellbeing Domains - 'Territories' - Interconnected areas of our lives							
		Mental Our thoughts	**Emotional** Our emotions	**Physical** Our actions	**Spiritual** Our spirit	**Social** Our communities	**Cultural** Our way	**Environmental** Our spaces	**Economic** Our trade
Wellbeing Dimensions 'Highways' Intertwined routes we use to navigate our lives	**Creating meaning**	Thinking	Feelings	Behaviour	Identity	Friendship	Way of life	Affinity	Needs
	Achieving potential	Focus	Control	Mastery	Motivation	Teamwork	Governance	Cultivation	Impact
	Nurturing relationships	Regard	Empathy	Interaction	Stories	Trust	Belonging	Cohesion	Fairness
	Building resilience	Flexibility	Agility	Health	Growth	Support	Diversity	Adaptation	Integrity
	Enriching lives	Imagination	Wisdom	Energy	Purpose	Empowerment	Integration	Renewal	Freedom
		Wellbeing Factors - 'Signposts' - Interconnected things that can help us improve wellbeing							

"If you think you can or you think you can't, you're probably right!"

HENRY FORD

How we think and understand things has a big influence on our well-being. Our thoughts and feelings determine our attitude which in turn drives our behaviour. If our thoughts and feelings are flawed then it can only follow that our behaviour and actions will follow suit.

And yet, so often, our thinking and understanding is flawed. We think we are right, that there is only one way. We see things only from our own perspective. We over emphasise and tell ourselves stories to reinforce our own narrative of the world.

The good thing is, we can learn to think and understand in ways that consider a wider spectrum of viewpoints and possibilities, which will enhance our critical thinking, ability to relate to others, and creativity. The starting point for broadening our thinking and understanding is awareness. As the great Walter Pater, 19th century art-critic and stylist, once said: "The first step towards seeing one's object as it really is, is to know one's own impression, to discriminate it, to realise it distinctly" (*The Renaissance*, 1873). In other words, we need to recognise our subjective opinion before we can begin to see the bigger picture.

So, what are some of the sticking points we should be looking out for and how can we develop better thinking and understanding? What follows is an exploration of some of the key areas where we might like to improve by looking at our thinking styles in the context of the past, present, and future. Often, our thinking can be too focused on worrying about what might happen in the future or what has happened in the past. As Einstein said, it is much better to: "Learn from yesterday, live for today, hope for tomorrow."

BIAS AND HEURISTICS

We have all been guilty of poor decision making or irrational behaviour due to bias. Bias is when we systematically make suboptimal decisions due to unconscious or automatic influences on our thinking. Among over 100 cognitive biases known to date this includes things such as:

- more readily recalling information that supports our existing beliefs (confirmation bias),

- a preference for maintaining the status quo (status quo bias),
- over-confidence in our decision making, contrary to what results actually tell us about their accuracy (confidence bias), and
- reacting to information in respect to how it is framed, rather than the actual facts (framing effect).

Heuristics are mental shortcuts we use to make decisions such as intuition, educated guesses, or the 'rule of thumb'. These can be extremely useful when making decisions where we have previous successful experience or the consequences of making a poor decision are very low. However, we need to be careful of not continuing to do things the way they have always been done without challenging our thinking from time to time.

It is not my aim to fully explore bias and heuristics: that would be a book in it's own right! My aim is to point out that poor thinking and understanding can impact our wellbeing and that of others.

If it is, then what can we do to mitigate bias and heuristics where they are having a negative effect? The first thing is awareness, although this in itself will not help us change. It can be difficult to become aware of our biases and heuristics. We need to read around the subject and get familiar with our strengths and weaknesses.

Once we've done this, we'll become familiar with key areas where we might like to focus to mitigate our own bias and the biases of those in our teams or organisations.

1. Reducing or increasing **Incentives** can be an effective way to change behaviour. Examples might be reducing the price of healthier alternative products to encourage consumption or taxing goods to reduce it.
2. **Nudging** is another approach where people are provided with information or options that encourage a

particular route. Having a default option is one example of this.

3. **Training** can be useful over the longer term
4. **Introducing processes** that seek to manage biases. For example, recruitment processes that include a diverse panel of interviewers.

Bias and heuristics are built on our experiences of the past but we can also think about the past itself in ways that either hinder or help our wellbeing. This brings us to reflection and rumination.

REFLECTION AND RUMINATION

Reflection is an intentional act of thinking about our past experiences and what we might do differently to achieve a better outcome next time. It is also often associated with thinking about who we are in respect to our values, goals, emotions, personality and even purpose in life. These are valuable activities to help us learn and they are associated with a growth mindset and a continuous journey of self improvement. *Reflection is productive.*

Rumination, on the other hand, is when we think over and over about past activities often with a negative mindset. There is little to no focus on learning and, rather than being intentional, rumination is often associated with mind wandering leading to stress or anxiety. *Rumination is unproductive.* Recognising when we are in this state and then focusing our thinking on activities which help us learn, or provide answers to problems, is a great way to overcome this.

This brings us to being more present minded.

MINDFULNESS AND MIND-WANDERING

For many of us, in this hectic world we live in, a focus on living in the moment is not as easy as it sounds. What were you thinking while brushing your teeth this morning? Was it the day ahead and issues you were likely to face or perhaps what happened yesterday? If you were mindful you would have been thinking about the water running through your fingers, the taste of the toothpaste, the sound of your toothbrush and perhaps how lucky you are to have running water, a toothbrush and a dentist that helps keep your teeth in good order!

In their excellent article in Harvard Business Review on "How to Bring Mindfulness to Your Company's Leadership"[1] Megan Reitz, Associate Professor of Leadership and Dialogue at Ashridge Executive Education and Michael Chaskalson, author of The Mindful Workplace and one of the pioneers of the application of mindfulness in leadership in the workplace describe their Mindful Leader program and study.

This research studied 57 senior business leaders in two cohorts and involved fortnightly workshops, 'buddying up' and daily home practice. Participants learned why mindfulness might be relevant to their leadership practice, how to practice it, and how to apply their learning to their individual leadership challenges.

They found that mindfulness training produces an improvement in three key leadership capacities: resilience, the capacity for collaboration, and the ability to lead in complex conditions, but that this was highly dependent on the level of practice that the leader undertook. The leaders that practiced for at least 10 minutes every day showed significantly better results than those that didn't. So mindfulness is no quick fix.

One leader summed up what this meant: "I now have moments of choice that I didn't have before."

Reitz and Chaskalson go on to recommend what they believe to be an effective approach to influencing mindfulness in the workplace. This includes daily personal practice, a supportive organisational system, formal 'taster sessions' to gauge interest and commitment, allocated quiet and private space, and encouraging group-based sessions. One example given is to start meetings with a "mindful minute" where attendees count their breath in silence and focus on working effectively with other attendees to get the most from the meeting.

Mindfulness clearly carries with it a host of benefits, and is extraordinarily simple. It is about using all of our senses to focus on the present and helps us better manage our emotions. Meditation is one approach to this. There are many different types of meditation, and some are connected to spiritual or religious practices, but perhaps the simplest of these - something you could put into practice this very moment - is mindful breathing. This involves focusing attention on the breath: the air moving through your nose, the rise and fall of your chest and stomach. If your mind wanders you simply bring attention back. In moments of stress, this is an excellent technique to perform, even if only for a few deep breaths.

But what about the times when we're not in the present moment? According to some estimates our mind is wandering for about 50% of our waking hours. That's right 50%! Something that takes up 50% of our day surely deserves more attention. So what exactly is our mind doing during this time and how can we make best use of it?

Recent research by Kalina Christoff, Professor of Psychology at the University of British Columbia, and her team provides us with a useful framework to consider this. They propose "that mind-wandering is best understood as a member of a family of spontaneous-thought phenomena that also includes creative thought and dreaming." Using this framework spontaneous thoughts are categorised as follows:

- Rumination and obsessive thoughts
- Spontaneous thoughts
- Dreaming
- Mind wandering
- Creative thinking
- Goal directed thoughts. These thoughts are directed at 'one's personal concerns'.

The good news is that many of these are related to helping us achieve our personal goals and concerns. As an example, whilst completing a mundane habitual task (driving to work on the same route you take every day), your mind might drift to key things you need to do to plan your forthcoming holiday. This could be perceived as 'good' mind wandering as it is helpful.

However, the bad news is that mind wandering can also be associated with negative affect and lower psychological well-being. In this respect there appears to be at least two significant drivers.

1. How distracted and emotionally 'caught up' we get with these passing thoughts. Mindful awareness is the ability to view thoughts as passing mental events and not get too caught up in them emotionally. Being more present focused.
2. The balance of our focus on self (self absorbed) and the external environment. This is referred to as 'encoding style' and is our tendency to pay more attention to the external environment (external) or internal mental processes (internal)

Research in this area is incomplete and ongoing, but if you find yourself getting too caught up in unhelpful past or future thinking, or too 'internally focused' whilst ignoring what's going on around you, then it is probably time to take action.

Mindfulness and meditation is an obvious starting place. However, we can also begin to challenge our thoughts. What evidence is there to support our thinking? If we're thinking too much about 'self' why not start noticing others a little more and taking more interest in the environment around us?

One of these debilitating thinking styles can be when we're overly worried or fearful.

OVERCOMING WORRY AND FEAR

Essex was an American whaling boat from Nantucket, Massachusetts. In 1820, while under the command of Captain George Pollard, Jr., a sperm whale attacked, ripping a catastrophic hole in the ship's hull that sank her. The twenty-man crew were stranded in the southern Pacific Ocean with little food and water.

The men, who only had limited supplies and rudimentary navigational equipment, were left with two options.

1. Sail to the nearest islands, the Marquesas, 1,200 mi (1,900 km) to the west or...
2. Sail to South America 3,000 mi (4,800 km) to the east. A much longer and arduous journey.

Captain Pollard intended to make for the Marquesas but the crew were terrified. They'd heard rumours of cannibals on these islands and voted instead to embark on the longer and much more difficult route to South America.

During the 95 days that the survivors were at sea, a total of seven crew members were cannibalised before eight survivors were rescued. First mate Owen Chase and cabin boy Thomas Nickerson wrote accounts of their ordeal which, in part, inspired Herman Melville to write his famous 1851 novel *Moby-Dick*.

It's clear in retrospect that their choice was based on fear. Which was more likely? Land on the Marquesas and get eaten by cannibals or head for South America and suffer almost certain starvation and dehydration. This decision, based on the lucid and vivid stories they had conjured in their heads, cost most of them their lives. It is also a tragic irony that seven of them were cannibalised by other crew members!

As Daniel Kahneman explains in *Thinking, Fast and Slow*[2] we can often make poor decisions by allowing our System 1 thinking to hijack System 2. For those who don't know, Kahneman's theory is that there are two principle styles of thought: System 1 thinking is fast, emotional, and instinctive; System 2 thinking is slow, deliberate, and logical. The novelist Vladimir Nabokov captures the same sentiment slightly differently. He said that the best reader combines two very different temperaments:

- 1. artistic passion and a willingness to get caught up in the story
- 2. the judgment of a scientist to temper these intuitive reactions.

Another example of where this combined thinking could actually have saved lives is given by Blalock, Kadiyali, & Simon in their paper "The Impact of 9/11 on Road Fatalities: The Other Lives Lost to Terrorism"[3].

In this they estimated that, due to people substituting air for more road travel after the terror attack, there were an additional 242 driving fatalities per month resulting in an additional 1,200 deaths. They conclude that the 'public response to terrorist threats can create unintended consequences that rival the attacks themselves in severity.' Of course we know air travel is safer than travelling by road but this didn't stop some people changing their mode of travel due to fear.

Our fears, then, are really the stories we tell ourselves. We are both the authors and the readers. As the reader, we should approach our story with two perspectives:

- an artistic, 'System 1' and
- scientific, 'System 2' mind-set.

As the author, we can always change the story. What harmful stories are holding us, our teams, or our organisations back?

One of the best ways of conquering a fear is to face up to it. In psychology, this is known as 'exposure therapy'. This can be done in small increments, gradually stepping further and further outside our comfort zone. So, for example, if you fear making a presentation, you might start by speaking up more in team meetings and then delivering a small session amongst known team members, gradually building confidence until such time as you can deliver something on a larger scale.

CONFIDENCE AND ARROGANCE

Confidence is a state of mind. It is the feeling or belief of being certain of your abilities. It can also be about having trust in people, plans, or the future. Whilst confidence is more about what we do, it is closely linked to our self-regard and self-esteem, or in other words, how we see ourselves.

It is good to have confidence as this inspires action. Can you think of a time when a lack of confidence has stopped you from doing something? A lack of confidence diminishes our lives. So how can we build confidence?

We can build confidence by working on the combination of our thoughts, feelings and actions. Here's how:

Thoughts

- Knowing who we are and what's important will help us focus on doing things that are intrinsically motivating.
- Focus on our skills, strengths, and successes. If we've done it before we can do it again!
- Reflecting on our failures. How did they help us move forward in life?
- Make some positive affirmations.
- Keep a healthy, balanced perspective.
- Set goals. Start small and build.

Feelings

- Regulating our emotions like fears and desires. Separating fact from fiction and challenging the stories we tell ourselves. Regulating emotions that might take us in a direction that could cause harm or excess. 'Giving in to our unhelpful desires' can erode confidence, making us feel helpless and out of control.
- Recording the feelings we have when others give us compliments. Asking for feedback about our strengths.

Actions

- A big factor in a lack of confidence is often fear of the unknown. By planning and preparing we can reduce this fear and think about actions we might take in different scenarios.
- For big overwhelming activities we can concentrate our efforts on small manageable goals that we've broken down into 'bite size chunks'.
- Resolving unfinished business. Leaving tasks unfinished creates a cluttered mind and erodes confidence.
- If we're feeling low, stand up. Changing our physiology and standing confidently helps shape our feelings and thoughts.
- Take care of our appearance including clothes, hair, shoes and make-up. If we look good we'll feel good. There's a reason for the saying 'dressed for the part'. It gets us in the right frame of mind for what we're about to do.
- Challenging a fear or trying something new and taking one small action to move forwards. Now take the next one, and then another.
- Focusing on the present through practicing mindfulness and meditation.
- Exercising can help build confidence through the release of endorphins and a sense of achievement

- Networking with others and learning from them. Supporting others. Sharing our knowledge and experience is a great way to build confidence.
- Where we don't yet have the necessary skills or capabilities to perform a task we can learn. Finding suitable training and development opportunities to help us prepare. Being creative.

Confidence is good for building our sense of wellbeing. However, when confidence is unwarranted it can be perceived as arrogance. When we think we can do anything, even without the necessary skills, capabilities and experience this can become problematic, or at its worst, even life threatening. Remember there are always ways for us to improve and nobody is perfect.

Another way we think about the future is in terms of optimism or pessimism.

OPTIMISM AND PESSIMISM

Whilst closely associated with confidence, optimism is different in that it tends towards a more general, outward looking view based more on the present and future. Confidence tends to be grounded in more reality, linked to more specific events, people or experiences and draws from the past, as well as influencing thoughts about the present and future. Optimism is more expectation oriented. Confidence is more action oriented.

An optimist might say, "I believe we'll have a rosy future".

Someone with confidence might say, "We're working to make sure the future is bright"

Is your "glass half-full or half-empty"? The "optimal" answer is probably both. If all we ever see is 'the best' then we may overlook dangers and threats. If, on the other hand, all we see is 'the worst', we will likely miss opportunities.

Based on the balance of research it is probably safe to say that a more optimistic outlook is perceived to have advantages over a more pessimistic one. For example, studies have shown that optimists set more challenging goals, put more effort into achieving those goals, and are more resilient in the face of obstacles, than pessimists[4].

However, some would argue that setting low expectations is the secret to happiness. The thinking goes that if we don't expect good things to happen to us, and are pleasantly surprised when they do, then we'll be happier. But this is just not true.

People with high expectations tend to feel better because, whether we succeed or fail, it is how we interpret the event that impacts on our wellbeing. Martin Seligman's work on 'Learned Optimism' describes the characteristics of personalisation, permanence and pervasiveness in how pessimists and optimists might differently interpret the causes of an event.

- Personalisation is how much a person believes in their own influence over the outcome of an event
- Permanence is the long or short term effect we believe events will have
- Pervasiveness is the degree that we believe an event will impact on, just a part of or, the whole of our lives

So, when successful a pessimist might attribute this to a 'one off' temporary (impermanent) achievement linked only to one aspect of their lives (not pervading their whole life). They would be more likely to cite external factors as contributing to their success than their own personal skills (de-personalising). On the contrary an optimist would be more likely to interpret their success as something to be expected repeatedly (permanence) due to their hard work (personalisation), in all areas of their life (pervasiveness).

Pessimists and optimists also tend to experience failure differently. A pessimist might say 'This always happens to me' whilst an optimist would argue that 'on this occasion the challenge has been particularly hard and that he/she will do better next time'.

Low expectations lead to less anticipation. Anticipation of a favourable event in the future is good for our wellbeing[5]. We have high expectations of our holidays and then look forward to the fun and enjoyment we will experience. Sometimes we will even delay instant gratification in anticipation of future enjoyment. Think of the bottle of champagne you are saving for that special occasion!

Finally, there are many studies which have shown that an optimistic outlook leads to better health outcomes and success in life, whereas there are stronger links between pessimism and depression.

But pessimism and optimism are not the opposite of each other. The opposite of optimism is lack of optimism, the opposite of pessimism is lack of pessimism. Working on reducing pessimism does not mean that you will instantly become more optimistic.

There are benefits and costs to both outlooks and they need to be viewed from different perspectives. A person's personality, character, social, cultural and environmental context will all have a bearing on which might be the most effective approach.

Take, for example, climate change. Is it better to be optimistic or pessimistic about this threat to the wellbeing of humanity? At present, I would argue that we need a little more pessimism. Until we accept the science for what it is, and become a little more concerned about the consequences, we may not be motivated enough to change. However, we also need a good dose of optimism. If we believe our efforts to change are futile then we may give up before we've even started.

Of course this also applies to our personal life. Sometimes a little pessimism might be useful to protect us from threats and help us consider dangers. But if all we do is remain pessimistic we might never make any plans to help overcome those dangers and threats. For this we will need optimism.

To make progress then, we need to imagine a different future and then believe that it is possible to get there. Other techniques for building optimism, which I'll cover in greater detail elsewhere in the book, include:

- Being *mindful* of negative thinking and disengaging from it when it is not helpful
- Noticing the positive things happening in our lives and being *grateful*
- *Visualising* a more positive future
- *Exercising* to boost our mood
- Building *confidence* through *goal setting* and taking *action*
- *Connecting* with others to hear different perspectives that might challenge our own

Another way of developing a more optimistic outlook is through improving our mental capability.

DEVELOPING MENTAL CAPABILITY

Recognising that work itself may provide significant opportunities for developing mental capability, here are some activities which could be introduced on the more positive spectrum of mental health:

- **Strategising** – Logic and reasoning skills help us make decisions and consider outcomes. We might like to think about including activities like video and board games or anything that includes logic and reasoning, encouraging debating and chess clubs for example. How about turning our projects into strategic games or finding other ways to incorporate 'strategising' into the work itself?
- **Memory challenges** – Every time we read, reason, or do any type of mental calculation, memory is important. Perhaps we can introduce memory games that could be work related or just for pure fun in team meetings? Why not encourage your team to learn the lyrics to a song for the Christmas party.
- **Focusing attention** – Attention decreases with age

and is fundamental to our cognitive ability. As outlined previously, much of what we do is routine and habit so by mixing things up a little from time to time we can force our brain to focus. This could be as simple as taking a different route to work from time to time or identifying tasks we do routinely and trying something different.

- **Relaxing** – Following the importance of attention and focus it is also important to give our brain a rest from time to time. Taking 5 minutes to stretch away from what we're doing can help us return to a task with renewed vigour and creativity.
- **Linguistic challenges** - Stimulating our brain to understand, remember, and recognise words. A few ideas here could involve reading more widely around industry topics, word games at team meetings, or building a library of shared books at work. What else can you think of?
- **Synthesising** – This involves linking, joining, and connecting information together to create new knowledge. Activities like mentoring and coaching would promote this type of activity, particularly where one person's learning is then shared with another. Asking a team member to produce a report that draws on multiple sources or encouraging an expert colleague to write a book, guide, or blog post!
- **Visualising** - Visual sense is one of our most dominant. Perhaps this could be combined with relaxation techniques. Thinking of our favourite place and visualising ourselves there bringing in other senses as we progress. Alternatively, why not visualise your team's goals and objectives. People learn differently, so having your team goals written down and in picture format may help some of your team members get more engaged with them.

By incorporating these types of activities into existing working practices or 'gamifying' them for team building we can send the message that mental health isn't just about prevention and recovery, but is also about growth.

HEAD, HEART & GUT

In respect to decision making most of us have been trained culturally to focus on our intellect. Research[6] has shown that intuition can have real impact and act as a fantastic complement to our intellect. In fact, the results of intuition are better than the results of aspirin prescribed for heart attack.

Is intuition always right? No, just like with our intellect, where we can absorb faulty information, intuition can be wrong. The point here is how often do we listen to our head, heart, and gut in order to help make decisions? Do we revert too much to one or the other?

The next time you have to make a low stakes decision, track the reaction in your head, heart, and gut. Notice what you feel and how that informs what you think. Build trust in the approach and develop it as you see fit.

A modern leader should be accessing all of this information through reading and/or the support of professionals. With the help of a coach these 'nuggets' can be incorporated into your leadership style for personal, team, and organisational benefit.

We've now taken a look at improving our thinking. By improving our collective thinking we will take one step towards improving our wellbeing. However, thinking is just one part of mental wellbeing. To achieve our true potential we also need to focus.

FOCUS

		Wellbeing Domains - 'Territories' - Interconnected areas of our lives							
		Mental Our thoughts	Emotional Our emotions	Physical Our actions	Spiritual Our spirit	Social Our communities	Cultural Our way	Environmental Our spaces	Economic Our trade
Wellbeing Dimensions 'Highways' Intertwined routes we use to navigate our lives	Creating meaning	Thinking	Feelings	Behaviour	Identity	Friendship	Way of life	Affinity	Needs
	Achieving potential	Focus	Control	Mastery	Motivation	Teamwork	Governance	Cultivation	Impact
	Nurturing relationships	Regard	Empathy	Interaction	Stories	Trust	Belonging	Cohesion	Fairness
	Building resilience	Flexibility	Agility	Health	Growth	Support	Diversity	Adaptation	Integrity
	Enriching lives	Imagination	Wisdom	Energy	Purpose	Empowerment	Integration	Renewal	Freedom
		Wellbeing Factors - 'Signposts' - Interconnected things that can help us improve wellbeing							

> "Begin with the end in mind...so that the steps you take are always in the right direction."
>
> STEPHEN COVEY

We need to know where we're going if we want to get there, and this requires focus. There are two primary definitions of *focus* in the dictionary. Firstly, it is a noun that refers to the centre of interest or activity. Secondly, it can be a verb that represents a state of mind: paying particular attention to something. Of course, we can also use focus to describe photographic principles. Is the shot 'in focus' or not?

In all of the above instances, focus provides clarity and direction. For individuals, depending where you are on the mental wellbeing spectrum, focus can be provided in a number of ways. For some this could be as simple as thinking about making your bed that morning, going out for a short walk, or talking to someone to ensure you aren't isolated. When people are overwhelmed or distressed a short term focus on daily activities and feeling good about completing them may be what's required. As confidence and capability improves the focus might shift to more medium and longer term goals and activity. The key is to choose the right level of focus for you.

In an organisational or group context focus is provided, in part, by an exciting vision that inspires people and generates enthusiasm to move in a new direction. Following this, people need to understand the plan and steps (objectives/goals) to get there.

THE BIG 'PICTURE'

As a leader, it's our role to paint the big picture and ***create a vision that everyone is excited about***. By aligning this with our purpose, we can create a motivating picture, somewhere where everyone would really like to be. The more vivid and exciting the vision, the more energy we will have to overcome any obstacles along the way. The key here is to make sure we're working on a vision that we all really want to move towards.

PLANNING & PREPARING

Once we've got a better idea of the 'big picture', we can think about planning and preparing how to get where we want to be. Using strategic analysis such as PESTLE and SWOT to *develop a strategy map* is an extremely useful way of capturing purpose, vision, and strategic goals all on one page and getting colleague alignment in the process. This will also help in prioritising key objectives and planning timescales so that we have goals with just the right amount of pressure, but not too much! Here is an example of how the CANBE Model can be used to create a strategy map:

Wellbeing strategy map

	People & purpose (employees, suppliers, customers, shareholders & other stakeholders)	Place Planet, facilities, community	Profit model Not-for-profit, profit, public
	Mental Emotional Physical Spiritual Social Cultural	Environmental	Economic
Creating meaning	Mission – thinking, feelings, identity, friendship, way of life, affinity & needs		
Achieving potential	Strategy – focus, control, mastery, motivation, teamwork, governance, cultivation & impact		
Nurturing relationships	Engagement – regard, empathy, interaction, stories, trust, belonging, cohesion & fairness		
Building resilience	Development – flexibility, agility health, growth, support, diversity, adapting & integrity		
Enriching lives	Experience – imagination, wisdom, energy, purpose, empowerment, integration, renewal & freedom		

We obviously then want to make sure that people are engaged in the strategy and understand the roles they have to play. Asking them to align their individual objectives to the strategic ones and encouraging discussions around this with colleagues and managers is an excellent way of checking understanding.

Linking back to the section on creating meaning, think about how you can set goals that are more in line with your personality, character, values, beliefs and purpose and they will mean more to you. People generally don't work to achieve organisational goals. People work to achieve personal goals. This goes back to thinking about 'who' we are and what we want as opposed to what we do.

These discussions can yield useful and creative insights. Obviously these goals need to be balanced with organisational ones, but taking this approach will make them SMARTER (Specific, Measureable, Achievable, Realistic, Timed, *Emotional/Exciting*, and Recorded). SMART goals just aren't enough. They miss a key element. Goals need to be **emotional** and **exciting** to make you want to achieve them in the first place!

This kind of thinking is far more prevalent in the creative industries. A colleague of mine is a novelist. He regularly gets people giving him suggestions of what to write his story about: "You should write a rom-com, because they're popular right now", "You should write about x trend or y news-story". My colleague's response is always simple and honest: "I could write about those things, but they don't really interest or excite me."

The reality is, he is not going to spend months writing 70,000 words or more purely to produce something commercial that 'might' sell; he knows he will not be able to produce quality where there is no passion. He is excited by certain types of story and those are the stories he works on. Whilst this might seem obvious in this example, it's amazing how we can forget this when we come to think about other less artistic businesses. Consider times when your organisation may have pursued a project but there was no passion in the team. Now, ask yourself how you could have made it more exciting and write down the answers! You might surprise yourself with your own innovation.

Finally, make sure goals are written down and on display to remind people what they are working towards.

THE RIGHT AMOUNT OF PRESSURE

When thinking about the timing element of goal setting it's worth reflecting on Parkinson's Law which says that "work expands so as to fill the time available for its completion"[1]. Wellbeing isn't about giving people more time than they need, but it is about setting challenging goals that stretch people. Obviously goals that are unachievable or consistently require overtime to complete will eventually lead to burn out for yourself and your people. It's about finding the right level of pressure for the individual. For some this could be very low and for others extremely high.

PRIORITISING

Building on this let's take a look at *time management*. The first point here is we can't manage time, we can only manage ourselves. However, there are many tips and tricks to help us use the time we have better. Richard Koch in *The 80/20 Principle – The Secret of Achieving More with Less* provides clear examples of how the *Pareto Principle* shows that 80% of results flow from just 20% of activities[2]. A good starting point, then, is to identify our most 'valuable' activities and give them more focus using tools such as 'important and urgent', which we'll come onto very shortly.

In terms of scheduling activity, the *concept of 'fixed' and 'variable' time* is also extremely useful. The idea here is that we try to 'fix' as many of our tasks as possible and schedule them into regular slots in our calendar. You'll find you can do this with more tasks than you think.

So, for example, emails can be 'fixed' into scheduled time slots rather than reactively responding to and sending them throughout the day. Leaving variable time to respond to unexpected activities or crises is always a good idea. If you find your calendar is fully booked day in, day out there's probably something wrong and you'll need to look at your priorities, workload, and think about opportunities to delegate. One tool you can use to help prioritise was kindly provided by President Eisenhower.

In a 1954 speech to the Second Assembly of the World Council of Churches, former U.S. President Eisenhower said: "I have two kinds of problems: the urgent and the important. The urgent are not important, and the important are never urgent." This "Eisenhower Principle" is said to be how he organised his workload and priorities.

Based on this principle, Stephen Covey developed a 4 box model which asks the user to categorise tasks as either 'Important and

Urgent', 'Important Not Urgent', 'Urgent Not Important' or 'Not Urgent or Important'. The idea being that we do the important and urgent tasks first with the ultimate aim being to focus more and more of our time on tasks that are deemed 'important not urgent'. These tasks are more likely to be 'strategic' and require greater thought.

Important and Urgent	**Important Not Urgent**
• Crises and pressing problems • Fire fighting • Deadlines	• Planning • Prevention • Opportunities • Learning/Development • Relationships
Urgent not Important • Interruptions • Other people's problems	**Not Urgent or Important** • Trivial • Time wasting

When used as part of a daily to do list and the 'pruning' methods, outlined next, this can be a powerful way to greater efficiency and effectiveness and can help with strategic, team, and personal prioritisation.

PRUNING

Sometimes it can be as much about what we *don't* do as opposed to what we do. We can play a role here by ***pruning*** personal, team, and organisational distractions. Models such as the 4Ds (Do, Ditch, Delegate, Dump), or SMOG (Should, Must, Ought, Got to), RAFT (Refer, Act, File, Throw) or Bank, Build, Bin can be used to facilitate discussions at personal, team, and organisational levels in these areas. Learning to say no by providing a REASON, politely REFUSING whilst suggesting options for a REMEDY or alternative solution, is also a great way to keep focused.

Another area worth covering here is the removal of distractions. An article on the BBC News website quotes Professor Gloria Mark of the Department of Informatics at the University of California who says "email, social media, notifications and countless other digital distractions are eroding our ability to concentrate on individual tasks in the 21st Century."[3]

Attention span is getting shorter, and whilst people do respond differently to distractions, it appears that loss of time is made up for by working quicker. This can often result in higher workload, more stress, higher frustration, more time pressure and effort. Tips like turning off RSS feeds, removing desktop shortcuts or any unnecessary choice in our workday, and setting rules such as only checking email once or twice a day can all help.

By helping people improve focus, planning, prioritisation and use of time they will be more effective. Ensuring they have the right resources and support gives them a greater chance of success. Helping them learn through feedback, measuring results and rewarding accomplishments leads to continual improvement.

Research has established that psychological wellbeing is directly correlated with performance[4]. Wright and Cropanzano report two field studies which both demonstrate positive relationships between levels of psychological wellbeing and job performance.

Using meta-analysis techniques, Harter et al. analysed data from nearly 8,000 separate business units in 36 companies. They found significant relationships between scores on an employee survey and business unit level outcomes, such as customer satisfaction, productivity, profitability, employee turnover and sickness/absence levels[5].

More recently, Robertson Cooper and the Bank Workers Charity found that psychological wellbeing does influence productivity, with survey results indicating that bank workers in the top 25% of reported psychological wellbeing are, on average, 30% more productive than those in the bottom quartile[6].

So it's clear that wellbeing influences performance. As a leader, we can improve wellbeing by using the CANBE Model, and this in turn can improve performance. Win, win!

So far, we've looked at how improving our thinking and focus can help build our mental wellbeing. Linked closely to these two topics is the regard we hold for ourselves and others.

REGARD

		Wellbeing Domains - 'Territories' - Interconnected areas of our lives							
		Mental Our thoughts	**Emotional** Our emotions	**Physical** Our actions	**Spiritual** Our spirit	**Social** Our communities	**Cultural** Our way	**Environmental** Our spaces	**Economic** Our trade
Wellbeing Dimensions 'Highways' Intertwined routes we use to navigate our lives	Creating meaning	Thinking	Feelings	Behaviour	Identity	Friendship	Way of life	Affinity	Needs
	Achieving potential	Focus	Control	Mastery	Motivation	Teamwork	Governance	Cultivation	Impact
	Nurturing relationships	Regard	Empathy	Interaction	Stories	Trust	Belonging	Cohesion	Fairness
	Building resilience	Flexibility	Agility	Health	Growth	Support	Diversity	Adaptation	Integrity
	Enriching lives	Imagination	Wisdom	Energy	Purpose	Empowerment	Integration	Renewal	Freedom
		Wellbeing Factors - 'Signposts' - Interconnected things that can help us improve wellbeing							

"Judge that ye be not judged."

MATTHEW 7:1

"I will speak ill of no man and all the good I know of everybody."

BENJAMIN FRANKLIN

Regard is really about how we think about ourselves and others. It is made up of a complex mixture of attitudes in our unconscious emotional brain and needs feeding with the right thoughts to stay healthy.

SELF-REGARD

This is about valuing ourselves as a person, for who we are, not what we do. It's about liking and accepting ourselves and can be described in terms of high or low self-esteem.

This links to character strengths which we look at in greater detail in the chapter on Spiritual Wellbeing. We are more likely to have higher self-esteem if we are living authentically in line with our character strengths, values, personality and beliefs, rather than constantly having to compromise them.

With high self-regard, we will more likely value diversity and accept others for who they are. We'll be more accurately aware of our personal strengths and weaknesses and open to honest feedback.

A good indication of self-regard is our reaction to feedback. When people say negative things, do we dwell on them, blow them out of proportion, or take it too personally? If you get positive feedback, do you dismiss it, feel embarrassed, or put it down to luck?

If this is the case, we can learn to change our self-image. If we feel good about ourselves, we'll perform better. We can do this by reminding ourselves about our strengths, learning to accept good feedback with humility, and understanding that no-one can make us feel good or bad. It's only the way we choose to react to what people say, or do, that makes us feel good or bad. We must choose carefully.

REGARD FOR OTHERS

Stephen Covey writes in *The 7 Habits of Highly Effective People*: "Who is the truly objective person, the person who knows that he is not."[1] When we can view the actions and words of people in respect to their values and not our own, we will be able to show them higher regard. We might not necessarily agree with them, but at least we'll have a better understanding.

If we're constantly judging people against our own set of values, how can we possibly hope to understand them better? Having high regard for others involves separating who they are from what they do and valuing them as people.

It also involves being more flexible by holding our personal values, beliefs, and attitudes more 'lightly' rather than being fixed and 'hard'.

FLEXIBILITY

		Wellbeing Domains - 'Territories' - Interconnected areas of our lives							
		Mental Our thoughts	Emotional Our emotions	Physical Our actions	Spiritual Our spirit	Social Our communities	Cultural Our way	Environmental Our spaces	Economic Our trade
Wellbeing Dimensions 'Highways' Intertwined routes we use to navigate our lives	Creating meaning	Thinking	Feelings	Behaviour	Identity	Friendship	Way of life	Affinity	Needs
	Achieving potential	Focus	Control	Mastery	Motivation	Teamwork	Governance	Cultivation	Impact
	Nurturing relationships	Regard	Empathy	Interaction	Stories	Trust	Belonging	Cohesion	Fairness
	Building resilience	Flexibility	Agility	Health	Growth	Support	Diversity	Adaptation	Integrity
	Enriching lives	Imagination	Wisdom	Energy	Purpose	Empowerment	Integration	Renewal	Freedom
		Wellbeing Factors - 'Signposts' - Interconnected things that can help us improve wellbeing							

'Failure is an event never a person.'

ZIG ZIGLAR

DEVELOPING A GROWTH MIND-SET

Carol Dweck is the Lewis and Virginia Eaton Professor of Psychology at Stanford University, best known for her work on mindset. In *Mindset: The New Psychology of Success,* she describes both a fixed and growth mindset[1].

A 'Fixed Mindset' is characterised by a belief that our qualities are carved in stone. If we have a fixed mindset, we'll work hard to hide our weaknesses, think things are the way they are, and be less resilient in the face of obstacles. Getting things right becomes our focus and we acquire a fear of failure. We might say things like: "I just can't remember people's names."

On the contrary a 'Growth Mindset' is characterised by a belief that our basic qualities are things that can be cultivated through effort. We embrace failure as an opportunity and focus on making progress and the processes that enable learning and growth. We might say: "I'm getting better at remembering people's names."

Skills and abilities are malleable. People aren't born as great leaders, elite athletes, or eminent scientists. Whilst Dweck argues that mindset does play a role in the development of "natural" talent, her book also dispels the myth about the lone, brilliant person suddenly producing amazing things. It demonstrates that behind every great person there is a lot of hard work, effort, and often a supportive team. Mozart, for example, worked for a decade before he wrote anything memorable.

It's clear that we can have a fixed mindset in regard to some traits and a growth mindset in regard to others. As a leader, we must listen to our inner voice to understand when we need to make adjustments. Where you identify opportunities for growth, try learning from others you admire, or that you feel are better at a particular task, or do something that stretches you out of your comfort zone. Change your language, rather than saying 'We failed' use 'We're not there yet.'

As outlined in 'Nurturing Relationships', in the section on feedback, use praise wisely. Praise the process a person has been through and the unique personality and characteristics they have applied to it and let the outcomes take care of themselves. I have heard many athletes talking about 'trusting in the process.' The ultimate outcome in their particular activity is outside of their control because of the actions of the referee, their competitors, the weather, and even spectators. What they can focus on is 'the process': their day to day training, reflecting and learning, small incremental improvements in their performance, diet, sleep, clothing, the build-up, acclimatising, preparing for their event, and all the other things they can do to be their best on the day.

Imagine if their coach only ever praised them if they won their race or achieved a personal best? How motivated do you think they would be to put in all of the hard work and effort it takes to be an Olympian? As a leader, if we praise the process and encourage our people to learn from mistakes, the results will surely follow. Developing a growth mind-set increases resilience, motivation, and productivity because it allows people to see failure as part of the process, pick themselves up and go again.

At an organisational level Dweck found that when she asked employees at Fortune 500 companies they could even name whether their company was characterised by a growth or fixed mind-set. Employees in the growth mind-set company were found to be more committed and more likely to take risks, as they knew their company would support them. These companies tend to seek employees who can address deficiencies and find solutions rather than employing for talent alone. They believe everyone can develop their abilities and provide opportunities for growth, mentoring, and coaching.

If we have a growth mindset, we also open ourselves up to new possibilities. This is the subject of our next section, imagination and creativity.

IMAGINATION

		Wellbeing Domains - 'Territories' - Interconnected areas of our lives							
		Mental Our thoughts	**Emotional** Our emotions	**Physical** Our actions	**Spiritual** Our spirit	**Social** Our communities	**Cultural** Our way	**Environmental** Our spaces	**Economic** Our trade
Wellbeing Dimensions 'Highways' Intertwined routes we use to navigate our lives	Creating meaning	Thinking	Feelings	Behaviour	Identity	Friendship	Way of life	Affinity	Needs
	Achieving potential	Focus	Control	Mastery	Motivation	Teamwork	Governance	Cultivation	Impact
	Nurturing relation-ships	Regard	Empathy	Interaction	Stories	Trust	Belonging	Cohesion	Fairness
	Building resilience	Flexibility	Agility	Health	Growth	Support	Diversity	Adaptation	Integrity
	Enriching lives	Imagination	Wisdom	Energy	Purpose	Empowerment	Integration	Renewal	Freedom
		Wellbeing Factors - 'Signposts' - Interconnected things that can help us improve wellbeing							

"There is nothing like a dream to create the future."

VICTOR HUGO

I'm using the terms creativity and imagination interchangeably here, but they are not really the same thing. Imagination is the tendency to think of new ideas and concepts. Creativity consists of divergent thinking, the ability to come up with lots of new ideas and concepts, and convergent thinking, the ability to sift and process those ideas into useful, functional solutions to the problem or opportunity at hand. It is clear that there is some overlap, but to be truly useful we need to turn our ideas into actions using creativity.

Imaginative and creative behaviour are both a cause and effect of positive emotions and wellbeing[1]. People feel good when they are able to create and imagine, but they are also often able to create and imagine better if they are in a good mood and have high levels of wellbeing.

We explored some of the ways to improve imagination and creative thinking earlier in the section on 'Thoughts', and in particular, developing mental capability. Let's explore these a little further and share some additional ideas.

CHANGING THE STORY

As the author of our stories, we are in the enviable position of being able to change them. Of course, we won't be able to change everything, and adaptability and flexibility involves recognising what we can and can't change and also thinking about things differently.

"If you see as you always see, and do as you always do, you'll get what you always get." What could you do to encourage greater flexibility and adaptability personally, in your team, and the wider organisation? One way of doing this is to put ourselves in the shoes of someone we admire, someone with expertise in the problem-area we face, and think about what they would do in this situation.

THINKING LIKE SOMEONE ELSE

Creativity in the business world is increasingly important and this often involves viewing things from different perspectives. New findings show that we are more creative when we think of others solving problems instead of ourselves. Professors Evan Polman and Kyle Emich asked 137 undergraduates the following riddle[2]:

"A prisoner was attempting to escape from a tower. He found a rope in his cell that was half as long enough to permit him to reach the ground safely. He divided the rope in half, tied the two parts together, and escaped. How could he have done this?"

They divided the participants into two groups. They asked the first group to imagine themselves as the prisoner locked inside the tower and the other half in a second group to imagine someone else trapped in the imaginary prison. In the first group, those locked in the tower, less than half (48%) of participants solved the riddle. In the second group, nearly two-thirds (66%) found the solution.

The answer: The prisoner split the rope in half lengthwise, tied the two halves together, and climbed down!

As a leader, we can use this approach to look at things differently in our business. Think of yourself as a supplier, customer, investor or competitor. What would they do in your situation?

6 THINKING HATS

A similar approach is that of Edward de Bono with his 6 thinking hats, each of a different colour. The hats are designed to encourage thinking from different perspectives including:

1. Blue – process, thinking about thinking, summarising, concluding and decision making.
2. Green – provocative, creative thinking and new ideas.
3. Yellow – harmony, positivity and benefits.
4. Red - feelings, intuition, and emotion without justification.
5. White - the facts, data and new information required.
6. Black – caution, critical judgement, practical and realistic.

The synchronicity with which the hats are worn, either literally or metaphorically, can be changed according to the needs of the group or individual. In groups, the hats can encourage greater collaboration through aligning the thoughts of team members at each thinking stage and getting everyone focused in the same direction.

MINDFULNESS

The myth of creativity being a right brain activity has long been dispelled. Creativity is a process which involves both open minded unconstrained thinking, to generate ideas and possibilities, and focused, critical attention to sift and whittle down those ideas and concepts into final solutions. As such it involves cooperation between large scale brain networks linked to cognitive control and spontaneous thought. So how can we increase the propensity for creative thinking and imagination in ourselves and others?

Certain types of mindfulness training such as open monitoring meditation can help increase connections between large scale networks in the brain that aid creative thinking. Forms of meditation, such as self-compassion, can also help us regulate and let go of emotions that may restrict creativity.

COMPASSION

Research has also demonstrated that increased self-compassion, through alleviating self-critical tendencies, can help to support creative expression among certain individuals[3]. I would speculate that if individuals are less worried about making mistakes, achieving perfection or judgement from others they can be more relaxed about generating new ideas. We'll explore compassion in more detail later in the book.

POSITIVE CONSTRUCTIVE DAYDREAMING

As we explored earlier, some of the research on mind wandering and daydreaming present them as activities which are detrimental to well-being. However, when used in the right way, they can help us become more self-aware, think of new ideas, improvise, refresh our memory, plan our future, reflect and think of others; so there are many benefits.

More recent research[4] has demonstrated the importance of the *context* and *content* of our daydreaming to whether it has a beneficial impact on our wellbeing. In essence, the greater our intention to daydream, and to remain non-judgmental of our thoughts as we do it, the more beneficial it may be. It would also seem to make sense that the contents of the daydream affect wellbeing and that these can be primed.

So, as leaders, rather than dismissing daydreaming perhaps we should be encouraging it more. Of course this needs to be managed carefully and research would lead us to believe that the following should be considered:

- Back it up with *mindfulness* training and support
- Make it more *intentional* through provision of time and appropriate space
- Create a positive *environment* and experience
- Carefully consider the *content* such as self-reflection, creative incubation, problem solving, goal planning and short breaks from tasks

One of the key personality traits linked closely with positive constructive daydreaming is 'openness to experience'. This has also been identified as a key contributor to creativity and here are a few ideas about how to develop it further.

OPENNESS TO NEW IDEAS AND EXPERIENCES

Different creative endeavours require different skills. Whilst linguistic skills are more relevant to creative writing, visual and spatial awareness are skills more aligned to artistic creativity. However across creative activities one trait has been found to be a common facilitator of creativity. Openness to new experiences is one of the Big Five Personality traits. We can develop this trait by changing our behaviours. If you're used to travelling the same way to work each day try a different route. If you eat the same things in the same places, try something different. Speak to new people, try a new hobby. Whatever it is, by opening yourself up to new experiences you can begin to open your mind to new possibilities.

CREATIVE TIME

Of course, all of the activities we've mentioned above require time. If we're constantly working on our project or trying to solve a particular problem we may have no time to think differently. Taking some time out and changing our environment can be a great way to give ourselves some space and time to think. Some well known companies have done this by providing employees with spaces and time which they can devote to creative activities or projects of their choice. These are times for experimentation, trial and error.

CHAPTER SUMMARY

Improving mental wellbeing is not just about managing stress, anxiety or depression. We must begin to think of mental wellbeing the way we do about physical wellbeing. There is a spectrum from *thriving* to *suffering* which everyone is on. Everyone can do work to improve in some way.

This starts with improving our *thinking*. We can learn to manage our bias, choose to reflect rather than ruminate, remove negative distractions and become more mindful. By overcoming worries and fears we can learn to build confidence and develop a more optimistic outlook. We can also develop our mental capability and begin using our head, heart, and gut to make better decisions.

Improving our *focus* through an engaging vision, strategy, goals and objectives can provide us with greater direction. Having high *regard* by thinking positively about ourselves and others will put us in the best position to develop strong personal relationships.

By thinking *flexibly*, we will be able to adapt to obstacles and overcome problems more effectively. And by using our *imagination* and creativity, we will enrich our lives and open up to new possibilities.

Imagine if we all improved our mental wellbeing by just 5%. What if we could remove much of the distress that many people in the world suffer today, whilst also improving our imagination? What could we create?

I think by re-evaluating mental wellbeing in this way, we can begin to create a better world. But better 'thinking' is just one part of our wellbeing. We also need to consider how we feel: our emotional wellbeing; what we do: our physical wellbeing; and who we are: our spiritual wellbeing. We'll come to these chapters in due course, but before we do, here are a few key concepts and thoughts to get you started on the road to better mental wellbeing:

KEY CONCEPTS TO IMPROVE MENTAL WELLBEING

Leaders should address the full spectrum of mental wellbeing at individual, team and group levels. In addition to supporting those people who are suffering with poor mental wellbeing you can do this by thinking about the key challenges and opportunities you and your people face in the following areas:

Improving Thinking:

- Understanding and managing bias and heuristics
- Reflecting rather than ruminating
- Being more present and mindful
- Avoiding unnecessary or unplanned distractions and mind wandering
- Overcoming anxieties, worry and fear

- Developing confidence
- Developing realistic optimism
- Exercising our minds like we do our bodies
- Using our head, heart, and gut to make decisions. Managing rational, emotional and intuitive thinking.

Improving Focus:

- Developing an exciting vision of where you want to be
- Producing a strategy for getting there
- Setting performance goals and objectives
- Role modelling and personal efficacy - being efficient, effective and organised
- Regular planning and refinement
- Ensuring that there are the right amounts of pressure
- Effective prioritisation

Improving Regard:

- Developing healthy levels of self esteem
- Having high levels of regard and respect for others

Improving Flexibility of our Mindset:

- Developing growth mindset
- Developing stress mindset

Improving Imagination:

- Being open to new ideas
- Changing our story - we are the authors
- Developing ideas through thinking differently
- Using mindfulness and compassion to imagine better futures

- Turning ideas into action through creativity
- Planning creative time and positive constructive daydreaming

KEY BEHAVIOURS:

Now we've reviewed and summarised the core concepts covered in this chapter where do you score on the following behaviours that contribute to personal, team and organisational mental wellbeing? Feel free to answer this on either an individual, team or organisational basis. Plot your score at each attribute on either the thriving, striving, surviving, struggling or suffering axis.

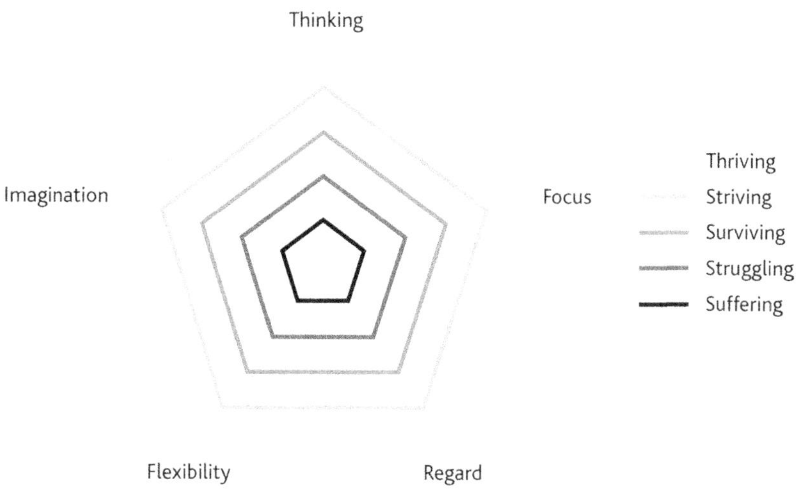

Now, what is the one most important or interesting thing you would like to do to improve?

CHAPTER SIX

IMPROVING EMOTIONAL WELLBEING

		Wellbeing Domains - 'Territories' - Interconnected areas of our lives							
		Mental Our thoughts	Emotional Our emotions	Physical Our actions	Spiritual Our spirit	Social Our communities	Cultural Our way	Environmental Our spaces	Economic Our trade
Wellbeing Dimensions 'Highways' Intertwined routes we use to navigate our lives	Creating meaning	Thinking	Feelings	Behaviour	Identity	Friendship	Way of life	Affinity	Needs
	Achieving potential	Focus	Control	Mastery	Motivation	Teamwork	Governance	Cultivation	Impact
	Nurturing relationships	Regard	Empathy	Interaction	Stories	Trust	Belonging	Cohesion	Fairness
	Building resilience	Flexibility	Agility	Health	Growth	Support	Diversity	Adaptation	Integrity
	Enriching lives	Imagination	Wisdom	Energy	Purpose	Empowerment	Integration	Renewal	Freedom
		Wellbeing Factors - 'Signposts' - Interconnected things that can help us improve wellbeing							

"When dealing with people, remember you are not dealing with creatures of logic, but with creatures of emotion."

DALE CARNEGIE

We outlined in the introduction that leadership is about *inspiring positive change in both people and process.* Providing people with a vision of a better place and then defining the best path to get there. Our role as leaders is to inspire relationships with and between people to help them move to this better place. To do this will require both intelligence (IQ) and emotional intelligence (EQ).

Emotional intelligence simply means being smarter with feelings. People who use their emotional intelligence skills do better at work, are more effective, have stronger relationships, and a higher quality of life.

The impact we can have by effectively managing our emotions both in and outside of the workplace is huge. Research undertaken by Fowler and Christakis[1] found that our own happiness influences the people we work with and the people they know. They found that the happiness of a close contact increases the chance of being happy by 15%. The happiness of a 2nd-degree contact (e.g. friend's friend) increases it by 10% and the happiness of a 3rd-degree contact (e.g. friend of a friend of a friend) by 6%. So as a leader we really can spread the love, or the fear! We can influence others with our negative emotions too.

Many leaders are promoted to their positions because of IQ and their technical ability and/or knowledge of the role. It's clear that a level of competence is required and expected for leaders to be successful. However, this isn't the full story, and EQ has been shown to contribute significantly, through numerous studies, to the success of managers and leaders.

Emotional wellbeing is about understanding and coping with the emotions we feel in reaction to circumstances and events that happen in our lives. This starts with **regard** for ourself and others, which we covered under mental wellbeing. Building on this, we need awareness of both our own **feelings** and those in other people. Understanding emotions helps us think about how to harness and **control** our response to achieve the best outcome.

Another key element of emotional intelligence is **empathy**, the ability to understand others and feel what they are feeling. Emotional wellbeing isn't just about positive emotions. It is great to feel happy, excited, or proud, for example, and these emotions help us develop a healthy emotional outlook. However, we won't feel good all the time, and nor should we expect to. Sometimes it is appropriate to feel angry, sad, or even fearful. These emotions can help protect us from harmful situations or recover during periods of mourning or loss.

So rather than just seeking to develop positive emotions we should be focusing on, what Susan David referred to in her book of the same name as, Emotional **Agility**. Emotional agility is the ability to manage our emotional response in the right way for the right person at the right time.

Finally through a combination of understanding our feelings, controlling our response, demonstrating empathy and emotional agility we can develop **wisdom** and maturity. Rather than appearing **impulsive** and reactionary we will be **composed** and calm in our emotional response to get the best out of each interaction.

Let's now take a look at each of these elements of emotional wellbeing in a little more detail.

FEELINGS

		Wellbeing Domains - 'Territories' - Interconnected areas of our lives							
		Mental Our thoughts	Emotional Our emotions	Physical Our actions	Spiritual Our spirit	Social Our communities	Cultural Our way	Environmental Our spaces	Economic Our trade
Wellbeing Dimensions 'Highways' Intertwined routes we use to navigate our lives	Creating meaning	Thinking	Feelings	Behaviour	Identity	Friendship	Way of life	Affinity	Needs
	Achieving potential	Focus	Control	Mastery	Motivation	Teamwork	Governance	Cultivation	Impact
	Nurturing relationships	Regard	Empathy	Interaction	Stories	Trust	Belonging	Cohesion	Fairness
	Building resilience	Flexibility	Agility	Health	Growth	Support	Diversity	Adaptation	Integrity
	Enriching lives	Imagination	Wisdom	Energy	Purpose	Empowerment	Integration	Renewal	Freedom
		Wellbeing Factors - 'Signposts' - Interconnected things that can help us improve wellbeing							

> "Our feelings are not there to be cast out or conquered. They're there to be engaged and expressed with imagination and intelligence."
>
> T.K. COLEMAN

The two words, feelings and emotions are often used interchangeably. Research in the area is evolving so at present there is no one accepted description of how they differ.

However there appears to be general support for the concept that feelings are how we create meaning from our emotions. Emotional reactions, which are coded in our genes, are biologically universally similar among humans and are linked more with our instincts, producing quick physical reactions to threats or rewards. Emotions have intensity. Higher intensity emotions may be harder to manage. Think of 'flying into a rage' versus feeling dis-satisfied with the customer service you just received.

Feelings on the other hand are the mental portrayal of our emotions such as when we experience pleasure or pain. In the short term they may influence our mood or, when experienced over the longer term, can develop into an attitude or established way of thinking.

Just as we need to learn how to think we also need to learn how to feel. Many people can be dismissive or avoidant of their feelings or project them onto others. But we can't learn from our feelings if we seek to bury or deflect them. We must learn to understand, hold and reflect on our feelings. Managed well, our feelings provide us with energy and motivation adding real colour and flavour to our lives.

One of the first things we can do to manage them better is to understand them.

SELF-AWARENESS

Self-awareness is about being in touch with our intuition and feelings, noticing what our body is telling us, and the impact of this on our behaviour.

Sayings like: 'I've got cold feet', 'Hot under the collar', 'I've got a gut feeling' might spring to mind. Another example could be when we feel energised by some people and not by others. How does this impact our behaviour?

As outlined previously, intuition, just as with intellect, can be both right and wrong. The key here is whether we are using all of the information, both intellectual and emotional, to help inform our behaviours. If we allow our emotions to hijack our thinking, then problems can arise. Equally if we intellectualise everything and never listen to our intuition, we could be missing out on some important signals.

We can improve self-awareness by beginning to give greater attention to our emotions. Naming them can really help in understanding and managing them before they manage us.

AWARENESS OF OTHERS

This is about tuning in to the feelings and states of others, picking up on what they say and other non-verbal cues like their body language. It's about showing genuine interest in and empathy with others.

CONTROL

		Wellbeing Domains - 'Territories' - Interconnected areas of our lives							
		Mental Our thoughts	Emotional Our emotions	Physical Our actions	Spiritual Our spirit	Social Our communities	Cultural Our way	Environmental Our spaces	Economic Our trade
Wellbeing Dimensions 'Highways' Intertwined routes we use to navigate our lives	Creating meaning	Thinking	Feelings	Behaviour	Identity	Friendship	Way of life	Affinity	Needs
	Achieving potential	Focus	Control	Mastery	Motivation	Teamwork	Governance	Cultivation	Impact
	Nurturing relationships	Regard	Empathy	Interaction	Stories	Trust	Belonging	Cohesion	Fairness
	Building resilience	Flexibility	Agility	Health	Growth	Support	Diversity	Adaptation	Integrity
	Enriching lives	Imagination	Wisdom	Energy	Purpose	Empowerment	Integration	Renewal	Freedom
		Wellbeing Factors - 'Signposts' - Interconnected things that can help us improve wellbeing							

"Any person capable of angering you becomes your master."

EPICTETUS

To be clear, I am not referring to controlling our emotions here, but rather how we *control the response to our emotions*. Daniel Goleman, author of the New York Times best seller *Emotional Intelligence*[1], coined the term 'emotional hijack' for the times when we allow our attitudes, and the emotions they generate, to take over from our thinking and behaviours.

When was the last time you allowed this to happen? Stuck in traffic when someone jumped the queue, a slow or crashed computer, or a disagreement with someone at work? What was the outcome? I'm guessing it was probably not as favourable as it could have been had you managed your response better. The fact is, being in control of our emotional response and able to empathise with others makes it easier to get on.

But how to control our emotional response? Earlier in the book we discussed embodiment, the concept that we experience wellbeing through the experience of our thoughts, feelings, and actions, and that each influences the other. It makes sense then that if we want to manage our feelings better we should look at their relationship with our thoughts and actions.

The first thing we can do is to think about the way we think about our feelings. Naming and noticing our emotions, including our physical response can be very helpful as outlined previously. Through this process we begin to understand the people, things, places and events that trigger our different emotions and can plan accordingly. For example, if we become irritated by a particular route on our commute to work then we can take action to leave earlier and avoid traffic, or go a different way. Or, if we feel a sense of enthusiasm and joy by being with a particular person we can plan to spend more time with them.

Our thinking may also be the thing leading to negative emotions in the first place. Leadership is demanding and often comes with high expectations. As a leader, it is easy to set expectations too high or too low. This in turn can lead to frustration, disillusionment or feeling disengaged and unmotivated. Changing the thinking and expectations of our team or individuals within it, including ourselves, may lead to better feelings. With better feelings we typically see better performance!

As we learned earlier our actions can also help us feel better. One simple technique is to learn to pause in the gap between the emotion we feel and the action we take. This small window of opportunity has played a huge part in history so shouldn't be underestimated.

One example of this came during the Battle of Gettysburg in the American Civil War. General Robert E. Lee's army was retreating but got held up due to a flood in the river. General George Meade, with 20,000 men, had failed to attack and almost certainly end the war. Shortly afterwards, Abraham Lincoln composed a letter in which he expressed his profound disappointment in Meade's inability. However, Lincoln did not send the letter. Writing such correspondence and storing it away was a favourite coping strategy he used. Lincoln knew how to pause.

Breathing exercises can also be an effective way to calm ourselves if we're feeling anxious, overwhelmed or overly excited. Placing our hand on our heart and feeling the rise and fall of our chest as we breathe in and exhale can help us remain in the present. Physiologically it gets more oxygen into our bloodstream, taking the pressure off our heart to pump blood quicker around our body.

Another simple action includes walking away from a situation where our emotional response might get the better of us in the short term. Similar to pausing, this can give us time to respond more effectively, or choose to stay away from the person or situation altogether.

Depending on the relationship we have with someone, effective communication can also be a great way to manage our emotional response. By effective I mean keeping the conversation centred on actions rather than personal comments. There is a reason that the Red Arrows, the elite performance team of the Royal Air Force, refer to each other as Red 1, Red 2 and so on when providing feedback. It makes it less personal. It becomes more about the actions that each pilot takes, rather than who they are as a person. A simple technique here is to talk about how we feel in response to the action of the other person - "When you do [that action] ... it makes me feel."

Finally, we can use actions like exercise or meditation to help release or manage emotions and feelings. These actions can be both proactive, helping us to manage emotions better in the future, and reactive, helping us let go of emotions from the past.

Of course, there are many other things you might like to try to help manage your emotions and feelings, but thinking about it in terms of how you can change the relationship between your thoughts, feelings, and actions is hopefully a useful pointer.

This is also relevant within a team and organisational context. When we see actions that need to change, what are the thoughts and feelings associated with those actions? How can we help our people think and feel differently about the actions we would like to see? Similarly, if people aren't thinking constructively, what are the feelings and actions that might be influencing their thoughts?

This brings us to understanding the feelings of others.

EMPATHY

		Wellbeing Domains - 'Territories' - Interconnected areas of our lives							
		Mental Our thoughts	Emotional Our emotions	Physical Our actions	Spiritual Our spirit	Social Our communities	Cultural Our way	Environmental Our spaces	Economic Our trade
Wellbeing Dimensions 'Highways' Intertwined routes we use to navigate our lives	Creating meaning	Thinking	Feelings	Behaviour	Identity	Friendship	Way of life	Affinity	Needs
	Achieving potential	Focus	Control	Mastery	Motivation	Teamwork	Governance	Cultivation	Impact
	Nurturing relationships	Regard	Empathy	Interaction	Stories	Trust	Belonging	Cohesion	Fairness
	Building resilience	Flexibility	Agility	Health	Growth	Support	Diversity	Adaptation	Integrity
	Enriching lives	Imagination	Wisdom	Energy	Purpose	Empowerment	Integration	Renewal	Freedom
		Wellbeing Factors - 'Signposts' - Interconnected things that can help us improve wellbeing							

"Seek first to understand, then to be understood."

STEPHEN COVEY

"When you listen with empathy to another person, you give that person psychological air."

STEPHEN COVEY

Empathy, from the Greek 'empatheia' meaning 'feeling into', is when others know you have a sense of what they are feeling through actively listening to what they are telling you. Sympathy is when we understand, on an intellectual level, the suffering of others without feeling what they feel. It is one step removed.

Empathy, on the other hand, is when we reach a stage of such deep sympathy that we feel the suffering of others as our own. This is far more powerful in building a connection with someone, and understanding the plight of people around us. It's about being moved by others.

Perhaps the most compelling evidence for the strength of empathy in animals came from a group of psychiatrists led by Jules Masserman at Northwestern University. In 1964, the researchers reported in the American Journal of Psychiatry, that rhesus monkeys refused to pull a chain that delivered food to themselves if doing so gave a shock to a companion. One monkey stopped pulling the chain for 12 days after witnessing another monkey receive a shock. The primates were literally starving themselves to avoid shocking another animal. We have a fantastic ability to empathise with others.

Alongside the following, *empathy* is a key part of our overall emotional intelligence:

- *Regard*, which we considered under Mental Wellbeing,
- Awareness of our *feelings* and the feelings of others and being able to *control* our emotional response, which we considered earlier in this chapter
- Key social skills which we'll consider when we look at *communications* under Physical Wellbeing

We can develop empathy by making sure we give people our full attention through active listening and avoiding distractions. We must put our own biases and perspectives to one side and try 'walking in their shoes'. Finally, by asking questions to really understand their point of view, we'll be better able to see and feel things the way they do.

Showing we know how someone feels is sometimes all that is required so they know we're on their side. However, there are also times when people need more, and this is the subject of compassion, which we'll come onto when we discuss support in the chapter on Social Wellbeing.

AGILITY

		Wellbeing Domains - 'Territories' - Interconnected areas of our lives							
		Mental Our thoughts	Emotional Our emotions	Physical Our actions	Spiritual Our spirit	Social Our communities	Cultural Our way	Environmental Our spaces	Economic Our trade
Wellbeing Dimensions 'Highways' Intertwined routes we use to navigate our lives	Creating meaning	Thinking	Feelings	Behaviour	Identity	Friendship	Way of life	Affinity	Needs
	Achieving potential	Focus	Control	Mastery	Motivation	Teamwork	Governance	Cultivation	Impact
	Nurturing relationships	Regard	Empathy	Interaction	Stories	Trust	Belonging	Cohesion	Fairness
	Building resilience	Flexibility	Agility	Health	Growth	Support	Diversity	Adaptation	Integrity
	Enriching lives	Imagination	Wisdom	Energy	Purpose	Empowerment	Integration	Renewal	Freedom
		Wellbeing Factors - 'Signposts' - Interconnected things that can help us improve wellbeing							

"Anyone can be angry—that is easy. But to be angry with the right person, to the right degree, at the right time, for the right purpose, and in the right way—that is not easy."

ARISTOTLE

"What counts in making a happy relationship is not so much how compatible you are, but how you deal with incompatibility."

DANIEL GOLEMAN

As outlined in the introduction to this chapter emotional agility is about context. With emotional agility we experience a full range of emotions and learn how to use them to our advantage. We begin to own and master our emotions rather than being under their control.

For example, depending on who, what, why, when and where it might be perfectly ok to feel and demonstrate anger. Many people have used anger constructively to do great things in life. So rather than seeing emotions as either good or bad, positive or negative it is good to think and feel more flexibly. When we develop rigid feelings and thoughts about our emotions as either good or bad, positive or negative this can be harmful, particularly when they turn into fixed beliefs, attitudes, mindsets or outlooks.

If, when we experience the emotion of fear, we always feel frightened this could result in avoidance behaviour. If we begin to allow this to permeate across all aspects of our lives we could become fearful of all challenges put before us and miss out on many potentially rewarding opportunities.

If, on the other hand, we become more nuanced about understanding fear we may find new opportunities open up to us. Consider your response to the fear of a venomous snake versus the fear of delivering a presentation to 300 people. In one situation, you might die and the fear would appear to be more rational. In the other, you won't die, and if managed appropriately, you may even benefit from opportunities for growth. Perhaps, if we are brave enough, even the fear of a snake could be re-positioned as healthy respect!

At other points on the spectrum, fear can also be experienced as adventure, enjoyment, or even exhilaration. 'Thrill seekers', horror movie fans and extreme sports participants all experience fear in these different ways.

We are only born with two innate fears, the fear of falling and the fear of loud noises. Both of these are instinctive fears linked to danger and designed for our survival. Other fears are learned based on our culture, experiences and environment. If they are learned then to a great extent they can also be unlearned.

The key to emotional agility is learning to experience, and accept, a full range of emotions and then tailoring our response in respect to the context in which we find ourselves. One way of facilitating this is to put a little distance between us and our emotions. Rather than saying 'I am angry' we say 'I notice that I'm feeling angry'.

WISDOM

		Wellbeing Domains - 'Territories' - Interconnected areas of our lives							
		Mental Our thoughts	Emotional Our emotions	Physical Our actions	Spiritual Our spirit	Social Our communities	Cultural Our way	Environmental Our spaces	Economic Our trade
Wellbeing Dimensions 'Highways' Intertwined routes we use to navigate our lives	Creating meaning	Thinking	Feelings	Behaviour	Identity	Friendship	Way of life	Affinity	Needs
	Achieving potential	Focus	Control	Mastery	Motivation	Teamwork	Governance	Cultivation	Impact
	Nurturing relationships	Regard	Empathy	Interaction	Stories	Trust	Belonging	Cohesion	Fairness
	Building resilience	Flexibility	Agility	Health	Growth	Support	Diversity	Adaptation	Integrity
	Enriching lives	Imagination	Wisdom	Energy	Purpose	Empowerment	Integration	Renewal	Freedom
		Wellbeing Factors - 'Signposts' - Interconnected things that can help us improve wellbeing							

"Yesterday I was clever, so I wanted to change the world. Today I am wise, so I am changing myself."

RUMI

I must point out that wisdom should not just be seen as just sitting in the domain of emotional wellbeing. However without feeling, emotional regulation, empathy for others and agility there is no wisdom.

Like many of the words used to describe the intersections it permeates many of the domains and dimensions of wellbeing. As such, balance is a key component of wisdom which comes through the combination of mind, body and spirit. It is based on experience, knowledge, and good judgement. In fact there is great reciprocity between the domains and dimensions of wellbeing and wisdom.

We become wiser when we consider many different perspectives and are open to new ways of thinking. We understand and manage our feelings and display great levels of empathy and agility. Through knowing themselves, continuous growth, and a sense of purpose wise people are self-aware but also deeply concerned about the welfare of others and the world around them. They empower people and seek to create acceptance for the reality of a situation, tolerance for ambiguity and harmony.

Throughout the ages wisdom has been contemplated by great philosophers as 'the way to live the good life' or what we would now refer to as wellbeing. It is related to the ideals of excellence in both individual and group human development.

Perhaps collective wisdom is a better way of viewing things from a leadership perspective. After all there are very few people who ascend to the position of truly wise or sage. However we need to 'wise up'. Relating back to the problems outlined in the Chapter 'Course Correction' it is clear that we are not being wise enough.

We have clever people looking at climate change. As far as I can tell the vast majority of these scientific experts tell us there is a problem. We now need leaders to use this knowledge and take action with character. This character and virtue is important. Knowing that carbon emissions need to decline by about 45%, on 2000 levels by 2030, and then only committing to reduce them by 20% is not wisdom. And yet this is the position we find ourselves in with our leaders today. Knowledge without virtuous action is not wisdom!

As leaders we must bring together the collective expertise of people around us to make wise decisions and take virtuous action. A wise decision and virtuous action is something that helps deliver personal, collective and planetary wellbeing. The CANBE Model is a framework to help us do this.

CHAPTER SUMMARY

Improving emotional wellbeing starts with understanding our feelings and emotions. It is about becoming more aware of these emotions and feelings in ourselves and others. The 'gap' or moment between these feelings and emotions, and the behaviour we choose as a result of them, is where we can apply emotional intelligence. By choosing our response we can ensure that our emotions work for us rather than against us.

By feeling what others are feeling we can communicate better with them, understand their needs and be more supportive. Emotional wellbeing is about being agile, it isn't about being positive all the time. Sometimes we will be angry, sad or frustrated and this is ok. True wisdom comes from being able to manage our emotions, in line with our thoughts, behaviours and character to deliver greater collective wellbeing.

Having said that emotional wellbeing is not just about positive emotions, there is significant research showing their benefits on performance and wellbeing. When we or our team members are positive, it is contagious, helping other colleagues feel good too. Research shows that positive emotions can even help people feel fitter, younger, and improve their memory!

According to Gallup's 142-country study on the "State of the Global Workplace", only 13% of employees worldwide are engaged at work. In fact, 24% are "actively disengaged," indicating they are unhappy and unproductive at work and liable to spread negativity to co-workers.

If that is the case, then considering the incredible benefits of improving positive emotions at work, shouldn't we invest a little more time and energy into cultivating them? Some of the benefits of improving positive emotions for individuals include: better health, longer life, increased creativity, improved resilience and stress management.

Some of the benefits of improving positive emotions for teams and businesses include: attracting better employees, less absenteeism, improved motivation and performance, increased customer satisfaction. Ultimately, better bottom line results!

KEY CONCEPTS TO IMPROVE EMOTIONAL WELLBEING:

Leaders should be more aware of emotions and how people feel. What people are thinking, feeling and doing can often be misaligned. We may say one thing and do another. By understanding the connections leaders will be more effective. We can do that by:

Improving our understanding of Feelings:

- Being aware of our full range of emotions and naming them
- Understanding the subtle difference between emotions and feelings
- Learning to understand, hold and reflect on our emotions and feelings
- Understanding the relationship between our thinking, feelings and behaviour

Improving Control of our response :

- Learning to regulate our response to emotions
- We can do this by pausing between feeling something and responding
- Breathing exercises and walking away from inflammatory situations are other techniques to remain calm

- Understand what 'triggers' our emotions
- When providing feedback, focus on how the actions of others make us feel, rather than who they are as a person

Improving Empathy:

- Actively listen and avoid distractions when doing so
- 'Walk in the other person's shoes'
- Ask more questions

Improving Emotional Agility:

- Understand that emotions are neither good or bad. Anger, for example, can be used either constructively or negatively.
- Choose the right emotion for the right time with the right person in the right place
- Other than the fear of falling and the fear of loud noises all other fears are learned. If we can learn them, we can also 'unlearn' them.

Wisdom:

- Consider different perspectives and be open to new ideas
- Bring together experts around us to make wiser decisions
- Being virtuous with our actions. Acting with true intent.

KEY BEHAVIOURS:

Where do you score on the following behaviours that contribute to emotional wellbeing? Consider this from a personal, team, and organisational perspective.

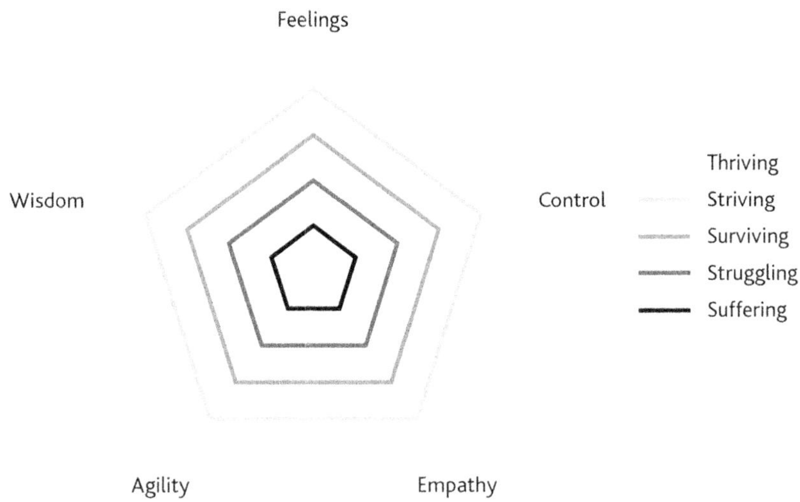

What would you like to improve on?

CHAPTER SEVEN

IMPROVING PHYSICAL WELLBEING

		Wellbeing Domains - 'Territories' - Interconnected areas of our lives							
		Mental Our thoughts	**Emotional** Our emotions	**Physical** Our actions	**Spiritual** Our spirit	**Social** Our communities	**Cultural** Our way	**Environmental** Our spaces	**Economic** Our trade
Wellbeing Dimensions 'Highways' Intertwined routes we use to navigate our lives	**Creating meaning**	Thinking	Feelings	Behaviour	Identity	Friendship	Way of life	Affinity	Needs
	Achieving potential	Focus	Control	Mastery	Motivation	Teamwork	Governance	Cultivation	Impact
	Nurturing relationships	Regard	Empathy	Interaction	Stories	Trust	Belonging	Cohesion	Fairness
	Building resilience	Flexibility	Agility	Health	Growth	Support	Diversity	Adaptation	Integrity
	Enriching lives	Imagination	Wisdom	Energy	Purpose	Empowerment	Integration	Renewal	Freedom
		Wellbeing Factors - 'Signposts' - Interconnected things that can help us improve wellbeing							

"To keep the body in good health is a duty...otherwise we shall not be able to keep the mind strong and clear."

BUDDHA

> "Keeping your body healthy is an expression of gratitude to the whole cosmos — the trees, the clouds, everything."
>
> THICH NHAT HANH

When we talk about physical wellbeing, I do not simply mean getting on an exercise bike. Whilst yes, your physical **health** in terms of fitness is exceptionally important, and often neglected in our modern age of convenience, it is not the only aspect of physical wellbeing. Of course, from a health perspective, there is a growing realisation of the importance of diet and sleep. What we put in our bodies and the time we take to relax are extremely important.

However, physical wellbeing is also impacted by our **behaviour** and actions. Think about your body in respect to being calm versus angry. If you are constantly angry, what impact do you think that has on your wellbeing? There is increasing evidence that our emotions and psychology have an even more direct influence on our physical wellbeing than we ever realised; in 1976 Louise Hays' book *Heal Your Body* directly correlated chronic illnesses with emotional and psychological issues.

The **mastery** of techniques to help us achieve what we want to, the way we **communicate** with others, and the **energy** we create are also important factors in our physical wellbeing.

When we express ourselves poorly, have little mastery over our actions, communicate ineffectively, disregard our health, and create lots of negative energy, our physical wellbeing is diminished. At worst, we can appear ***drained***.

With clear expression, skillful action, effective communication, good health, and high levels of positive energy we demonstrate ***vitality***. This is when we have good physical wellbeing.

BEHAVIOUR

		Wellbeing Domains - 'Territories' - Interconnected areas of our lives							
		Mental Our thoughts	Emotional Our emotions	Physical Our actions	Spiritual Our spirit	Social Our communities	Cultural Our way	Environmental Our spaces	Economic Our trade
Wellbeing Dimensions 'Highways' Intertwined routes we use to navigate our lives	Creating meaning	Thinking	Feelings	Behaviour	Identity	Friendship	Way of life	Affinity	Needs
	Achieving potential	Focus	Control	Mastery	Motivation	Teamwork	Governance	Cultivation	Impact
	Nurturing relationships	Regard	Empathy	Interaction	Stories	Trust	Belonging	Cohesion	Fairness
	Building resilience	Flexibility	Agility	Health	Growth	Support	Diversity	Adaptation	Integrity
	Enriching lives	Imagination	Wisdom	Energy	Purpose	Empowerment	Integration	Renewal	Freedom
		Wellbeing Factors - 'Signposts' - Interconnected things that can help us improve wellbeing							

"A journey of a thousand leagues begins with a single step."

CONFUCIOUS

"A tree is known by its fruit; a man by his deeds. A good deed is never lost; he who sows courtesy reaps friendship, and he who plants kindness gathers love."

ST. BASIL

"The way to do, is to be."

LAO TZU

A man's favourite donkey fell into a deep precipice. No matter how hard he tried, he couldn't pull it out. Whilst it was his favourite donkey, he knew that the best thing was to put it out of its misery. So he began to bury it alive pouring soil on to the donkey from above. As he did so, the donkey shook off the soil and stepped on it. As each further shovel of soil was poured, the donkey shook it off and stepped up. The more soil was poured, the higher it rose, and after much shaking off and stepping up, the donkey was eventually back out of the hole, grazing in green pastures.

This is a great example of emotional wisdom and positivity in action. In terms of ***emotions***, the donkey was likely scared and fearful for its life. It would have been easy to ***feel*** despondent and give up. However rather than cower and suffer the intended fate it ***thought*** optimistically and chose positive ***action***.

Creating good energy for ourselves and others is about being constructive. It's not about viewing everything with 'rose tinted' glasses but it is about how we deal with both good and bad things that happen. Just like this donkey, by 'shaking off' bad events or feelings, we can take more positive actions. By 'stepping up' and learning from them, we can improve our situation.

This book is full of actions we can take to help improve personal, team, organisational and community wellbeing. Some of these we'll need to work on and some may already be habitual.

But habits can be both good and bad. Sometimes it's worth reviewing habits to see which ones are helping and which ones are detracting from our wellbeing.

HABITS

Shawn Achor, in *The Happiness Advantage*[1] describes habits like 'financial capital. Forming one today is an investment that will automatically give out returns for years to come.' A few less calories each day leads to less pounds and stones in the future. So forming good habits today, whether as a business, team or individual can lead to great returns in the future. We are what we repeatedly do. It's often the seemingly small, insignificant daily actions that add up to the sum of our lives.

If *we're overweight*: Perhaps we're taking the lift rather than the stairs, sitting on the couch rather than going to the gym, eating a larger portion than we really need.

If *we're adrift financially*: Perhaps we don't have a budget or don't stick to it, we're spending on frivolous items, money is sitting in accounts that we're not earning interest on.

On the other hand if *our relationships at work are fantastic*: Perhaps we're giving our full attention to listening, we always fulfil our promises no matter how small, and we always show appreciation when a colleague has done us a favour.

Habits are extremely powerful for individuals, teams and organisations. Charles Duhigg in his book *The Power of Habit: Why We Do What We Do and How To Change*[2] describes the habits of successful individuals, organisations and societies.

The great thing is that we know that habits can be changed. In his work, Duhigg describes the habit loop. All habits consist of a *cue* or *trigger*, followed by a *routine* and then a *reward*. The key to breaking a habit is to change the routine whilst keeping the cue and reward the same.

Another key learning point is that habits can't be eradicated; they can only be changed. If you think about it a habit is like an impression on your brain. You've heard the saying 'cells that fire together wire together'. Each time you perform an action it becomes more deeply embedded as a pattern on your brain until eventually it becomes a habit. The pattern is so strong that you don't even need to think about it. Think cleaning your teeth, driving to work and putting on your pants!

Now, if you drive a different way to work one morning your brain has to work harder, but it doesn't mean the pattern of your usual journey has been wiped away. It's still there and you'll pick it up quickly if you go back to your normal routine.

Duhigg offers the following process for helping to change a habit and this involves identifying the elements of the habit loop and replacing the routine.

- Identify the routine. This is the behaviour we want to change.
- Next, identify and experiment with *rewards*. To identify the reward Duhigg suggests a little experimentation. Rewards satisfy our cravings and can range from physical sensations such as hunger to emotional payoffs like feelings of pride. We're often not conscious of the cravings that drive our behaviours so we need to figure out which cravings are driving particular habits and experiment a little.
- Isolate the cue. Duhigg explains that experiments have shown that almost all habitual cues fit into one of five categories: location, time, emotional state, other people and the immediately preceding action. If we record when we perform the habit, we should start to see patterns that relate to one, or a combination of, these categories.

As an example you should end up with an understanding of your habit recorded as follows:

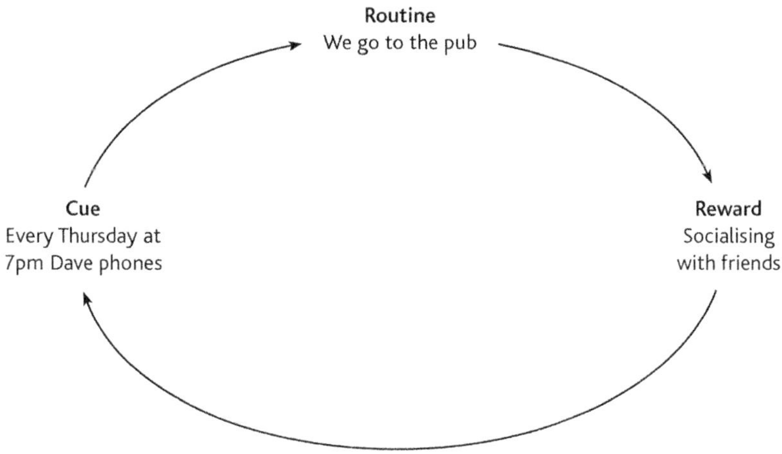

Have a plan. The next step is to develop a plan to replace the habit you don't want with the one that you do, keeping the cue and reward the same:

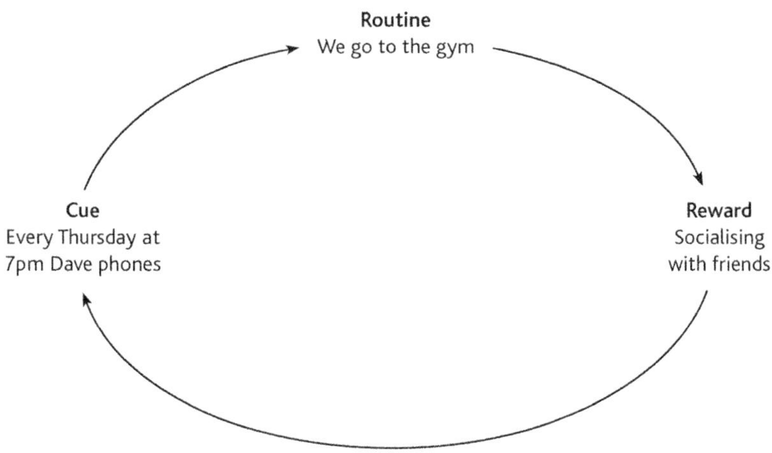

Obviously habits are complex and the example shown is simplified. You may need to persevere with understanding the various triggers and rewards that are motivating you. However, now you have a better understanding of what makes a habit and how to change one here's a

7 step plan to replace the ones you want to. This will hopefully link with some of the learning you take away from this book!

1. **Make a list of bad habits you'd like to change and good ones you'd like to keep** - Write down what the bad habits are costing you. Think about the attitudes and emotions associated with them. What has stopped you changing until now? How will you make sure this doesn't stop you going forward? What could you do to build on your positive habits?

2. **Now think about and visualise some new successful habits** - It's generally better to think positively as our subconscious brain is wired to support what we want rather than what we don't. For example, I'm exercising 3 times per week for 20 mins rather than I'm not spending so much time watching television. What are the benefits of adopting this new habit? Visualise the specific behaviour change you will achieve. How do you feel? What are you thinking? How is your behaviour different? Repeat this visualisation until you can picture the new successful habit really clearly and feel motivated by it.

3. **Set a SMARTER plan to change the habit** - Sometimes you can get 'stuck in a rut'. You know your habits and behaviours aren't moving you in the direction you'd like to go but you have difficulty changing. Everything is hard before it becomes easy. Behaviours and habits are like a well-trodden path. Initially they take a while to form. Well, the good news is, you can choose a new path. It just takes time. Research[3] has shown that the time it takes to change a habit depends on many things including the habit you're changing, the people involved and your circumstances. So set a timescale that is realistic and commit to repeated daily activity. Eventually after repeating them for a while it gets easier and easier as the path in your brain becomes well-formed. Eventually you just do things naturally without even thinking.

4. **Make things easy for yourself -** "Psychic entropy" is a term used to describe the listless, apathetic feeling you get when you take the easy route and just watch TV or 'browse' on Facebook for

example. It's just so easy, convenient and, well, habitual isn't it?. This is also evident in the 'path of least resistance' which is used by marketeers through things like 'opt outs' playing on our inertia. Use this knowledge to your advantage.

As an extreme example: in the film *Confessions Of A Shopaholic,* Rebecca Bloomwood freezes her credit cards in blocks of ice to help prevent her from spending more and more. What tricks or ideas can you think of to make it easier to develop a good habit, and harder to develop a bad one? For example, if you want to learn to play the guitar put it in a place where you'll see it often and it's easy to pick up and play. Set up visual reminders to prompt you in places you're bound to see them like the fridge or the bathroom mirror.

Another key area where you can help yourself is through enrolling the help of others. Duhigg's book reflects clear evidence that shows the support of others, even just one person, can help improve belief in your chances of success. Of course if that person is working on the same habit as you then the moral support and sharing of experiences can be invaluable.

5. **Eliminate negative thinking** - Everyone has negative thoughts from time to time and these are destructive and unhelpful. A positive affirmation could be one way to counter these negative thoughts and replace them with positive ones. Remind yourself of your successes to date or when you've changed a habit successfully in the past. Visualise your new successful habit and what it brings you.

6. **Plan for slip ups** - The research previously mentioned also shows that it doesn't matter if you mess up here and there[4]. If you do make a slip up don't beat yourself up, just get back into your plan as quickly as you can. Having said that forewarned is forearmed. What might get in your way? How could you overcome this? Whose support could you rely on to help you?

7. **Monitor and reward your progress** - Use free tools like Toodledo to record, monitor and measure your progress. It's also important to reward yourself along the way. How about using your new habit for the benefit of the community or to raise money for char-

ity? These added incentives will give you greater motivation and help you achieve your goals. The other important element here is that changing a habit isn't always easy. The amount of effort you need to put in will vary according to how long you've been doing it, how big a task it is, your motives and many other factors. Remember sustainable change takes time.

We've looked at habits on an individual basis but what about at a team or organisational level? What are the habits in your team and organisation? Which ones have been engrained and might need revising? Which ones are holding you back? Which ones can you build on?

Let's start with one question that could transform your working life forever. **Could I/We do in 30 hours what I/We do in 40 hours and still get paid the same amount?** Where did the arbitrary 40 hour week even come from? Is it just a nasty habit that we've failed to question? The 20th-century British economist John Hicks said, "It has probably never entered the heads of most economists ... that hours could be shortened and output maintained."

This won't be right for every individual, team or business but that's not the point. The point is, have you asked the question or are you just accepting usual practice because it's easier to do? Are you really leading or are you just wearing out the same old path? Some organisations and leadership teams that have asked the question have been pleasantly surprised.

Sweden, in particular, is a country that seems to be challenging the norm. In a Forbes contributors article entitled "Sweden's Intriguing 6-Hour Workday Experiment"[5], the results of a 2 year test to 'turn shorter work days into bigger gains' at Sahlgrenska University Hospital's orthopaedics unit proved positive as of June, 2016. The unit switched 89 nurses and doctors to a six-hour day in 2015, hiring 15 staffers to ensure the hospital work got done. The test was expensive — costing the hospital $123,000 a month — but no one has called in sick since it began and the nurses and doctors have been more efficient.

In a similar test, the Svartedalens nursing home has let 80 nurses work six-hour shifts with the result that nurses are happier, sick leave is half the average absenteeism rate in Gothenburg city and the level of care is better.

In the private sector a Toyota service centre and the Background AB digital production company have switched to six-hour workdays, and report less staff turnover, more productivity and increased creativity.

In another article entitled "What Happened When I Moved My Company To A 5-Hour Workday"[6] Stephan Aarstol describes how he has successfully moved his company from an 8 hour to 5 hour day by applying great time management principles, shifting to a production mind-set with the introduction of a profit share scheme, using technology to automate processes and not being too rigid with the 25 hours per week principle. Employees sometimes do work longer hours to 'get the job out the door' when required. The results: happier, more engaged employees, unsolicited resumes from people eager to work at the company, increased productivity and revenues up in 2015 by over 40%!

It should be noted that in some of these examples above public expense needs to be weighed against the potential gains. But that in itself raises a bigger question for leadership about how best to balance the wellbeing of your people and the communities in which they live with the efficiency and profitability of your organisation. However, overall there are clear examples that reducing hours, improving employee wellbeing and increasing productivity can work.

If reducing hours isn't for you, then looking at how you can redistribute them might be another approach. Serps Invaders, a digital marketing agency based in Edinburgh, has noticed an increase in productivity after moving to a 4 day week, introducing 'duvet days', where employees can call in and take a day off at short notice, and remote working[7].

It should also be stated here that productivity is clearly linked to employee engagement so reducing working hours isn't a silver bullet in itself. However reviewing your working hours in line with other elements in the CANBE Model will enable you to take a strategic approach to embedding wellbeing and increasing engagement and productivity in your organisation.

Of course not everything is habitual and sometimes new skills are required. This brings us onto mastery.

MASTERY

		Wellbeing Domains - 'Territories' - Interconnected areas of our lives							
		Mental Our thoughts	**Emotional** Our emotions	**Physical** Our actions	**Spiritual** Our spirit	**Social** Our communities	**Cultural** Our way	**Environmental** Our spaces	**Economic** Our trade
Wellbeing Dimensions 'Highways' Intertwined routes we use to navigate our lives	Creating meaning	Thinking	Feelings	Behaviour	Identity	Friendship	Way of life	Affinity	Needs
	Achieving potential	Focus	Control	Mastery	Motivation	Teamwork	Governance	Cultivation	Impact
	Nurturing relationships	Regard	Empathy	Interaction	Stories	Trust	Belonging	Cohesion	Fairness
	Building resilience	Flexibility	Agility	Health	Growth	Support	Diversity	Adaptation	Integrity
	Enriching lives	Imagination	Wisdom	Energy	Purpose	Empowerment	Integration	Renewal	Freedom
		Wellbeing Factors - 'Signposts' - Interconnected things that can help us improve wellbeing							

"Ah, mastery… what a profoundly satisfying feeling when one finally gets on top of a new set of skills… and then sees the light under the new door those skills can open, even as another door is closing."

GAIL SHEEHY

In order to progress and achieve we must grow. Learning and mastering new things helps us feel competent and in control. When we're stretched and have the resources and capabilities to deliver, we experience what Mihaly Csikszentmihalyi determined as 'flow'.

Mastery is developed over time when people overcome challenging tasks or activities and develop new skills and confidence as a result. It is recognised as the possession of great skill and technique in a particular field.

On one end of the scale, comfort and boredom are the enemies of mastery. On the other end is feeling over-whelmed. Supporting the growth of people through learning and development, ensuring workloads are manageable and that the necessary information and resources are in place are all key here. Pairing people with strong support networks and successful role models will also help.

The importance of good goal setting is paramount. Set goals that are too hard and there is potential to damage and erode self-esteem. Too easy, and growth will be limited.

GOAL SETTING

It's also worth mentioning the value that coaching can bring to this area. Without apology, the importance of coaching as a tool for increasing wellbeing is a common theme throughout this book. By working to the coachee's agenda and asking skillful and challenging questions, a good coach can ensure that personal goals are stretching. The coach will also help the coachee explore obstacles, provide support, and build esteem to provide the best chance of success. This coaching approach will also help with identifying goals which are more linked with an individual's identity, motivations and purpose. By doing this the chances of the goals being achieved will be much greater. As a leader, if you want to build mastery and wellbeing in your organisation, you should consider coaching both personally, for your team and organisation.

The emphasis and balance of goals can also be important here. Too many short term performance goals focused on results and outputs can lead to an overly competitive environment where burn-out and one upmanship pervade. Balancing these short term goals with long term goals focused on learning, mastery and the journey being taken will help to keep perspective and create an environment of greater collaboration, trust and sense of growth.

PERFORMING

Performance can be defined as: potential minus interference.

As a leader, it is our role to remove as much interference as possible at a personal, team, and organisational level. Interference can come in a number of different forms. This includes everything from too much bureaucracy, literal interruptions, trying too hard, lack of confidence, fear of failure, lack of focus, clash of personalities, boredom, and expecting perfection, to name just a few. Hopefully it is clear to see the connections here between mastery and other elements of wellbeing, which again reinforces the point that they are all interconnected.

Our performance will be affected by how we think, our levels of focus, the regard we have for those we work with, our flexible mindset, the imagination we use to overcome problems, how we feel about the task, the control we have over our emotions, the empathy we display for others and many other aspects of our overall wellbeing.

What if we could improve performance by 10% by removing just one of these obstacles?

PERFECTING IMPERFECTION

Mastery is not perfection. It is the realisation that we will never be perfect but carrying on despite that. Expecting perfection is a common interference, particularly amongst leaders who may have risen to the top because of the high standards and expectations they set for themselves and others. *Perfecting imperfection is about knowing what is good enough.* Sometimes only the best will be good enough and striving for excellence will be the right approach.

However, on other occasions perhaps this might be too much and could even take valuable people, resources, and time away from priorities that need attention. Helping people understand what standards are expected at the beginning of a project is a key role of the leader.

PERSONAL EFFICACY

Employees have an expectation that leaders will both 'talk the talk' and 'walk the walk'. Acting as a *role model* will help you achieve potential and inspire those around you. The things you need to role model? Well they are all of the 'signposts' outlined in the CANBE Model with one of those being the way we interact with others.

INTERACTION

		Wellbeing Domains - 'Territories' - Interconnected areas of our lives							
		Mental Our thoughts	Emotional Our emotions	Physical Our actions	Spiritual Our spirit	Social Our communities	Cultural Our way	Environmental Our spaces	Economic Our trade
Wellbeing Dimensions 'Highways' Intertwined routes we use to navigate our lives	Creating meaning	Thinking	Feelings	Behaviour	Identity	Friendship	Way of life	Affinity	Needs
	Achieving potential	Focus	Control	Mastery	Motivation	Teamwork	Governance	Cultivation	Impact
	Nurturing relationships	Regard	Empathy	Interaction	Stories	Trust	Belonging	Cohesion	Fairness
	Building resilience	Flexibility	Agility	Health	Growth	Support	Diversity	Adaptation	Integrity
	Enriching lives	Imagination	Wisdom	Energy	Purpose	Empowerment	Integration	Renewal	Freedom
		Wellbeing Factors - 'Signposts' - Interconnected things that can help us improve wellbeing							

"Your words control your life, your progress, your results, even your mental and physical health. You cannot talk like a failure and expect to be successful."

GERMANY KENT

"Wise men talk because they have something to say; fools, because they have to say something."

PLATO

"Everything that irritates us about others can lead us to an understanding of ourselves."

CARL JUNG

Interactions are all about how we affect each other. It is important to remember the two sides to this coin. We often get so wrapped up in our own feelings that we neglect the feelings of others. Let's firstly look at how we affect others. It is rather ironic that one of the best ways to have a positive affect on others is to listen.

People will like you better when you listen, ask them effective questions, and can see things from their perspective. You will communicate more effectively, be more influential, and garner respect. Remember, respect must be earned, it doesn't come de facto with your job title or even experience!

GOOD LISTENING - YOU JUST MIGHT GET TO KNOW SOMETHING!

The benefits of good listening are highlighted well by Wilson Mizner, an American playwright, who said: "A good listener is not only popular everywhere, but after a while they get to know something."

Stephen Covey, in habit five of his *7 Habits of Highly Effective People*[1], wrote 'seek first to understand and then to be understood' highlighting the importance of listening first. You've also probably heard someone saying 'there's a reason we have two ears and one mouth', yet the importance of good listening continues to be underestimated. Thinking back to the hours we spent at school learning to read and write. How much time did we spend on learning to listen?

There are different types of listening; these include:

- *peripheral,* or unfocused listening. We might be earwigging or just overhearing a conversation;
- *factual* or *apparent listening,* where we're hearing the words and facts the other person tells us but our thoughts are elsewhere and we're still focused on ourselves; the next step up is
- *emotional* or *active listening,* where our focus is on the other person's emotions, hearing what, why and how things are being said, (and critically what *isn't* being said). Lastly, there's
- *intuitive* or *global listening,* when we'll be using all of our senses and intuition to really understand the person speaking.

Which of these types of listening do you employ the most? Hopefully, it's the latter, but if it isn't perhaps you've got some work to do on your listening skills! The key to good listening is an understanding that communication is a subtle mixture of verbal (the words), non-verbal (the tone of voice and pace), and para-verbal (body language).

Research is mixed about the influence of each of these three elements. However, each of them does have an influence on the overall message delivered, and if one element is out of line with the others it can give us important clues. Picking up on these clues means we're going to need to become a great *HEERER*.

***H**ead* – Going into a conversation expecting to be interested really helps and yet it's so easy to choose a mind-set where we have already switched off. The other person will pick up subtle clues and will either 'close down' or 'open up' depending on our approach. This is the most important part of listening which really does start before any words are spoken.

In the busy office or home environment, distractions are everywhere and the stimulus or motivation to listen well may be harder to muster. Remove as many distractions as possible and move to a quiet space. We must set listening up so that we can give the other person our full attention.

It is also no coincidence that in order to *LISTEN* well, we must be *SILENT*. One of the key distractions for listening is thinking of the next question we would like to ask and then interrupting the speaker. Asking questions is a great way of showing our interest, we just need to do it at the appropriate time when we've given the person speaking plenty of 'airtime'.

***E**yes* – Both ours and theirs. Maintaining comfortable eye contact. Showing we're interested. Those with children will be familiar with the feeling that we may as well be 'talking to the wall' as they look away into the distance whilst we're getting across what we believe to be a very important point. Eyes also give away important clues about what both we and the person speaking might be feeling or thinking. Are they happy, sad, angry, or calm?

***E**ars* – Listening is not just about the words. The tone of voice and pace of conversation can tell us a great deal. Someone who is nervous is likely to speak much quicker in a higher pitch, whereas someone who speaks at a more standard pace and tone is likely more assured and confident. What isn't being said? What might the tone of voice be communicating? What emotions are we picking up on?

***R**est of the body* – Be attentive, respectful and encouraging. Facing the person we're listening to helps. How many times in the workplace have you seen a conversation between people where they're not even facing each other?

It is no secret that we tend to like people that are like us. In this respect, mirroring and matching is a technique associated with Neuro Linguistic Programming where we can help build rapport quickly with someone by matching their body language and use of words. This generally occurs subconsciously and is best done when it comes from a genuine and authentic desire to 'get along'.

***E**mpathy* – By checking our understanding of what someone is saying to us we demonstrate empathy. Paraphrasing, summarising, questioning and imagining what it might be like from their perspective can all help us gain a deeper understanding of what is being communicated. Be cautious here about making assumptions. Who hasn't heard someone say: 'I know how you are feeling' and thought: 'No, you don't.' A better approach might be: 'Tell me, how are you feeling?' or 'I'm sensing something. What is it?'

Rapport – Finally, rapport is what we build through developing an understanding of the other person. By listening first and using the techniques outlined above, we'll be well on our way to developing a greater understanding of the other person. Now, it's just up to them to listen to what we've got to say!

As a leader, we need to understand our strengths and weaknesses as a listener and seek to build on them. But we can also help encourage better listening in our organisation by becoming a role model, emphasising the importance of listening, removing distractions, and, if needed, getting some training or coaching on being a better listener.

Of course, listening also has a wider context than just interpersonal. How well does our team or organisation listen to customers, suppliers, and other stakeholders? What mechanisms have we got in place to listen to them?

Social media is a good example of the 'two ears one mouth' saying. I'd hazard a guess that most companies' social media activity is at least 80/20 biased towards talking rather than listening. Everyone is so keen to promote themselves and tell everyone how great they are they forget to listen to what customers are saying.

In a similar vein, how well does our organisation listen to employees? Obviously day to day conversations between leaders and employees are paramount here but what else could our organisation do to listen better to employees?

FEEDBACK

In his best-selling book *How to Win Friends and Influence People* (1936), Dale Carnegie's first principle is 'Don't criticise, condemn or complain'. He explains that instead of condemning people we should try to understand them and why they do what they do. In doing this, we can develop greater empathy, tolerance, and kindness.

This starts with listening: 'seeking first to understand'. As part of this, we'll also need to ask effective questions that help increase awareness and understanding and we'll look at this shortly. We'll also undoubtedly be in the position of both providing and receiving feedback at some point.

When providing feedback, we should make it as specific and constructive as possible. Otherwise, it could appear as disingenuous and more importantly there is no learning. Telling a colleague: 'Your report was great' might make them feel good but it isn't specific enough to provide them with any real learning opportunities. Why was it great? Helping a colleague understand that their report was great because of the way they had broken down complex information into simple to understand diagrams and tables will encourage them to do likewise on the next occasion.

Building on this we might also like to compliment them as a person. 'I love your thorough approach to producing reports...' 'It was great because of the way you broke down complex information into simple diagrams...' Through this approach, as outlined in the table below, you can help build confidence (what a person does) and self-esteem (who a person is).

Criticism of who you are as a person e.g. 'You are clumsy'	**Positive enthusiastic feedback on your actions** e.g. 'your presentation was excellent because...'
Criticism of your actions e.g. 'your presentation would have been better if...'	**Positive enthusiastic feedback on who you are as a person** e.g. 'I love your energy and enthusiasm'

Of course, there will also be occasions when we need to deliver negative feedback. Research has indicated that a key thing to consider here is the *ratio* of positive to negative comments[2]. A ratio of 6 positive comments to 1 negative has been associated with the highest performing teams and, interestingly enough, marriages! The lower the positive to negative ratio becomes the poorer the performance of the team and, in the case of marriage, the higher the likelihood of divorce.

The 6-to-1 ratio is simply staggering if we consider the way feedback is generally delivered, particularly in British companies. It is more like the reverse of this statistic: 6 negatives to 1 positive! Imagine the overall impact that is having on the wellbeing of the nation's workforce?

Here are some key points to think about when we engage in feedback.

1. Provide plenty of positive, specific feedback to colleagues on their personal qualities and what they have done.
2. Choose carefully when providing negative feedback. Is it really important? If not it might be worth saving up our feedback for an alternative occasion when the stakes are much higher.
3. When delivering negative comments, ensure our

> feedback is specific and constructive. We should base our feedback on actions and not on them as a person.

Much of this comes back to the spirit in which the feedback is given. Is our feedback provided with the aim of helping the person succeed? Or, is it points-scoring and destructive with a view to making us feel better? Following Dale Carnegie's advice, it's worth remembering that even well-intentioned criticism can undermine and erode relationships.

Leaders have a responsibility to encourage feedback within their teams and organisation. Helping others understand the principles of giving and receiving constructive feedback is one way we can help here. We could do this through role modelling or, of course, through organising more formal coaching and training. Perhaps someone in our team is particularly good at providing feedback and would be comfortable in mentoring others?

Of course, feedback can also be gathered collectively at a team and organisational level through processes such as 360° feedback, customer surveys, net promoter score, and even anecdotally. I believe leaders have a responsibility to ensure there is an appropriate level of feedback being given and received across all of these areas and, more importantly, that the feedback is being acted on.

Another approach to raising our colleague's awareness of strengths and weaknesses is to ask better questions. However, this is not as straightforward as it sounds. There are specific ways of questioning people that can be helpful and motivating, and ways which can be off-putting and disruptive. Through asking questions, we don't have to provide feedback but can achieve the same result. Let's take a look at this.

QUESTIONING

Using the preceding example of a colleague producing a report, we've already explored how we can provide them with specific and constructive feedback. But what about asking them questions instead? Imagine our colleague has provided us with the report which we have now read through. They know we've had a chance to have a look and ask us for some feedback.

What if, rather than giving our own views straight away, we were to respond with 'Thanks for asking for my feedback but I'm actually more interested in understanding how well you think you tackled the report first.' 'Tell me... 'What do you think went well with the report?' 'What could be better?', 'What would you do differently next time?'

In which scenario do you think the person you are talking with would have greater understanding, awareness, ownership, and responsibility?

1. When you give them your feedback
2. When you ask them questions to solicit their own views and thoughts first?

Asking questions provides the creator of the report an opportunity to raise concerns before receiving feedback. There is nothing more frustrating than being aware of a fault prior to a feedback session, and then having it relentlessly penalised. The creator of the report may well be aware of flaws in the report, but ran out of time to rectify them, or required more guidance to address them. Asking questions first gives them the opportunity to raise these and may lead to very interesting conversations.

In addition, this ties in with a problem many leaders face. How often, as a leader, do you feel responsibility for providing the answer when you're asked a question by a colleague? 100% of the time? 80% of the time? Less?

Of course, there are times when we need to provide an answer and feedback. However, could we help others more by asking questions rather than always giving them OUR answer?

Think about the following for a moment and write down your answers. On which occasions do you think you could ask more questions of your colleagues rather than providing them with answers? Now choose one, perhaps your next opportunity, and ask more questions to see what happens.

So, what type of questions should we ask? There are many types but the main distinction is between open and closed questions. Open questions such as *what, when, who* and *how* solicit a descriptive answer. They require the person being asked to think more deeply, creatively, and to explore options. They are great questions to start conversations and open things up. Closed questions such as *did, can, have, will, has, are, do* and *is,* can be answered with yes and no responses. They're generally great for the latter part of conversations when it's time to narrow in on the specifics.

Why questions should be treated with caution. Asking "Why did you do that?" particularly if asked in the wrong tone of voice, can be perceived as critical. An alternative could be: "What were you aiming to achieve?"

Leading questions, such as "Don't you think that...?" and "What about trying...?" should also be treated with caution. The more we're seen to provide answers the less responsibility and ownership our colleagues will have. In a situation where they've run out of ideas and have asked for our input, sharing our thoughts with these types of questions may be more appropriate.

Questions can also be used to challenge beliefs that are limiting us, our colleagues, team or organisation. Questions like, "What's stopping us?" "How could you...?" "What if...?" are really useful in this situation.

We can use questions to check commitment. Once we've explored a topic with colleagues, we'll want to know that things will get done. Questions like: "On a scale of 1-10 how enthusiastic are you about achieving this?" or "What will you do as a result...?" or "When will you get this done by..?" help to build commitment. Obviously, if the answers we receive flag concerns we can explore them further. For example, if people only answer 6 out of 10 for enthusiasm we might like to ask the question: "What would increase that to 7 or 8 out of 10?" You get the picture!

Questions aren't just about helping people with tasks, however. They can serve the more profound purpose of building great relationships. Encouraging people to talk about their own interests and lives, so we can get to know a little more about what motivates them, is not only a great joy, but an important part of turning a 'group of people' into a functioning team. If we have a tendency to be very task and project focused, we must remember that people have lives outside of their work, and in many instances, they do not live to work, but work to live. Thinking about how we can get to know people better through asking questions not just about what they do, but who they are is a great way to build relationships!

We'll now look at presenting ideas and influencing others, but at this point it's probably worth emphasising that if we are emotionally aware, listening well, giving and receiving good feedback, and asking great questions, we're probably already well on our way to becoming more influential!

So, what else can help when presenting our ideas and influencing others?

INFLUENCING

In defining what leadership is all about, we have already established that a key component is inspiring positive change in both people and processes. Through listening, questioning, and generally seeking to understand others better, we're already one step ahead of the game as a leader. It's clear that a lot of influence can be built before we even say a word.

Following from this, it's worth highlighting the subtle difference between influence, persuasion, and manipulation. Persuasion and influence aren't about getting our own way. They're about finding common ground and beliefs to move in a direction where everyone can see the benefit. With manipulation, it's often the case that one party benefits whilst the other loses. We need to think about how the people we're communicating with will benefit.

If you apply the listening and questioning techniques we have discussed, you will already have a good idea of the direction people want to travel, what inspires, motivates and/or scares them. You'll understand what they see as the key challenges or obstacles along the way and at least some clues as to the relationships that might help or hinder the process. As Dale Carnegie suggests: by becoming genuinely interested in others, they'll become more interested in you.

Other simple, yet often neglected, principles suggested by Carnegie include remembering people's names and smiling more. Can you recall a time when someone took the time and trouble to remember your name? Perhaps you hadn't seen this person for a while and yet they still remembered. How did it make you feel about them?

Through these common sense, but less commonly practiced, actions, we can start to create connections and bonds that can be built on when we present our own ideas, thoughts, and feelings about a subject.

These habits are re-enforced by Dr Robert Cialdini, Regents' Professor Emeritus of Psychology and Marketing at Arizona State University, who, in his best-selling book *Influence – The Psychology of Persuasion*[3] describes 6 principles for interacting with others. These principles of influence include, Liking, Reciprocation, Social Proof, Consistency, Authority, and Scarcity.

In the first of these principles, '*Liking*', Cialdini describes how: "People prefer to say yes to individuals they know and like." By applying some of the thinking we've previously covered, including showing a genuine interest in others through listening, questioning, remembering their names, and giving them positive feedback, we are already increasing our chances of being liked! In fact, Cialdini cites 'uncovering similarities and offering genuine praise' as two key factors that reliably increase the connection between people.

This is backed by another of Cialdini's principles: '*Reciprocity*' which states that people feel indebted to others who do something for them or offer them a gift. In a similar vein, Stephen Covey talks about having an 'emotional bank account' with your friends, colleagues, and acquaintances. This is also why marketing departments often use free samples as an effective way of introducing customers to products and services. Getting something for nothing makes you feel obligated to purchase from them in the future.

As a leader, we can apply this thinking in a variety of ways. Perhaps the first, most basic way, is to live up to our promises no matter how small. If we promise to do something for someone, then we must make sure we deliver. Each time we don't, we are withdrawing from the 'emotional bank account' we hold with that other person.

This is the right time to talk about trust. Influence and persuasion can often be less about words and more about our actions. If we've consistently 'lived up to our word' then people are much more likely to trust what we tell them in the future. Whilst this might seem obvious, it is remarkable how often leadership and organisations fail to live up to their promises.

Demonstrating our ideas or requirements by relating back to times when we've previously delivered can be a powerful way to influence and persuade others. In other words, we need to remind others of when we have come through for them in the past to remove any doubts.

We should also think about opportunities to give more. When could you freely give more of your time or knowledge to others? Taking this more literally: what opportunities are there for you to provide your colleagues with 'gifts' - a small token or handwritten note of appreciation, a birthday gift. What others can you think of? Obviously in this area you need to be careful and mindful of your organisation's policies around corporate gifts, bribery, and corruption - especially if you are thinking of gifting externally. The point is: the more we give to others, the more likely they will give back and provide support when it is needed. Of course, if we give with expectations of receiving in return, this principle can backfire. The value of the gifts we give will be quickly eroded if people see that we expect something in return. Give freely and openly without expectation.

'Authority' is another of Cialdini's principles which explains that people defer to experts. It makes their decision-making easier and there is also strong pressure in society for people to obey authority figures and experts. Rather than imposing our authority on another, it is much more subtle to build it by establishing our knowledgeability, practical skills, or other valuable expert trait. From explaining our experience and expertise in conversations, through to writing blogs and social media posts, we can build our authority and credibility. What is your expertise and how can you demonstrate it to build trust in others?

Whether they realise it or not, people look to others for cues on how to behave and what to believe. In his principle *'Social Proof'*, Cialdini outlines how people tend to follow people that are like themselves. Testimonials and reviews are one example of this. A customer who reads a testimonial or review from someone they consider to be like themselves is much more likely to be convinced than if they read one from someone who is nothing like them. So, if we're trying to convince a senior colleague to change their views, enroll another supportive senior colleague to help persuade them. Another example might be providing colleagues with proof of other people like them who've done this before.

Following on from this, in his principle, *'Consistency'*, Caldini describes that once people make an active, public, and voluntary commitment, they tend to stick with it. People are more likely to follow through with something if they have committed to it, verbally or in writing. This isn't to say that we should be coercing our colleagues into making public commitments that they will later renege on in private. But by asking great questions, checking commitment, and getting written confirmation, we will become far more influential and persuasive.

Finally, according to the *'Scarcity'* principle, people assign more value to objects and opportunities that come in limited quantities or are more difficult to obtain. Giving colleagues an early heads up with exclusive information will carry greater weight. Explaining that an opportunity is only available for a limited time frame, and what your colleague might lose if they don't take it up, will influence their decision. In fact, framing a decision in terms of what people might lose, as opposed to what they gain, has been shown to increase chances of success.

An important point in regard to these principles is to use them ethically. The balance between persuasion and manipulation can be a fine line. We have to think carefully about our intentions. It is worth reiterating the work of Daniel Kahneman in his book *Thinking, Fast and Slow*[4]. As outlined previously, Kahneman describes our thinking in respect to two systems in the brain. System 1 is fast and automatic, based on learned patterns, principles, and the habits we've developed. This is associated more with the limbic (emotional) brain. System 2 is slower and more considered, linked with the cerebral cortex (cognitive or executive) brain.

The point here is that some of the principles described by Caldini are more like mental shortcuts linked with the System 1 part of the brain. These are likely to be even more effective when the decisions are lower-stake and simpler. That's not to say that they won't help influence others in high-stake circumstances but in these situations the people you are trying to influence are likely to want thorough data to support any decision making. These people will be engaging both the System 1 and System 2 parts of their brain in these situations.

To wrap up this section, I'd like to come back to what I believe to be the key source of influence and persuasion: the focus on others. UC Berkeley psychologist Dacher Keltner in his book *The Power Paradox: The Surprising and Sobering Science of How We Gain and Lose Influence*[5] conducted twenty years of research exploring what power is, what confers it upon an individual, and how it shapes the structure of groups.

A key point made by Keltner is the ability of our routine day-to-day actions in helping to either build or erode our power: "Power defines the waking life of every human being. It is found not only in extraordinary acts but also in quotidian acts, indeed in every interaction and every relationship, be it an attempt to get a two-year-old to eat green vegetables or to inspire a stubborn colleague to do her best work."

Keltner's central point is that power in the modern world is: "gained and maintained through a focus on others" and he offers the four practices of empathising, giving, expressing gratitude, and telling stories, as ways to enable this. He adds: "All four of these practices dignify and delight others. They constitute the basis of strong, mutually empowered ties. You can lean on them to enhance your power at any moment of the day by stirring others to effective action."

It's clear through reviewing the work of Covey, Carnegie, Caldini, Kahneman, and Keltner that true enduring power and influence are attained through a focus on others and the integrity of our everyday actions.

This is as true for individuals as it is for teams and organisations. So, as a leader you can apply these principles systematically across all of these areas.

PERSUADING

So far, quite rightly, we've covered more in this chapter about how we can build relationships through talking less and a focus on others. However, as a leader, the time will come when it is time to talk and engage people in a compelling story that they believe in. However, if you're working in an organisation that you struggle to connect with and clashes with your personality, beliefs, character, and values, then no matter how good a communicator, it will impact on your ability to influence and persuade others.

Most people will not be lucky enough to work in a place where their beliefs are totally congruent with those of the organisation. But this is why it is so important to think about it in a deeper way. By understanding our own character, personality, values, and beliefs we can consider where these are aligned and where they differ from the organisation, and then plan accordingly.

I previously coached a manager in a financial institution which, in his opinion, had become overly sales and target focused at the expense of customer service. This focus on sales and targets was alien to many of the front line staff, who had joined the organisation to help customers, not sell insurance. As a result of these targets, the manager was having difficult performance conversations with some staff members, which didn't sit well with his own values and beliefs or those of his colleagues.

By coaching around this topic, he was able to re-frame the conversations more in line with his own beliefs and those of his staff, which was to serve customers to the best of their ability. He gained a promotion and his branch performed extremely well, achieving the targets that were set. Re-framing conversations around shared beliefs can have a powerful effect on your ability to influence.

If you haven't already thought about where your character, personality, values and beliefs do and don't align with those of your organisation, then now is the time to do it. Where can you build on the strengths of alignment? How can you close gaps? Where can you re-frame your conversations?

Sometimes, however, we need to recognise that these gaps are just too big. I've also coached a Head of Department whose beliefs weren't aligned with those of his organisation. In this situation coaching conversations turned to what an alternative career path might look like for him!

The point here is that our power, influence, and ability to communicate effectively will come from a place of authenticity if our values are aligned with those of the organisation we work for. Not only that but we'll feel better about it. We'll have greater belief.

So, now that we're more understanding of others and working

from a place of personal power, how can we package and communicate our messages most effectively?

In the previous sections we've already covered many of the ways that we can build credibility and trust with people. On some occasions, however, particularly when presenting to unfamiliar audiences, we may need to win credibility very quickly. Demonstrating knowledge, experience, and achievements through a short introduction will help, as will stories of when we've helped people—like our audience—in similar situations. Another way to achieve this is through acquiring testimonials and introductions from people already respected in a particular field.

For example, when talking to a team of colleagues we might say: "I've worked in every department across this business and have over 20 years experience..."

Whether you are thinking about writing an email, a one-to-one, or planning for a presentation to hundreds: preparation is so important. Understanding our audience is the first step. What will they gain from us? What are their problems, issues, concerns? What do we know about what they like and don't like? The better we understand our audience, the more we can adapt our message and style to communicate in a language they can relate to. This will also help us anticipate any concerns or arguments that they might put forward. Plan for these potential differences, be flexible, and show that you respect others' opinions.

Practicing/Drafting will also help. Think about headlines, key messages, and summary. Through practicing we can refine our communication to keep it concise.

DELEGATION

When delegating, a key mistake is being too prescriptive with the 'inputs'. These are the things that **you** think need to be done to achieve the 'output' or result required. Notice the emphasis on 'you' here. Where there is scope, provide the person you are delegating to with room to decide *how they will deliver* the end result required. You never know: they might come up with better ideas and ways of doing something than you had ever thought of!

Effective delegation involves painting a clear picture of the desired results, discussing any No/Nos, who else might help them, how they'll report back to you, and any consequences, both good and bad. Then you need to let them get on with it. Of course, this is also a great opportunity to demonstrate you know your people for who they are, rather than just what they do. Who best fits the task based on their personality, values, character and beliefs as well as their skills?

BODY LANGUAGE

Body language is another way of conveying your credibility, authority, and emotion. Dressing to impress is a simple way to build some authority. Standing tall, making eye contact, smiling and managing stress will also help. If you suffer from pre-presentation nerves, some simple exercises can help you prepare.

Deep breathing before you present helps increase oxygen levels in your blood with a resulting slowing of your heart rate. Repeatedly visualising your success beforehand will get you in the right frame of mind.

Amy Cuddy, Social Psychologist, has conducted research[6] on body language, revealing we can change our own body chemistry, and other people's perceptions of us, simply by changing body positions. Her excellent video on TED, which at the time of writing has received over 38 million views, describes how assuming a power pose, standing tall with hands on hips, for just two minutes, can affect testosterone and cortisol levels in the brain and increase confidence levels.

COACHING

This is probably a good point to expand further on coaching. Leaders can benefit from coaching, adopting a coaching style, and implementing a coaching culture in their organisation. In his book *Coaching For Performance*[7] Sir John Whitmore expresses the multiple benefits of coaching as improved performance and productivity, staff development, improved learning, improved relationships, quality of life, more time, more creativity, better use of people and resources, faster and more effective emergency response, and greater flexibility and adaptability to change.

When we relate this back to some of the key challenges facing leaders today, it is easy to see how coaching can be so beneficial. When you ask people a great *question* that raises their *awareness* and gets them to take *responsibility* (all key elements of coaching) you help them **C**reate meaning, **A**chieve their potential, **N**urture relationships, **B**uild resilience and **E**nrich their lives. In other words, a coaching approach helps facilitate the CANBE Model.

The importance of this 'coaching style' of leadership is emphasised in Judith E. Glaser's book *Conversation Intelligence: How Great Leaders Build Trust & Get Extraordinary Results*[8]. This describes how your day-to-day conversations can either trigger the lower, more primitive brain, resulting in releases of cortisol (the stress hormone), or activate higher-level intelligences such as trust, integrity, empathy, and good judgment associated with oxytocin, sometimes referred to as the "love" hormone.

Working this through, it becomes clear that organisational performance relies on the quality of the culture, which relies on the quality of relationships that, in turn, depend on the quality of your conversations. The lessons are clear, be careful with both what you say and how you say it!

Suffice it to say that good coaching, through its propensity to open up conversations and help the 'coachee' come to their own realisations, is well aligned with activating higher brain activity and achieving better results than providing all the answers for your people. Leaders who think they need to have all the answers really need to think again.

OTHERS' AFFECT ON US

So far in this section I've focused on how what we say and do affects others. These skills will impact how others perceive us and provide the best chance for them to reciprocate with positive behaviours.

This is important as the affect others have on us can play a big part in our wellbeing. Bullying in the workplace and domestic abuse are two extreme examples of the negative impact others can have but people can also inspire and energise us.

Have you ever worried about what someone thinks about you?

Been concerned that others must know exactly what you're thinking about them?

The thing is, we're the only ones who ever really know what it is that we're thinking. We often really don't know what others truly think about us. The best advice here is to think about patterns. Due to the biases, heuristics, lack of self-esteem, fixed thinking, lack of empathy and many of the other factors outlined in this book, other people's individual impression of us may be distorted to fit their own goals. However, if lots of people are reacting to us in a similar fashion, over a period of time, that may be a warning sign for us to look at our own behaviours in a different light!

We are all impressionable. We often follow trends (what other people do), conform to culture (wear certain types of clothes to certain types of occasions) or imitate others (picking up traits from a close friend). We are influenced more than we realise and often this is a good thing. Being like others helps us to fit in. Weight Watchers and Alcoholics Anonymous are two organisations based on the power of social influence. It's easier to give up alcohol or lose weight when we have 'people like us' for support. We can use this information to our advantage. Trying to get fit or become a better leader. Find other people like you who are trying to do the same. The social support will provide you with a better chance of success.

However, being like others can also cause harm. Racism and discrimination are two types of extreme negative outcomes that can be based on the influence of those around us, but there are many others. One of the simplest strategies for reducing this negative influence is to avoid the 'influencers' or give them less of your time. By taking responsibility and choosing our own thoughts, feelings and actions we can also disarm these negative influencers by directing the course of conversation to more positive territories. Finding more like minded people with a constructive approach can also help us to balance out any interactions that leave us feeling drained of energy.

When interactions turn into conflict it is worth considering impartial, objective support to help us resolve situations. I'll talk more about this in the Chapter on Social Wellbeing. After all, unresolved conflict can be bad for our health.

HEALTH

		Wellbeing Domains - 'Territories' - Interconnected areas of our lives							
		Mental Our thoughts	**Emotional** Our emotions	**Physical** Our actions	**Spiritual** Our spirit	**Social** Our communities	**Cultural** Our way	**Environmental** Our spaces	**Economic** Our trade
Wellbeing Dimensions **'Highways'** **Intertwined routes we use to navigate our lives**	**Creating meaning**	Thinking	Feelings	Behaviour	Identity	Friendship	Way of life	Affinity	Needs
	Achieving potential	Focus	Control	Mastery	Motivation	Teamwork	Governance	Cultivation	Impact
	Nurturing relationships	Regard	Empathy	Interaction	Stories	Trust	Belonging	Cohesion	Fairness
	Building resilience	Flexibility	Agility	Health	Growth	Support	Diversity	Adaptation	Integrity
	Enriching lives	Imagination	Wisdom	Energy	Purpose	Empowerment	Integration	Renewal	Freedom
		Wellbeing Factors - 'Signposts' - Interconnected things that can help us improve wellbeing							

"Health is a state of complete mental, social and physical well-being, not merely the absence of disease or infirmity."

WORLD HEALTH ORGANISATION

"Healthy citizens are the greatest asset any country can have."

WINSTON CHURCHILL

Sleep, diet and exercise are the biggest contributors to resilience in this area and there has been an explosion of apps, companies, and devices looking to serve the market. This means that whether you are a multi-national or a sole trader there is support out there to tap into, at varying degrees of cost. In fact, many of the apps are free or offer free 'lite' versions.

As a leader, you have a responsibility to yourself and those around you to develop and encourage good physical resilience. Obviously, your colleagues are responsible for their own health and there is danger of becoming too 'paternalistic' here. However, by acting as a role model and creating an environment where people can discuss and feel supported in achieving good physical health, you can demonstrate a caring approach. The best thing to do here is to talk with them about these topics and see what support is required.

At an organisational level your workplace can be proactive in encouraging and promoting good physical health and resilience through policies and practices like health and safety, personal safety training, health promotion, health checks and benefits, health insurance protection, managing disability, occupational health support, employee assistance programmes, and safe working practices and equipment.

A good approach to sickness/absence management, return to work interviews, and rehabilitation practices can help in highlighting the key health issues of your workforce and further organisational support can then be tailored accordingly. Even a simple activity like encouraging employees to take a lunch break away from their desk can work wonders and help set the correct tone.

SLEEP

Most scientists agree that between seven to eight hours of sleep are optimal, but many of us aren't getting this. So a great way to improve physical resilience is to change your habit and make sure you get the right amount of sleep.

Circadian rhythm is our natural reaction to changes in temperature, light, and other variables during the normal 24 hour cycle each day. Disruption to this rhythm usually has a negative effect and over the longer term is believed to have significant adverse health consequences. By finding your own natural rhythm, and sticking to this as closely as possible, you will have the best chance of good quality sleep.

Irregular sleeping patterns or long lay-ins at the weekend won't be helping and will make getting up on Monday much harder. There's a reason it's called 'Blue Monday'! Commit yourself to a regular wake up time and if you do miss sleep, go to bed earlier rather than having a lay in. Other tips here include having a cool down period from technology at least an hour before you go to bed and ensuring your bedroom is cool, dark, and free from technological disruptions.

Short power naps have also been found to be effective at decreasing stress and improving productivity, whilst not having a detrimental effect on the circadian rhythm. In fact, certain forward thinking businesses have started to recognise the simplicity and benefits of helping employees with sleep. Staff at insurance group Aetna get paid up to $300 (£225) a year for having a good night's sleep[1] and Google, Uber, Zappos, Ben & Jerry's, Huffington Post and PwC all have facilities for power naps. It doesn't take a rocket scientist to understand the benefits which include less health and safety issues, increased levels of concentration, and a reduction in anxiety and stress.

DIET

Along with sleep and exercise, diet is one of the most highly cited poor habits. There are many theories and outlooks and opinions on what constitutes a healthy diet, and it is likely that a healthy diet is in some ways unique to each person. However, to give a brief definition: a healthy diet is a balanced diet which includes food from all the major food groups in the right proportions, and in quantities which maintain a healthy body weight. The benefits of a healthy diet are manifold, including a lower risk of certain chronic diseases, increased energy levels, better sleep, improved mobility and more. In fact, new research is emerging all the time on the wider benefits of a healthy diet; it is truly extraordinary the difference what we eat can make to virtually all facets of our lives.

There are a variety of options for individual, team, and organisational support in this area including apps like MyFitnessPal, which has a database of over 6 million foods and a barcode scanner function that makes it easy to track what you are eating. Alternatives include online challenges such as those promoted by the British Heart Foundation[2], including the 'Food Labels', 'Waist Watchers' and a 'Hydration' challenge. Taking this a step further you could consult a nutritionist for expert advice to help inform personal, team, and organisational eating habits. This could be at a workshop level, or for a more thorough approach, a review of the menu in your workplace canteen to offer healthier options.

EXERCISE & STRETCHING

Exercise makes people more resilient not only to physical stress, but also to emotional and cognitive stress due to the unique combination of demands it puts on the body, brain, and the physiological changes it elicits (such as decreased blood pressure). As outlined earlier, it is often seen as a keystone habit that can lead to positive change in other areas of life.

In moderate doses, regular exercise helps build up your immune system so that you are better prepared when confronted with psychological stress. It also blunts the hormonal stress response to sudden psychological stress. Of course, if over-done, it can lead to greater stress, so the key is to ensure you are exercising regularly with the appropriate recovery periods.

As with diet, the explosion of technology in this area can be used to support healthier lifestyles. Devices like 'Fitbit' and associated apps can be used at an individual, team, or organisational level to measure physical activity, sleep, and other variables. Aside from technology: walking or cycling to work, lunchtime walking, exercise classes, yoga and group volunteering exercises are all simple ways to encourage exercise in the workplace.

Perhaps some of the simplest activities, particularly for desk-based workers, are to encourage stretching at the desk every hour for 5 minutes and just getting up and moving about. Changing your physiology releases hormones and endorphins that positively influence the way you feel. For ideas on stretching, there are plenty of guides online if you type in 'desk based stretches'. This is just a jumping off point, of course. How far you wish to take it is up to you.

RELAXATION

Just as with elite athletes, we need periods of relaxation for both our mind and body. Listening to your body and taking a break from things where you have become bored, tired, or stressed is one way to help remain resilient. In the workplace, this might mean getting up and having a break for 5 minutes, taking your (full) lunch break, getting out for a walk, listening to music, reading a book or even taking a power nap. Your organisation should have policies which encourage employees to relax at appropriate points in the day. As a leader, you should be a role model in this area.

Often we think the world will end with a moment of inattention, but in actuality, many of us can walk away and things will keep running as usual. Or, at worst, nothing drastic will happen. Of course, there are professions where there is a higher risk, such as nursing. Relaxation periods in these kinds of environments should be more structured so as to maximise restoration for the team whilst not compromising service or 'coverage'.

ENERGY

		Wellbeing Domains - 'Territories' - Interconnected areas of our lives							
		Mental Our thoughts	Emotional Our emotions	Physical Our actions	Spiritual Our spirit	Social Our communities	Cultural Our way	Environmental Our spaces	Economic Our trade
Wellbeing Dimensions 'Highways' Intertwined routes we use to navigate our lives	Creating meaning	Thinking	Feelings	Behaviour	Identity	Friendship	Way of life	Affinity	Needs
	Achieving potential	Focus	Control	Mastery	Motivation	Teamwork	Governance	Cultivation	Impact
	Nurturing relationships	Regard	Empathy	Interaction	Stories	Trust	Belonging	Cohesion	Fairness
	Building resilience	Flexibility	Agility	Health	Growth	Support	Diversity	Adaptation	Integrity
	Enriching lives	Imagination	Wisdom	Energy	Purpose	Empowerment	Integration	Renewal	Freedom
		Wellbeing Factors - 'Signposts' - Interconnected things that can help us improve wellbeing							

"You give life to what you give energy to."

ANONYMOUS

Our energy is really about our intentions, our commitment and the 'heart' we put into things. It draws from all the other areas of wellbeing. It's hard to describe but you know when you see and feel it in yourself and others. As such it is perhaps a good barometer of our overall personal wellbeing.

You can probably think about times when you've done things half heartedly or just 'gone through the motions'. We add power to our actions through the energy we put into them. You can forgive someone, but if you don't really mean it then the action becomes less meaningful, if carrying any meaning at all. On the contrary, think about a time when your actions were fully in tune with your thoughts, feelings and who you are. I'm guessing your energy levels were much higher.

Energy, intention and commitment are so important. Sometimes, if not always, they are more important than the action itself. Eddie The Eagle is perhaps one famous example from the UK. You may have seen the film. If not I fully recommend it!

In 1988 Eddie became the first ski-jumper since 1928 to represent Great Britain in the Olympics. He finished last in the 70 and 90 metre events. It wasn't what Eddie did, so much as the way he did it and the way he made people feel, which endeared him to the British public and fans across the World.

Everyone knew he stood little chance, including Eddie, but his enthusiasm, spirit and dedication to his sport were infectious. People loved him for that. So much so that Frank King, President of the Organising Committee speaking at the closing ceremony of the 1988 Winter Olympics said "At these Games, some competitors have won gold, some have broken records, and some of you have even soared like an eagle."

So how do we generate the levels of energy that enrich our lives and the lives of others? Let's test the CANBE Model.

MENTALLY

From an early age Eddie dreamt of becoming an Olympian and he had the **imagination** to change his story. His goal was to compete for Britain at the Calgary Winter Olympics and he had a plan and **focus** for getting there.

However there were doubters all around him in the media, the sport itself and the general public. He overcame this negative **thinking,** and any worries or doubts, and in doing so had to develop high **regard** for himself and a healthy respect for the other athletes he was competing against.

Eddie had originally intended to enter as a skier in the Calgary Olympics. So, to improve his chances of qualifying, he moved to Lake Placid in the USA to train and enter higher standard races. However, due to a lack of funds, he had to demonstrate a **flexible mind-set** and switched to ski jumping which offered lower costs and easier qualification!

EMOTIONALLY

Eddie had been written off throughout his life. It would have been easy to let his **feelings** get the better of him and quit. But he had high levels of self-awareness and knew both his limitations and his strengths. Of course the event itself was filled with adrenaline and hurtling down the ski slope was a scary prospect. Managing these emotions to perform skillfully was a feat in itself. Throughout both the highs and lows he had to **control** his emotional response and build relationships with people around him with **empathy**, humour and **agility**. With all of the criticism, barbed comments and even obstacles put in his way Eddie showed great emotional **wisdom** to navigate to his end goal. Even after the Olympics he had to demonstrate this wisdom after almost being banned from Olympic competition. His accusers said he was making a mockery of the sport and was too popular for someone who wasn't at the top of their field!

PHYSICALLY

The **actions** Eddie took propelled him forward and with practice and perseverance he began to master his event. Perhaps though, this was the area where Eddie was most limited. It is clear that his skills were not the equivalent of his competitors and his levels of **mastery** not the same. In respect to his **health** he was also handicapped by his weight, being more than 9 kg (20 lb) heavier than the next heaviest competitor. But success for Eddie wasn't to win the Olympics, only to compete. Through his endeavours he managed to **communicate** a story around ski jumping that took it from page 50 to page 1.

SPIRITUALLY

It was perhaps in this domain of wellbeing where Eddie excelled most. His popularity was largely due to him exemplifying the 'Olympic Spirit' and it could be said that he had more of it than any of the other jumpers out there. He had **identity** and **purpose**. Can you remember any of the other jumpers from the 1988 Olympics? He was, and still is, Eddie The Eagle, the *story* of 'David versus Goliath' that captured the imagination of people across the World.

He has described his **motivation** as proving the doubters wrong, representing Great Britain and using the Calgary Olympics as a way of getting attention and sponsorship so he could continue ski jumping to get 'better and better and better'.

Through this combination of mental, emotional, physical and spiritual wellbeing Eddie has enriched the lives of many. The World would be a poorer place without him. He created a great deal of energy, and continues to do so.

In this story I've focused mainly on the more 'personal' elements of wellbeing. However it is clear that there are strong social, cultural, environmental and economic elements too. The key message here is that to create energy we need to focus on our wellbeing in a balanced way.

Using the CANBE Model, where can you identify gaps and strengths in your energy levels? Think about your identity, purpose and story. How well do your thoughts, feelings and actions match up? Where are you doing things habitually that might need re-thinking?

As a leader you will lead through the intentions of your thoughts, feelings, actions and spirit. If these are mis-aligned your leadership will be poorer for it. However, if you focus on improving your personal wellbeing, and can lead with intention and commitment, you will be a leader with charisma and aura. You will be a leader who creates energy.

CHAPTER SUMMARY

Physical wellbeing is entwined with all other domains of wellbeing and particularly mental, emotional and spiritual. Who you are as a person, how you think and feel, all interplay with your actions and behaviours. Encapsulated in your daily habits, it is these ***actions*** that lead to the current life you are living.

If you want to lead a different life you need to change these habits. The CANBE Model provides 'signposts' for many things you can do to improve your wellbeing and that of your team and organisation.

To improve our physical wellbeing we must also learn to ***master*** new skills. This involves stepping outside our comfort zone. Setting goals and standards is a great place to start and then making sure we manage any obstacles that might get in the way. Role modelling the behaviours we expect to see by 'talking the talk' and 'walking the walk' will help us gain the trust and respect of people.

Poor ***interactions with others*** can often have a negative effect on physical health by causing feelings of anxiety, uncertainty, nervousness and reduced optimism. A leader has a responsibility to communicate well by listening, providing effective feedback, asking great questions, influencing, persuading, delegating and coaching. Through effective body language, using emotions, character and logic appropriate to the situation and audience, leaders will communicate with greater impact.

Physical wellbeing is about more than just ***health,*** but without good physical health wellbeing is diminished and performance reduced. A combination of good sleep, diet, exercise and relaxation help set us up for the challenges and opportunities we face each day.

Finally, the ***energy*** and intent we create as leaders are more important, sometimes, than the action itself. If intent and commitment are strong, failure can be overcome and motivation maintained to succeed next time.

KEY CONCEPTS TO IMPROVE PHYSICAL WELLBEING:

Leaders should think more broadly about physical wellbeing as all the things we do, not just exercise, sleep and diet. Our daily habits and behaviours contribute significantly to our wellbeing. We can improve through the following:

Improving our daily actions:

- Changing bad habits and building on good ones

Mastery of new skills:

- Learning new skills
- Getting into 'flow' states more often

Improving interactions with others

- Actively listening
- Constructive feedback
- Using effective questioning techniques more often
- Coaching more
- Using the patterns others see in us as signposts for improvement

Improving health

- Eating a better diet and good hydration
- Good levels of exercise
- Getting better sleep
- Ensuring we have periods of relaxation

Improving energy

- Inspiring others with intent and commitment

KEY BEHAVIOURS:

Where do you score on following behaviours that contribute to personal, team and organisational physical wellbeing?

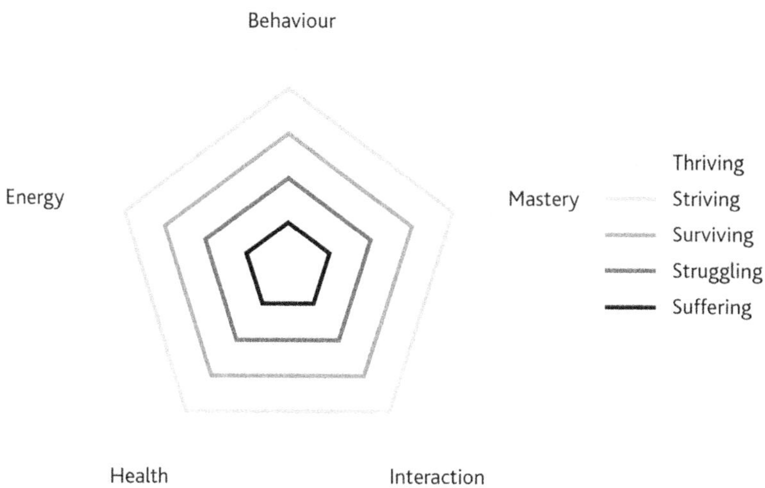

What would you like to improve on?

CHAPTER EIGHT

IMPROVING SPIRITUAL WELLBEING

Wellbeing Domains - 'Territories' - Interconnected areas of our lives

Wellbeing Dimensions 'Highways' Intertwined routes we use to navigate our lives		Mental Our thoughts	Emotional Our emotions	Physical Our actions	Spiritual Our spirit	Social Our communities	Cultural Our way	Environmental Our spaces	Economic Our trade
	Creating meaning	Thinking	Feelings	Behaviour	Identity	Friendship	Way of life	Affinity	Needs
	Achieving potential	Focus	Control	Mastery	Motivation	Teamwork	Governance	Cultivation	Impact
	Nurturing relationships	Regard	Empathy	Interaction	Stories	Trust	Belonging	Cohesion	Fairness
	Building resilience	Flexibility	Agility	Health	Growth	Support	Diversity	Adaptation	Integrity
	Enriching lives	Imagination	Wisdom	Energy	Purpose	Empowerment	Integration	Renewal	Freedom

Wellbeing Factors - 'Signposts' - Interconnected things that can help us improve wellbeing

---

"Life isn't about finding yourself. Life is about creating yourself."

GEORGE BERNARD SHAW

If mental and emotional wellbeing are largely about how we think and feel, and physical wellbeing is about what we do and how we express ourselves, then spiritual wellbeing is who we are as individuals and groups. Often described as 'our soul', this is acquired genetically and through a sense of **identity** based on values, beliefs, personality and character, or virtues.

By understanding ourselves better, we can live in alignment with our true self. Not being true to ourselves can constantly feel like having to wear a mask. When we go against our true values or ideals (for example, continuing to work for a company where we don't agree with the values and policies), we can become demotivated, stressed, or even depressed. When we *are* aligned with our true self it feels easier and gives us more **motivation**.

Our **stories** describe who we are and connect us through shared beliefs, values, hopes, dreams, and experiences. Of course, these stories are based on our experiences. The more we push outside our comfort zones and grow, the richer our stories become. Things don't always go to plan and we often need to change direction which adds to our **growth.**

Finally, spiritual wellbeing is about understanding that we are part of something bigger than ourselves defined by our sense of **purpose**.

If we have a poor understanding of who we are and feel disconnected from anything bigger, we can become **'unfulfilled'**. With greater self-awareness and meaning in life we are **'fulfilled'**.

IDENTITY

		Wellbeing Domains - 'Territories' - Interconnected areas of our lives							
		Mental Our thoughts	Emotional Our emotions	Physical Our actions	Spiritual Our spirit	Social Our communities	Cultural Our way	Environmental Our spaces	Economic Our trade
Wellbeing Dimensions 'Highways' Intertwined routes we use to navigate our lives	Creating meaning	Thinking	Feelings	Behaviour	Identity	Friendship	Way of life	Affinity	Needs
	Achieving potential	Focus	Control	Mastery	Motivation	Teamwork	Governance	Cultivation	Impact
	Nurturing relationships	Regard	Empathy	Interaction	Stories	Trust	Belonging	Cohesion	Fairness
	Building resilience	Flexibility	Agility	Health	Growth	Support	Diversity	Adaptation	Integrity
	Enriching lives	Imagination	Wisdom	Energy	Purpose	Empowerment	Integration	Renewal	Freedom
		Wellbeing Factors - 'Signposts' - Interconnected things that can help us improve wellbeing							

"Be yourself; everyone else is already taken."

OSCAR WILDE

This point in the book brings us to the age old argument of 'nature versus nurture'. How much does our wellbeing depend on our environment and circumstances versus our genes? As you can imagine, with the increasing recognition of the importance of wellbeing to policy development, business performance and the mapping of the genome, research in this area is growing significantly.

One of the most recent meta studies[1] looking at how genes impact wellbeing concluded 'results indicate that genetic factors contribute significantly by explaining about 35 % of the variance'. Other studies have linked extroversion to 'positive affect' (how often we feel positive emotions over a short time frame) which is one of the key elements used to measure wellbeing. Similarly there are studies linking neuroticism with anxiety and depression. Genes do influence our wellbeing, by about a third according to the meta study mentioned above. However it is clear that our circumstances and environment also play a part.

Another salient point to mention here is that, contrary to popular belief, our personality and character aren't fixed. We can change. 'Old dogs can be taught to learn new tricks.' This is the concept of Neuroplasticity - our experience of thinking, feeling, and doing changes the physical structure of our brain, and the function of different brain circuits.

Neuroscientific investigations[2] have recently begun to explore how wellbeing is created and changed by our brains. We mentioned previously, 'cells that fire together, wire together'. This describes the way that pathways and connections in our brain's circuitry are created the more we use them. Identifying these 'pathways' and understanding interventions that can induce changes in them will help us lead happier, healthier lives.

So whilst some of our wellbeing is determined by our genes, there is still real scope to change and improve. Certainly one way to do this is through knowing ourselves better. Understanding ourselves is fundamental to our wellbeing and is an ongoing quest worthy of a large investment of time and energy. It can help us in all areas of our lives including career-planning, friendships, choosing life partners, and just simple day-to-day decision making.

It is surprising, then, that many people, if asked the following questions, might struggle to answer.

- What are your values?
- What are your core beliefs?
- How would you describe your personality?
- What are your character strengths?

Getting to know ourselves better is not easy. Our experiences are the best way to understand ourselves, so a little reflection each day - or capturing the way we thought, felt, and acted in a diary - can be an excellent exercise to learn more about ourselves.

We also often learn a great deal about ourselves during key events in our lives, such as crises or even major successes. How did we react at these key points? What does this tell us about ourselves?

Life is made up of this ongoing learning. However, we can also take a snapshot from time to time, and this can be helpful to assess where we are (and who we are). Some useful exercises include: reviewing our values, beliefs, character, and personality.

Of course, these principles can also operate effectively at an organisational level. If we think of our department or organisation as the cumulative representation of all the people in it, then it's hopefully clear that everyone needs to understand how their individual values, beliefs, characteristics, and personality can be harnessed for personal, team, and organisational benefit. If everyone is pushing and pulling in different directions, then it will be very difficult for our customers, suppliers, and other external parties to get a true feel for what our organisation stands for.

This is the role of branding. By helping employees leverage personal attributes with those that have been aggregated at the departmental and organisational level, we can get everyone driving in the same direction. In doing so, we will deliver a much more consistent and powerful customer experience, whilst still satisfying the needs of our individual employees.

Of course, the previous paragraphs make an assumption that we have defined organisational values, purpose, beliefs and culture already. If these are absent or misunderstood, then how will people get behind them? One great way of getting people engaged, particularly in smaller companies where it is more feasible, is to involve them in the development of the company's purpose, beliefs, and culture. Organisations are made by people, after all. Even ones that rely heavily on algorithms or technology.

Many companies have 'stated' values and purpose, with posters displayed around the central office, but this is often where it stops. To truly engage with company values and to give people a reason 'why', values must be 'lived'.

They must be embedded in every element of the organisation's operations from recruitment, through performance management, pay, reward and recognition, to product development, pricing, and customer service. Demonstrating and communicating how they are being used to inform company decision-making is another excellent way to do this. Actions speak louder than words!

Once these values, character, beliefs, and personality are embedded throughout the organisation, they will begin to get recognised by customers who will, hopefully, have more of a 'reason why' to do business with you.

Another way to extend them further is to think about how our organisation can help build wellbeing in the community and the world at large. A genuine and authentic sponsorship, volunteering effort, or campaign that comes from our organisations 'heart' can be a great way of building pride amongst employees and better connections externally.

Developing pride in the organisational purpose and aligning activity to our brand are important, but this should be balanced with providing people the freedom and skills to get the job done.

Let's now take a look at each of these key identity elements in turn.

VALUES

Values are like having a compass for your life and help you remain true to yourself. They are hugely important in providing motivation and direction, and yet many people go through their lives without knowing what their values are. When you know your values, you focus on what really matters rather than wasting time on activities that aren't a priority.

We all have different values that make us unique and distinct, so understanding our values, and those of others, can help us build regard for ourselves and the people around us resulting in greater respect and stronger relationships.

Values, attitudes, and beliefs have a strong connection to our thoughts, feelings, and behaviours. When we are in-line with our values, life will feel easier. In contrast, when we are doing things that are out of line with our values, we may feel stressed, frustrated, or dissatisfied and this can, in extreme situations, affect our health.

Here are a few questions to help you think about your values if you haven't already. Write down your answers.

- What things hold the greatest meaning for you in life?
- What are you likely to be doing when you feel the best about yourself?
- What things do you hold the strongest beliefs about?
- What are your key priorities in life?

Now, ask yourself what each of the things you've written down gives you. So, for example, you may have written down 'family'. What does family give you? Is it security, love, friendship, support? Which of those is most important to you?

Using your list of values, you can assess how well aligned these are with those of the organisation you work for. Where are there synergies? Where are the gaps? Where are the conflicts?

Thinking this through should provide a better understanding of where any frictions and strengths lie to help you get on better in your workplace. Of course, this might require you to take action and make some adjustments.

I hope you can also see how this type of exercise would be useful for a team and how some of these questions might prove helpful in your recruitment processes.

BELIEFS

Whilst values are the principles or standards of an individual or group, beliefs are what they hold to be true. People can hold extremely strong beliefs, but that doesn't mean they are right. We once believed the world was flat but subsequently found out we were wrong!

Beliefs are the 'scripts' we have developed throughout our lives. They result in the 'stories' we tell ourselves that either propel us forward, or hold us back. Most of us can remember the power of the monsters we told ourselves were in the cupboard at the end of our bed when we were a child!

As a leader, beliefs will have an impact on personal, team, and organisational performance. What are your own personal beliefs? Are they helping you move forward or holding you back? What are the beliefs in your leadership team or amongst your people?

We can listen out for beliefs in our language and the language of the people around you. 'Shouldn't', 'can't', 'won't be able', 'impossible', are all examples of language that might be holding us, our team, or our organisation back. There are many other examples, but these are some common ones that crop up.

The great thing is: these stories and scripts can be changed over time. Our subconscious mind is unable to distinguish between what is genuine and what is false. That is why dreams hold such power over us, and we may even experience physical reactions when dreaming. To the brain, the experience is real. And this is why what we expect to happen often does. Henry Ford put it this way:

"If you think you can, or you think you can't, you're probably right."

By feeding the subconscious mind with positive thoughts, we can start challenging these beliefs. Asking questions like: 'What evidence have you got to support that?', 'What makes you think that?' and then opening up the minds of people around us with questions like: 'What if we could do it?', 'What would you do if you knew you couldn't fail?' is one way of helping here.

Whilst the importance of 'values' are well discussed and understood in the workplace, it's my experience that 'beliefs' and their power receive less emphasis. As a leader, we can change this by starting the conversation and asking questions like the ones mentioned above. Having a 'vision', using positive language, and setting goals that increasingly challenge us and our team to step outside our 'comfort zone' are also great ways to build belief and confidence.

PERSONALITY

Our personality is a reflection of the way we behave and has its roots in character. It is the mask we choose to wear in any given situation and the way we present ourselves to the world. There are no good or bad, right or wrong personality styles. They are what they are.

There are many different personality profiling exercises including tools like MBTI or DISC. By completing one of these, it can help us understand ourselves and others better. Perhaps one of the most dominant models today is the 'Big 5 Personality Traits Test' which was derived from gathering all relevant words from the dictionary and using factor analysis to group them together in ways that most effectively described the differences between people. Some of the biggest differentiators used among many of these tools is the distinction between being introverted and extroverted, and people-versus task-focused. Which do you tend towards the most?

Some of the benefits of taking a test include: building higher levels of rapport through adapting our style, fostering greater understanding and co-operation with others, understanding why certain conflict situations may have occurred, identifying areas for training and development and gaining insight into how our personality fits with our organisation.

Just as we would describe an individual as having a certain type of personality, so too can we describe a team or organisation. Defining personality at these levels can help employees, customers, suppliers, and other stakeholders relate to our team and organisation and develop more meaningful connections.

While this all seems obvious, it is amazing how dis-engaged and de-motivated many employees are. Gallup in its Global Great Jobs 2016[3] report says 'what the whole world wants is a good job' which it defines as '30+ hours per week of consistent work with a paycheck from an employer'.

Gallup goes on to outline the importance of the quality of a job. One way of quantifying this is through employee engagement metrics. Between 2013 and 2015, Gallup asked engagement questions worldwide and found that only 14% of people with good jobs were also engaged. This is staggering, but also provides a fantastic opportunity for modern leaders to ensure a greater number of people are engaged and motivated in their work.

CHARACTER

Our virtues, otherwise called character, come from learned behaviour, starting from early relationships. They are a set of behaviour traits that define what type of person you are. It has been described as one's soul, the real you.

Research[4] emerging from over three years of rigorous and comprehensive historical analysis by more than 50 leading scientists identified six virtues – wisdom, courage, humanity, justice, temperance, and transcendence. These are seen as the basic building blocks of human goodness and flourishing; valued by philosophers and great thinkers across time and world cultures.

Below these virtues sit 24 character strengths. Research has shown that using your 'signature' or core character strengths can actually have a significant positive impact on your life, helping to build resilience, improve relationships, and enhance health and overall wellbeing.

Using character strengths helps people tap into their 'intrinsic' motivation and channel natural energy and passion. In addition to reasons driven by increasing motivation, research[5, 6] also shows that when you see more of a fit between yourself and your job you are more likely to experience work as personally meaningful and respond with enhanced job performance, find satisfaction, and stay longer.

Understanding character can also help with team building and communication by encouraging people to understand each other better and take on roles more aligned to their strengths. There are also clear links here with levels of autonomy and control which both help to contribute to higher levels of wellbeing.

As a leader, exploring your own personal character strengths and helping your people and teams do likewise is one way you can 'humanise' the workplace. Using character strengths can also lead to more balanced decision-making and supports a more sustainable business model.

The key thing here is seeing people not just for what they do but more for who they are. The greater confidence people have in being true to themselves at work, the happier they'll be and the better they'll perform.

MOTIVATION

		Wellbeing Domains - 'Territories' - Interconnected areas of our lives							
		Mental Our thoughts	Emotional Our emotions	Physical Our actions	Spiritual Our spirit	Social Our communities	Cultural Our way	Environmental Our spaces	Economic Our trade
Wellbeing Dimensions 'Highways' Intertwined routes we use to navigate our lives	Creating meaning	Thinking	Feelings	Behaviour	Identity	Friendship	Way of life	Affinity	Needs
	Achieving potential	Focus	Control	Mastery	Motivation	Teamwork	Governance	Cultivation	Impact
	Nurturing relationships	Regard	Empathy	Interaction	Stories	Trust	Belonging	Cohesion	Fairness
	Building resilience	Flexibility	Agility	Health	Growth	Support	Diversity	Adaptation	Integrity
	Enriching lives	Imagination	Wisdom	Energy	Purpose	Empowerment	Integration	Renewal	Freedom
		Wellbeing Factors - 'Signposts' - Interconnected things that can help us improve wellbeing							

> "Motivation is part of our future, and our ability to realise that future. No motivation means no energy; and no energy means, at best, a deeply unsatisfying life."
>
> JAMES SALE, *MAPPING MOTIVATION*

Hopefully it is clear that by understanding our identity better, we are more likely to take on activities that are aligned with who we are. 'Intrinsic' motivation is doing things because they are interesting and satisfying and reflect who we are as a person. We do them for their own sake and not because of external influence. How can leaders create the best conditions for motivated colleagues? Well, Figure 1 shows the relationship between Maslow's Hierarchy of Needs, engagement, and wellbeing.

Whilst there is, at the time of writing, no empirical research that clearly links engagement with wellbeing, the diagram takes a common sense approach to the relationships and those with Maslow's Hierarchy of Needs.

For example, someone who sees a larger purpose in their work is likely to be more highly engaged and have higher wellbeing, providing their other needs are also satisfied. This illustrates the point that a more holistic approach to all elements of the model needs to be taken. It's probably worth pointing out that whilst these needs have been presented over time as a hierarchy, they were never deliberately intended to be presented that way by Maslow. Rather than seeing them as a hierarchy it may be better to view them as inter-connected. In fact, by using the CANBE Model you'll be doing this anyway!

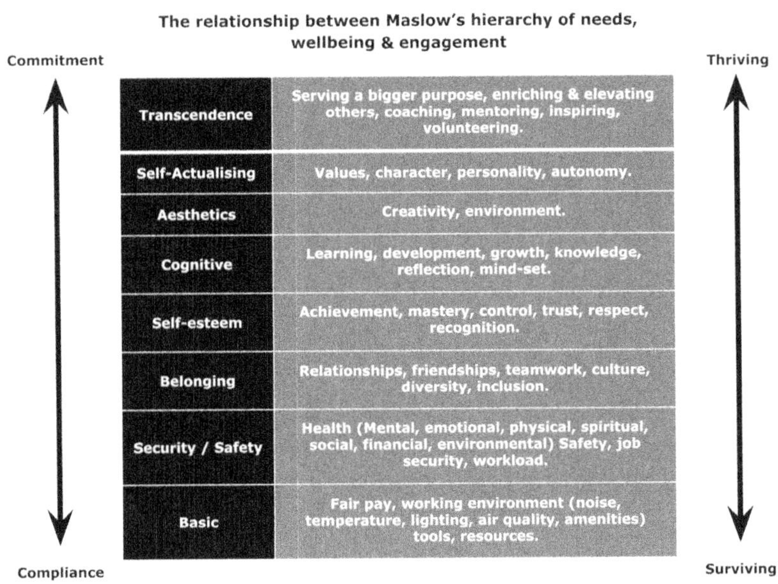

Simon Sinek in his TED talk "How Great Leaders Inspire Action"[1], talks about the importance of people knowing *why*. With a better understanding of 'why' we're doing something we have greater motivation and connection.

This 'why' will be different for each individual and will be linked to the criteria in Figure 1. However, higher level motivators like values, beliefs, character, and personality fit are more likely to have a greater influence on engagement than some of the lower level motivators like pay. Research[2] generally shows that these lower level motivators play an important role in retention but have less impact on effort and commitment.

As a leader, these higher level motivators are a great starting place if you haven't already reflected on them personally. Once you've done this you'll be better placed to answer the question 'What motivates me to want to be a leader'?

SELF-DETERMINATION

Bridging the topics of motivation and wellbeing is the theory of self-determination developed by Deci and Ryan[3]. The theory identifies three innate, universal and psychological needs seen across time, gender and culture. These needs influence human motivation and focus on the degree to which an individual's behaviour is self-motivated and self-determined. They include autonomy, competence and relatedness, with the research suggesting that higher levels of each will lead to greater motivation and wellbeing.

Autonomy, which we have already mentioned on several occasions throughout the book, is our need to self-determine, perceive that we have choices and do things of our own volition. It is the desire to act in harmony with our beliefs, values and who we are. This does not, however, mean we need to act independently. When we feel forced, pressured, controlled, compelled, influenced or manipulated, then we have lost at least some, if not all, of our autonomy. When we volunteer, offer, choose, accept, support, consent, willingly conform or decide, then we have retained most, if not all of our autonomy. Autonomy is the difference between feeling forced to accept guidance or willingly accepting it.

Competence is our need to feel capable of meeting every-day challenges and opportunities, and feeling a sense of growth and mastery which we have already explored.

Relatedness is our need to connect, interact, care about, and be cared for by others, and the feeling that we are contributing to something greater than ourselves. This could be who we are doing an activity for or with. It could also be the person or people who benefit, for example our managers, team mates, friends, neighbours or customers. It is closely linked with purpose, which we'll come onto later in this chapter, and our next chapter Social Wellbeing.

Leaders can create the best conditions for high levels of motivation and wellbeing by enabling greater autonomy, competence and relatedness. As we explored earlier in this section, this is normally when leaders tap into who a person is and facilitate circumstances where they are intrinsically motivated. Some examples of how leaders can achieve this include:

Autonomy

- Really understanding a person's values, beliefs, character, skills, strengths, personality and ensuring tasks and projects provide an individual with opportunities to express themselves
- Removing barriers and obstacles
- Explaining the outcome required and leaving people to come up with their own ways of delivering
- Providing people with choices

Competence

- Matching tasks with skill sets

- Providing training and growth opportunities
- Coaching people to stretch outside their comfort zones
- Ensuring people aren't overstretched in terms of their skill set or overwhelmed with too much to do
- Providing positive feedback

Relatedness

- Getting teams working well together
- Helping people understand and get to know each other better
- Explaining how the task will impact on people's lives
- Having a higher purpose

Not all tasks will be intrinsically motivating. Motivation may also be extrinsic or lie anywhere on a spectrum between these two polarities. Externally motivated behaviour can become closer to intrinsic motivation when it is linked to higher levels of autonomy, competence or relatedness. For example, when a boring task set by a manager is congruent with the beliefs of a person (autonomy) or a person sees a chance to grow skills (competence) or feels caring for the people they are doing the task with, for, or to benefit (relatedness).

I'd like to highlight, at this point, the importance of these concepts to the following domains of wellbeing. Social, cultural, environmental and economic events can positively and negatively impact people's autonomy, competence and relatedness and therefore their wellbeing. For example:

Socially, when someone is intrinsically motivated but is working in a team where there is little friendship, minimal trust, they feel unsupported or disempowered.

Culturally if their way of life is threatened, governance is weak, policies and procedures are restrictive, they feel like they don't belong, there is little respect for diversity and poor integration.

Environmentally if they don't feel at home, have a place which doesn't help them achieve their goals or interact effectively with others. If they are unable to adapt to changes in the environment or don't have opportunities for renewal.

Economically if they don't have access to information and resources, or understand the impact of their work for others, if rewards are unfair or used inappropriately. If the system lacks integrity and there is little progress.

All of the above examples demonstrate the clear links between these four domains and wellbeing. As you read through the chapters please keep these in mind and think about how you can create more autonomy, relatedness and competence.

REWARD & RECOGNITION

We know from neuroscience that the things we choose to do are often because of the anticipated reward, whether these are intrinsic or extrinsic. Therefore, how you choose to celebrate and reward success as a leader can have a big impact on the types of behaviours, culture, and outcomes you develop.

Knowing how to get the best out of people as a leader means providing them with the rewards and motivation that matter most. It is my contention that if you align your reward and recognition scheme to the CANBE Model it will provide an excellent framework that helps to create greater wellbeing. I hope, as you read through the following sections, you can see the links with autonomy, competence, and relatedness!

Creating meaning – We've already seen how values, beliefs, personality and character can help create meaning. Rewarding people for 'living' the values and delivering in alignment with the purpose will help reinforce this meaning. Going further and recognising people for their character is a great opportunity for a leader to make this even more personal.

Putting people in control and giving them greater autonomy will increase the meaning of reward and recognition. The trend to develop "menu-style" reward schemes, where people can choose from an increasingly diverse set of financial and non-financial rewards, does this fantastically. Let's face it, the person who knows what motivates them best is the person receiving the reward!

This balance between financial and non-financial rewards is worth expanding on here. Research[4] has shown that, up to a point, pay has a positive impact on emotions such as joy, stress, sadness, anger, and affection that make one's life pleasant or unpleasant. That point is circa $75,000 or £58,000[5]. So for a large percentage of employees, pay is still a significant motivator. But past that point, non-financial rewards may have an increasingly significant impact on day-to-day emotions. So a key point here is ensuring people are getting paid fairly for the work they do. Benchmarking versus competitors and against industry standards and then communicating the outcomes internally is one way of demonstrating transparency and fairness.

Achieving potential – In the past, organisations awarded people for 'long service', in effect just being there. The increasing trend is to award people for performance linked to the organisational goals and objectives. Your scheme needs to have clear objectives to ensure people understand 'what' they need to do to be successful. More than this, the scheme should also reward people for 'how' they do it and reflect the values of your organisation.

Nurturing relationships - The *fairness and transparency* of the reward and recognition scheme will have a big impact here. A good reward and recognition scheme should promote stronger cohesion amongst the staff, rather than instilling jealousy or competition. Good examples include peer-to-peer recognition where staff can send each other a 'thank you', linked perhaps to company values, or even award each other 'points for prizes'. Be careful that employees don't see this as a needless additional bureaucracy (or worse, a system to be gamed). The sincerity with which this scheme is implemented will have a tremendous effect on the outcome, and the way it is received.

Building resilience – This is an interesting area in respect to the focus of rewarding success versus failure. Penalising and condemning failure can stifle innovation and keep people from trying new ideas.

An increasing number of companies reward their employees for failure. This includes P&G, with their "heroic failure award" and Google with its innovation lab. This isn't to say these companies are rewarding bad work, or recklessly promoting failure, but they are encouraging it in a structured way. After all, breakthroughs are only possible with experimentation and attempts to do things that have never been done before. Thomas Edison, the serial inventor, famously said: "I have not failed. I've just found 10,000 ways that won't work." As a leader, you can help promote innovation and engagement by setting aside some budget that encourages calculated risk-taking.

This also links with learning and growth. Rewarding someone with an opportunity to go on a course or learn something new to develop their career is an excellent incentive. In fact, the absence of career development and learning opportunities are often cited as key reasons for people leaving an organisation.

Perhaps also thinking of a more long term approach to reward and recognition rather than instant gratification might go some way to encouraging greater sustainability. We have seen this approach being taken increasingly at board and senior level, with executives being rewarded for sustained performance over time, as opposed to large yearly bonuses linked to annual performance.

Enriching lives – Finally, reward and recognition schemes should enrich the lives of employees through encouraging forgiveness, gratitude, enjoyment, fun, confidence, and optimism. If you don't have the resources to set aside a budget for failure or experimentation, then the very least you can do is show forgiveness when people do fail. Encouraging people to learn from mistakes and try again will set the right tone for new ideas and innovation to rise to the surface.

A simple 'thanks' can go a long way and it is surprising how often this can be neglected. Doing this in a way that recognises the individual can enhance the benefit. Let me share a brief story to explain fully what I mean. There was an organisation a friend of mine used to work with, and indeed there are many like it, that would always recognise great performance by calling someone up on stage, making everyone else applaud, and presenting them with a public award. This was a very big ostentatious occasion. What the organisation found, however, after years of running this award, was that the same names kept winning over and over. At first, they thought that made sense. The highest performers were the highest performers, surely? But over time they came to realise that this wasn't the case, it was that others were avoiding meeting the criteria to be selected for the reward. They talked to their people and found most of their staff *hated* being called up on stage. They were introverted, didn't like being the centre of attention, and in fact would go so far as to either conceal their good performance, or actively sabotage their chances of getting the award to *avoid* having to get up on stage. When the organisation realised this, they were aghast. They thought they were doing something really great for their staff. In reality, only a small handful of people liked the public attention, and the rest came to be terrorised by the reward scheme!

Now, we have come a long way from those slightly old school days, and most organisations now recognise that every individual is different and one size does not fit all. However, it's worth bearing in mind how important it is to think through reward schemes. Whilst one person might like public praise, another may prefer their recognition face-to-face. Expressing thanks through a written note can also be a great way to show you care.

Social events at work, fun and enjoyment, is another area that will benefit from a considered approach that puts people in control and provides them with choice. Fun to one person might be a complete 'drag' to another. How many Christmas work-dos are orientated towards drinking? In today's world, many people drink less, and so it's important to consider options that include others. Fun and enjoyment at the workplace shouldn't just be a once a year event, or even necessarily organised at all: spontaneously buying the team ice creams on a hot sunny day, or just having a laugh together between tasks, is what makes the workplace a welcoming and great place to be.

Reminding people of what they are good at and praising their character will help build their confidence. Encouraging your team to discuss what they've done well this week/month can also help. Unsurprisingly, it's often the neglected little things that can really make a big difference.

STORIES

		Wellbeing Domains - 'Territories' - Interconnected areas of our lives							
		Mental Our thoughts	Emotional Our emotions	Physical Our actions	Spiritual Our spirit	Social Our communities	Cultural Our way	Environmental Our spaces	Economic Our trade
Wellbeing Dimensions 'Highways' Intertwined routes we use to navigate our lives	Creating meaning	Thinking	Feelings	Behaviour	Identity	Friendship	Way of life	Affinity	Needs
	Achieving potential	Focus	Control	Mastery	Motivation	Teamwork	Governance	Cultivation	Impact
	Nurturing relationships	Regard	Empathy	Interaction	Stories	Trust	Belonging	Cohesion	Fairness
	Building resilience	Flexibility	Agility	Health	Growth	Support	Diversity	Adaptation	Integrity
	Enriching lives	Imagination	Wisdom	Energy	Purpose	Empowerment	Integration	Renewal	Freedom
		Wellbeing Factors - 'Signposts' - Interconnected things that can help us improve wellbeing							

"Stories are a communal currency of humanity."

TAHIR SHAH, ARABIAN NIGHTS

"The stories we tell literally make the world. If you want to change the world, you need to change your story. This truth applies both to individuals and institutions."

MICHAEL MARGOLIS

"Those who tell the stories rule the world."

HOPI AMERICAN INDIAN PROVERB

Stories have been told since the beginning of time, even before humans learnt to read and write. But they are also part of our everyday lives from the advertising we see, political campaigns, the books we read, the anecdotes we tell friends, through to the films we watch.

Storytelling is useful in every avenue of our individual and collective wellbeing, appealing to both our hearts and our minds. Stories help us create meaning, achieve our potential, nurture relationships, build resilience and enrich our lives.

The domains, dimensions and signposts we've covered through this book help us see and act systemically. Stories help us make meaning out of these connections and patterns. They are a direct route to our emotions and changing the values, mindsets, rules, and goals to help us get where we want to be.

A powerful example of this came at the height of the Blitz in the UK, when World War II was about to be lost. Winston Churchill urged Londoners to "Keep Calm and Carry On." These five words framed the stoic attitude and grit of a battered city and nation to help change the course of history.

This is also a great example of keeping your eyes on the prize. When telling stories it is far better to focus on where you want to be and not on what's stopping you getting there. When you read lots of stories about how bad things are likely to be, the bad thing literally becomes more likely.

As a leader stories can help you paint the big picture, but they are also implicitly good for our wellbeing. Mentally, our vocabulary, comprehension, focus, memory and creativity all grow when we tell stories. They strengthen or challenge our thoughts and opinions, and we experience them in our imagination as if they were real.

Emotionally they inspire and evoke deeper feelings to help us understand more complex concepts, thoughts and ideas. We grasp a greater understanding of the full range of emotions from stories, and this helps us empathise and understand others better. For those struggling to express or understand their own emotions, storytelling within their own lives through journaling, blogging or video can be a great way to help process and work through these challenges. Of course consuming too many bad stories can be bad for our emotional and mental wellbeing, just as consuming too much junk food can be bad for our physical wellbeing. If these stories or bad news are getting you riled up, or feeling anxious or depressed, then stop.

Instead practice telling and listening to good stories. See and celebrate the best in others. Tell good stories about your spouse, boss, colleagues, clients or whoever you can. When you change the story you're telling about them, they will change too.

For our physical wellbeing stories are central to the way we communicate. They help us to listen better and inspire us to take action and try new things. Sometimes we get stuck or overwhelmed in a story. By taking action and doing one small thing we can create momentum. An example is when people with huge financial debts are encouraged to pay off their smallest bill. This small act creates a positive step forward, and it is known that they are much more likely to ultimately become debt free. Of course, physically, stories can also play a part in the way we relax and even sleep!

Spiritually, stories are inherently linked to our own identities. We see ourselves in the stories, or who we would like to be, and our experiences form part of our own story. Stories have always helped us connect with others socially and through preserving knowledge, traditions and legends they are also culturally important. Environmentally they help us understand, explore and imagine places and finally, economically, through stories we understand the world as it is and as we would like it to be.

Stories are important to our personal and collective wellbeing so we need to make sure we're telling and listening to the best ones. In the section on 'Persuading' we outlined the importance of authenticity, the consistency between who you are and the story you're telling. This is built on the congruence of your story with your values, beliefs, personality and character, which we explored earlier in this chapter. If you can't believe in the story you're telling how can you expect others to?

For now let's assume that you do believe in the story you're telling. What are the mechanics for telling a good one? Aristotle coined the terms Ethos, Pathos, and Logos as the three artistic proofs; and they are the key modes of persuasion used to convince audiences. 'Ethos' is about convincing the audience of your credibility and *character*. 'Pathos' means persuading an audience through *emotion*. Finally 'logos' is about providing an audience with facts and *logic* to back up your argument. A good story contains an element of each depending on the context.

Through linking back to personal, team, or organisational vision and goals you can appeal to people's emotions and focus on higher motives. Stories that cause us to pay attention and also involve us emotionally are the ones that move us to action.

Example: 'If we innovate and change quickly we can all thrive and prosper to make this organisation the champion of our industry it once was.'

Using meaningful language, tone of voice, metaphors, analogy, visualisation, stories of emotional events, and implied meanings are all ways you can do this. Pausing, enunciating, enthusing, showing appreciation, using gestures and selling the benefits can also be used to dramatic effect.

The latest neuroscience research supports this. Studies[1] by Paul J. Zak, Ph.D. scientist, author, and public speaker have found that oxytocin, a peptide synthesised in the hypothalamus region of our brain, is released during social interactions and increases prosocial behaviours such as empathy, trust, and generosity.

In one experiment, he showed research participants a short video clip of a father talking to the camera, while his two-year-old son, Ben, who has terminal brain cancer, plays in the background. The father is struggling to connect to his son, all the while knowing that he has only a few months to live. The clip concludes with the father finding the strength to stay emotionally close to his son "until he takes his last breath."

Zak found that this story caused an increase in cortisol and oxytocin release and that this had a positive correlation with the participants' feelings of empathy for Ben and his father. This heightened empathy resulted in participants offering money to a stranger who was part of the experiment.

When the audience, or you for that matter, have little at stake and any respective decisions or actions are easy to make, you might like to focus more on character, values, and emotions in your story. Where decisions are increasingly complex, you will need to use more 'logos' which is about appealing to an audience's logic (System 2 thinking). This will require providing them with more facts, figures, citations, and using historical precedent or analogy.

Example: 'Our market share has reduced over the last year from 15 to 12%'.

Grabbing an audience's attention and keeping it is also important! Asking a provocative or thoughtful question right up front is one way to grab attention. Building suspense through a story that finishes with a 'big reveal' is one way of keeping it. Involve people in your communications by asking questions and giving them space to talk, helping them see how they can become part of the answer. Throw down some challenges and you'll ensure you keep them interested. Use first-person narratives in your stories. This is always more compelling in helping us see people as individuals, rather than as a group, like 'patients', 'refugees' or 'the homeless'.

Now what's your actual story as a leader? What's the story you would really like to tell? Another great thing with stories is that they help us to grow.

GROWTH

		Wellbeing Domains - 'Territories' - Interconnected areas of our lives							
		Mental Our thoughts	Emotional Our emotions	Physical Our actions	Spiritual Our spirit	Social Our communities	Cultural Our way	Environmental Our spaces	Economic Our trade
Wellbeing Dimensions 'Highways' Intertwined routes we use to navigate our lives	Creating meaning	Thinking	Feelings	Behaviour	Identity	Friendship	Way of life	Affinity	Needs
	Achieving potential	Focus	Control	Mastery	Motivation	Teamwork	Governance	Cultivation	Impact
	Nurturing relationships	Regard	Empathy	Interaction	Stories	Trust	Belonging	Cohesion	Fairness
	Building resilience	Flexibility	Agility	Health	Growth	Support	Diversity	Adaptation	Integrity
	Enriching lives	Imagination	Wisdom	Energy	Purpose	Empowerment	Integration	Renewal	Freedom
		Wellbeing Factors - 'Signposts' - Interconnected things that can help us improve wellbeing							

"Don't grow old, grow up."

DALE CARNEGIE

To be resilient spiritually, we need to keep growing, we need to become a 'lifelong learner'. Dale Carnegie wrote the book *Don't Grow Old, Grow Up* with the overarching story that we need to keep learning. We grow old when we stop learning and trying new things.

We can grow in all areas of wellbeing and this is really what this book is about.

Spiritual growth in an organisation really starts at the intersection between an individual's values, personality, character and beliefs, and those of the organisation. If these are incongruent, and there is little flexibility on either side making concessions then there will be no growth. In fact growth, in these situations, should probably include a parting of ways.

Where there is greater congruence then spiritual growth is about enabling each individual to grow for the benefit of the wider group. It's about enabling a person to bring their whole selves to work. Again the CANBE Wellbeing Model comes to our aid. In the domain of Mental Wellbeing, this can be in encouraging people to develop their thinking, focus, and regard for others, or encouraging creativity based on individual strengths, experiences, and qualities.

People should feel comfortable sharing emotions and feelings in a safe, supportive environment. Emotions are often a taboo subject in the workplace, and this is probably a big area for spiritual growth. Starting discussions about how people are feeling about work, without fear of recrimination, as well as what they are actually doing, is one way to facilitate this. Training and coaching in emotional intelligence is another.

Encouraging people to express themselves physically and spiritually through how they look, what they say, and what they do, needs to be balanced with the organisation's requirements. This is a fine balance. Too many rules and regulations that stifle individual expression will lead to a dull, uninspiring workplace; $1+1 = 1$. Get this right, in combination with the other ideas mentioned here, and leaders can unleash the power of creativity and imagination, $1+1 = 3$.

Dress code, practices in meditation, religious and spiritual beliefs and personal development to learn new technical skills would fit into these categories. Encouraging good health through diet, sleep, exercise and relaxation are other areas. Perhaps the main link to spiritual growth is that of purpose. Ensuring each individual understands opportunities to grow and contribute to society in a meaningful way is key here.

Social and cultural practices unique to individuals can also be supported. Initiatives such as buddying, mentoring and coaching are good examples of this in practice. How can you encourage greater sharing of culture in your organisation? Linking this to food and health practices is one area to explore, but anything that helps to develop the quality and depth of interpersonal relationships would qualify.

Growth in respect to the environment can be as simple as empowering employees to decorate their work stations in a way that is fully representative of them as a person. How might this encourage conversations between employees and foster stronger relationships? On a wider level the facilities themselves should also cater for the different cultures, friendships, groups and individuals that form your workforce. Basically, this is about fostering a sense of individual affinity with the environment, which we'll explore in more detail later.

Economically, do you know how each person in your organisation would like to be rewarded to reflect them as an individual? Whilst some might want more money, others may prefer time off. Some might prefer to own shares in your company, whilst others might prefer cash. Offering alternatives that reflect individual preferences for economic growth will enable greater wellbeing.

PURPOSE

		Wellbeing Domains - 'Territories' - Interconnected areas of our lives							
		Mental Our thoughts	Emotional Our emotions	Physical Our actions	Spiritual Our spirit	Social Our communities	Cultural Our way	Environmental Our spaces	Economic Our trade
Wellbeing Dimensions 'Highways' Intertwined routes we use to navigate our lives	Creating meaning	Thinking	Feelings	Behaviour	Identity	Friendship	Way of life	Affinity	Needs
	Achieving potential	Focus	Control	Mastery	Motivation	Teamwork	Governance	Cultivation	Impact
	Nurturing relationships	Regard	Empathy	Interaction	Stories	Trust	Belonging	Cohesion	Fairness
	Building resilience	Flexibility	Agility	Health	Growth	Support	Diversity	Adaptation	Integrity
	Enriching lives	Imagination	Wisdom	Energy	Purpose	Empowerment	Integration	Renewal	Freedom
		Wellbeing Factors - 'Signposts' - Interconnected things that can help us improve wellbeing							

"The person without a purpose is like a ship without a rudder."

THOMAS CARLYLE

"True happiness... is not attained through self-gratification, but through fidelity to a worthy purpose."

HELEN KELLER

"Musicians must make music, artists must paint, poets must write if they are ultimately to be at peace with themselves. What humans can be, they must be."

ABRAHAM MASLOW

Purpose is the way we bring together an understanding of our self or group to determine how we can best serve others. When an organisation has a clear, motivating purpose that teams and individuals can align with, there will be more commitment.

In his 2009 book *Drive: The Surprising Truth About What Motivates Us*[1], Dan Pink, best-selling business, work, and management author describes three important factors for satisfying work:

- *Purpose*: the feeling that what you do is worthwhile and part of some wider whole
- *Mastery*: doing work which is challenging but which you can manage successfully
- *Control*: having enough discretion in how you do the job

When people 'fit' with an organisation they will be more relaxed, authentic, and will perform better. However, they also need to know how their work is connected to the bigger picture, how they're making the world a better place. This famous story from 1962 is a great example of an employee understanding a higher purpose.

When President Kennedy visited NASA space center and noticed a janitor carrying a broom, he interrupted his tour, walked over to the man and said: "Hi, I'm Jack Kennedy. What are you doing?" "Well, Mr. President," the janitor responded, "I'm helping to put a man on the moon."

Helping people connect with the bigger picture like this can be as simple as having conversations about what they do, and how the widget they make or the service they provide improves customers' lives. Emphasising team performance, and how one role can help the success of another, ensures all people see the part they play as worthwhile.

Purpose can be explored at an individual, team, and organisational level and will be linked to values, beliefs, character, strengths, personality, skills, and passions. Looking at these things from a personal level, what themes or patterns do you notice? Where have you had the most success? What things do you want to be remembered for?

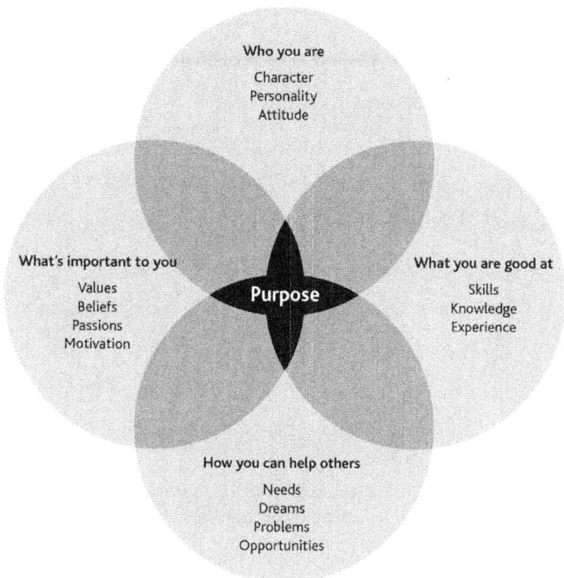

In his book *Good To Great*[2], Jim Collins described this slightly differently for organisations as the intersection between:

- What the business is deeply passionate about
- Understanding what the business can be 'best in the world' at
- The driver of the economic engine

Whatever approach you take, understanding your purpose is a valuable exercise for individuals, teams and organisations. It gives you your reason 'why', which we explored earlier, and helps build motivation and commitment. When people work together with a shared purpose it can help build friendships, teamwork, trust, support and empowerment, which we'll move onto shortly in our next chapter.

CHAPTER SUMMARY

Spiritual wellbeing is really about knowing who we are as individuals and groups and continuing to learn through our experiences. Understanding who we are, our ***identity***, helps us in all areas of our lives, from personal relationships through to career choices. It helps bind groups of people together. By acting in ways which help build autonomy, competence, and relatedness we can develop higher levels of ***motivation*** to achieve our full potential.

When we use ***stories*** to communicate, and are clear on our own story, we create more meaning. This helps inspire others to achieve their potential, come together, and keep focused on the end goal so we are better able to overcome obstacles along our path.

To be resilient we must keep ***growing*** and the CANBE Model provides opportunities to identify and plan for areas where we would like to improve.

Finally, by understanding how we can use our unique skills, strengths, character, personality and values to enrich the lives of others, we develop more ***purpose***.

KEY CONCEPTS TO IMPROVE SPIRITUAL WELLBEING:

As leaders we can cultivate more spiritual wellbeing by really getting to know ourselves, our team and the people we are leading. Knowing who we are helps with the why and the how we do things. Here are some ideas for improving in this area:

Understanding our identity better

- Review values
- Review beliefs
- Understand our personality
- Understand our character strengths
- Understand our core skills

Improving motivation

- Align activities with our identity

Paint, write, tell, visualise our stories

- Review our story so far
- Think about what we want the next chapters in our story to be
- Write down what we want our legacy to be

Take opportunities to grow

- Step outside our comfort zones
- Say yes more often

Define our purpose

- Record it. Share it. Tell people about it

KEY BEHAVIOURS:

Where do you score on following attributes that contribute to personal, team and organisational physical wellbeing?

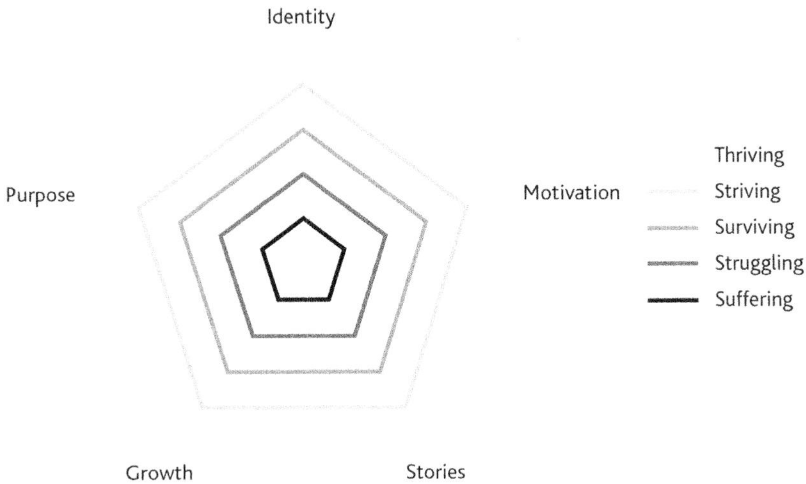

What would you like to do differently?

CHAPTER NINE

IMPROVING SOCIAL WELLBEING

		Wellbeing Domains - 'Territories' - Interconnected areas of our lives							
		Mental Our thoughts	**Emotional** Our emotions	**Physical** Our actions	**Spiritual** Our spirit	**Social** Our communities	**Cultural** Our way	**Environmental** Our spaces	**Economic** Our trade
Wellbeing Dimensions 'Highways' Intertwined routes we use to navigate our lives	Creating meaning	Thinking	Feelings	Behaviour	Identity	Friendship	Way of life	Affinity	Needs
	Achieving potential	Focus	Control	Mastery	Motivation	Teamwork	Governance	Cultivation	Impact
	Nurturing relationships	Regard	Empathy	Interaction	Stories	Trust	Belonging	Cohesion	Fairness
	Building resilience	Flexibility	Agility	Health	Growth	Support	Diversity	Adaptation	Integrity
	Enriching lives	Imagination	Wisdom	Energy	Purpose	Empowerment	Integration	Renewal	Freedom
		Wellbeing Factors - 'Signposts' - Interconnected things that can help us improve wellbeing							

"Too often we underestimate the power of a touch, a smile, a kind word, a listening ear, an honest compliment, or the smallest act of caring, all of which have the potential to turn a life around."

LEO BUSCAGLIA

"No one cares how much you know, until they know how much you care."

THEODORE ROOSEVELT

Social wellbeing is about connections and positive relationships between people. These relationships operate with varying degrees of closeness and objectives such as family, **friends**, **team** mates, neighbours and relations. However they are all based on **trust**, **support,** and **power**.

Without these close connections, we can become separated from others, groups, or even whole countries. Feelings of **isolation** and being dis-connected are damaging to our wellbeing. When we feel **engaged** on the other hand, through having close relationships and benefiting from strong support networks, our wellbeing is improved.

George Valliant, the psychologist who directed the Harvard Men study for over 40 years, described it as: "70 years of evidence that our relationships with other people matter, and matter more than anything else in the world." In fact, the strength of our social network has been found to be by far the most significant predictor of our happiness and wellbeing.

FRIENDSHIP

		Wellbeing Domains - 'Territories' - Interconnected areas of our lives							
		Mental Our thoughts	Emotional Our emotions	Physical Our actions	Spiritual Our spirit	Social Our communities	Cultural Our way	Environmental Our spaces	Economic Our trade
Wellbeing Dimensions 'Highways' Intertwined routes we use to navigate our lives	Creating meaning	Thinking	Feelings	Behaviour	Identity	Friendship	Way of life	Affinity	Needs
	Achieving potential	Focus	Control	Mastery	Motivation	Teamwork	Governance	Cultivation	Impact
	Nurturing relationships	Regard	Empathy	Interaction	Stories	Trust	Belonging	Cohesion	Fairness
	Building resilience	Flexibility	Agility	Health	Growth	Support	Diversity	Adaptation	Integrity
	Enriching lives	Imagination	Wisdom	Energy	Purpose	Empowerment	Integration	Renewal	Freedom
		Wellbeing Factors - 'Signposts' - Interconnected things that can help us improve wellbeing							

> "Friendship makes prosperity more brilliant, and lightens adversity by dividing and sharing it."
>
> CICERO

We have evolved as social animals. In Social Baseline Theory, several studies inspecting brain activity suggest the brain looks more 'at rest' when social resources are obviously available to us[1]. "Indeed evidence suggests that hills literally appear less steep when standing next to a friend." This ability for the brain to rest is due to the perceived reduced risk, and potential distribution of effort, when we have people around us that can help.

Friendships are diverse and can change in shape and form due to class, gender, age, status, ethnicity and personality, amongst other dimensions. They help us create meaning in our own lives. We tend to make friends with people who are like ourselves and therefore help to reinforce our own identity. They help us understand ourselves and are influenced by both social and cultural norms, such as when a family member subtly, or less subtly, provides their acceptance or disapproval of our friends!

Aristotle defined friendships in four different categories. I share this information about friendships not because we need to delve deeply into what constitutes friendship but because it provides clues as to how leaders might help create the environments and circumstances for friendships to develop. He described friendships based on:

1. Usefulness and shared interests. This might be neighbours who help each other out from time to time
2. Pleasure. People who enjoy each other's company. This could be people who like to share a drink at their local cafe or pub, but perhaps have very different values, beliefs, and character
3. Shared character, values, beliefs and therefore greater mutual affection.
4. Shared experiences. Alumni or previous work colleagues might fit into this category

As far as I am aware more recent research hasn't particularly advanced this categorisation of friendship, although what is clear is that friendships are good for our wellbeing. They help us share problems and "A problem shared is a problem halved". In itself this can help us feel more secure and protect us against stress.

Along the same theme friends can provide us with new perspectives and different ideas about how to approach challenges and opportunities in our lives. In their simplest form friends can just be good fun. They can help us laugh, play, raise our spirits and provide us with a distraction from problems in our lives. But friendship is also about give and take. When we give to others it makes us feel good.

Friendships develop naturally and they can't be forced, but leaders can play a role in creating circumstances where friendships can evolve. In the community, starting a neighbourhood watch or befriending scheme might be one example. In the workplace, creating a meeting place or mechanism for ex-employees to connect might be another.

The point is that friendships are good for our wellbeing so as a leader we can help facilitate them by creating the right circumstances and environment. Of course, friendships can sometimes deteriorate and cause conflict, so as a leader we also need to be prepared.

MANAGING CONFLICT

There will always be times when relationships come into conflict. As a leader, we require effective strategies for managing personal, team, and organisational conflicts. Both Covey and Carnegie reflect the importance of apologising, and as a leader this is one simple way to set the tone and manage conflict before it escalates. Be prepared to apologise quickly if you are the source of the problem.

The CIPD Survey report April 2015 "Getting Under The Skin of Conflict: Tracing the Experiences of Employees"[2] found that: "nearly four in ten UK employees (38%) report some form of interpersonal conflict at work in the last year. This includes an isolated dispute or incident of conflict (29% of UK employees reporting at least one case), and ongoing difficult relationships (28%)." Whilst the report only cites 1 in 10 of these conflicts resulting in an employee leaving the organisation, when you combine this with the obvious impacts that there will be on stress, motivation, sickness absence, and productivity, the costs to our organisations can be significant.

This survey found that the largest contributor to incidents of conflict was personality or styles of working, noted as "relational issues". However task-based issues were also prevalent, particularly in the areas of individual performance, target setting, and the level of support or resources.

Interestingly, these conflicts are most common with one's superiors, indicating the importance of power dynamics between different levels in an organisation. It is paramount that leaders and managers understand how to manage and navigate these situations to diffuse them before they escalate.

The report also highlights a requirement for both formal and informal processes to provide flexible solutions to conflict resolution. Whilst a formal process can be seen as more legalistic, encouraging entrenched thinking, it can also be seen as fair and objective, providing a degree of closure.

It is clear that whilst there isn't only one way to resolve a conflict, the skills previously mentioned (including emotional intelligence, active listening, questioning, providing constructive non-personal feedback and understanding body language) are all ways to improve relationships and turn a conflict into something positive.

This is reflected in the Interest Based Relational Approach to conflict resolution, as developed by Roger Fisher and William Ury and published in their 1981 book, *Getting To Yes*[3]. The book provides principles based around respect, separating people from problems, listening to understand, focusing on interests not positions, working together to find creative and fair options, and basing discussion on facts.

Cultivating a culture of emotional intelligence is one way a leader can seek to prevent rather than cure. Having said that, even if a situation does escalate, these same skills are the ones required to resolve the situation.

Conflict is generally perceived with negative connotations and is a useful sign that there is a lack of tolerance and harmony. It can demonstrate, amongst other things:

- Poor thinking - biases, lack of regard, closed or fixed mindsets
- Lack of emotional control - frustration with a lack of change, or a pace of change that is too fast, uncontrolled emotional responses, and a lack of empathy
- Poor communication and habitual responses
- An unwillingness to grow and learn
- Lack of trust, support and empowerment

It may not have escaped your attention that these are all things that impact on our individual and collective wellbeing. I'm not saying conflict will never happen, we're all human after all, but the aim for leaders, as we'll discuss further in Cultural Wellbeing, is to turn conflict into tolerance and even harmony. Conflict is a sign that things aren't as good as they can be, and can be a significant deterrent to people working effectively together.

TEAMWORK

		Wellbeing Domains - 'Territories' - Interconnected areas of our lives							
		Mental Our thoughts	**Emotional** Our emotions	**Physical** Our actions	**Spiritual** Our spirit	**Social** Our communities	**Cultural** Our way	**Environmental** Our spaces	**Economic** Our trade
Wellbeing Dimensions 'Highways' Intertwined routes we use to navigate our lives	Creating meaning	Thinking	Feelings	Behaviour	Identity	Friendship	Way of life	Affinity	Needs
	Achieving potential	Focus	Control	Mastery	Motivation	Teamwork	Governance	Cultivation	Impact
	Nurturing relationships	Regard	Empathy	Interaction	Stories	Trust	Belonging	Cohesion	Fairness
	Building resilience	Flexibility	Agility	Health	Growth	Support	Diversity	Adaptation	Integrity
	Enriching lives	Imagination	Wisdom	Energy	Purpose	Empowerment	Integration	Renewal	Freedom
		Wellbeing Factors - 'Signposts' - Interconnected things that can help us improve wellbeing							

"Alone we can do so little; together we can do so much."

HELEN KELLER

"Talent wins games, but teamwork and intelligence win championships."

MICHAEL JORDAN

As outlined in the previous section, good teams don't always need to be friends, but they can be. The focus on improving performance in organisations is often directed at individuals. But how often do we focus on team performance? I'd argue that the latter is much more important as a key driver of organisational success.

So what constitutes a high performing team? As outlined previously, the strength of the CANBE Model is that it works for teams as much as it does for individuals, organisations, or the human race as a whole.

Creating meaning - This is about your team ***identity*** aligning around a common set of values, behaviours, and beliefs that support the organisation's mission. As a leader, your role is to provide individuals with the right level of autonomy and freedom to get the job done without micro-managing and stifling creativity. Team members that feel confident to be themselves as part of the team will perform better. Encouraging ***friendships*** to develop naturally over time will bond team members closer together. Teams have ***'ways of doing things'*** and by ensuring team members know what these are they will be able to better fit in with others. The team environment can help to create ***affinity*** through celebrating individuals and the team as a whole. The team should also understand its own ***needs*** and the needs of others.

Achieving potential - Teams need **focus**. How does the team strategy and vision support organisational objectives? You must provide a clear understanding of team direction and individual roles. Emotionally team members must learn to **control** their response to each other, colleagues and customers to achieve the best outcomes. Team members need to develop SMARTER personal goals, and manage time and resources effectively. **Mastery** means team members having the necessary skills to deliver, whilst also understanding the relevance of the products and services to customers. When this is combined with tasks that bring out team members intrinsic skills, character, and personality there will be higher levels of **motivation**. Good **governance and leadership** removes obstacles, provides clear direction, policies and procedures that empower people. Of course, the spaces in which the team works must also be conducive to high performance. This can be achieved by **cultivating the environment** to support performance. Finally, to achieve true potential, the team should clearly understand their **impact**. When all these attributes are put together we get great **teamwork**.

Nurturing relationships - This starts with each team member having high levels of ***regard*** for themselves and each other. Team members need to develop skills in listening, questioning, communicating, ***interacting*** and giving/receiving feedback with each other, other teams, and especially customers. Shared understanding, delivering on promises (no matter how small) helps to build ***empathy***, ***trust***, and loyalty. Being included and feeling part of the team ***story*** through having their voice heard, their ideas implemented, and a chance to influence decisions will help them ***belong***, as will an environment that encourages team members to ***collaborate*** through shared spaces, being valued through ***fair*** pay, processes, and access to resources.

Building resilience – The team must have a ***flexible*** growth mind-set. With this approach, teams approach change with ***agility***, looking for solutions and options rather than putting up barriers. Of course, without good mental and physical ***health***, a team can't perform effectively, so there must be encouragement, support, and access provided in these areas. ***Growth***, through learning and reflection must be embedded to continue development and facilitate improvement. A key element of effective resilience is the ***support*** of colleagues, so this must be encouraged through mentoring, buddying, and coaching. Teams consisting of more ***diverse*** members will provide different perspectives and experiences that enable better problem solving. This is also about creating an environment that is physically and mentally stimulating, where stress levels are carefully managed, and teams are able to ***adapt*** to change. From an economic perspective, a team must operate with moral and financial ***integrity***.

Enriching lives – This is probably one of the areas in the workplace that receives least focus. Team members must be stretched to ***imagine*** better solutions that deliver greater ***freedom*** to colleagues and customers. This can be achieved through harnessing the collective ***wisdom*** of team members, and developing a positive approach to risk-taking where people aren't blamed but encouraged to learn from mistakes. It's also about developing a workplace where thanks, gratitude, and celebration of other team mate's success is commonplace. The ***energy*** of the team should be greater than the sum of its parts and as a leader you should be encouraging team members to find the fun and enjoyment in work whilst also ***empowering*** each other through difficult times with compassion and kindness. This will be enhanced if the team environment encourages opportunities for ***renewal.*** Helping the team manage its impact on the environment will also create pride. Our role as a leader is to ***integrate*** individuals with varying backgrounds into a collective whole where respect and understanding of differences is central to the way of working. Great team managers help individuals play to their strengths and virtues whilst ensuring that they understand their role in delivering on the team and organisational ***purpose***.

TRUST

		Wellbeing Domains - 'Territories' - Interconnected areas of our lives							
		Mental Our thoughts	Emotional Our emotions	Physical Our actions	Spiritual Our spirit	Social Our communities	Cultural Our way	Environmental Our spaces	Economic Our trade
Wellbeing Dimensions 'Highways' Intertwined routes we use to navigate our lives	Creating meaning	Thinking	Feelings	Behaviour	Identity	Friendship	Way of life	Affinity	Needs
	Achieving potential	Focus	Control	Mastery	Motivation	Teamwork	Governance	Cultivation	Impact
	Nurturing relationships	Regard	Empathy	Interaction	Stories	Trust	Belonging	Cohesion	Fairness
	Building resilience	Flexibility	Agility	Health	Growth	Support	Diversity	Adaptation	Integrity
	Enriching lives	Imagination	Wisdom	Energy	Purpose	Empowerment	Integration	Renewal	Freedom
		Wellbeing Factors - 'Signposts' - Interconnected things that can help us improve wellbeing							

> "Make small commitments and keep them. Be a light, not a judge. Be a model, not a critic. Be a part of the solution, not the problem."
>
> STEPHEN COVEY

In well-functioning groups, organisations and even countries there are high levels of trust. Studies suggest that trust causes people to be more satisfied with their lives. However, reviewing World Happiness

Reports, it is also clear that trust has fallen over time in countries like the UK and USA, whilst in Denmark and Italy, for example, it has risen. As outlined in the Chapter on 'Course Correction' this is supported by waning levels of trust as reported in the Edelman Trust Barometer.

This is particularly true of people's trust in government and politics, where polarisation and populism have caused large divides. People are also fearful of automation and losing their jobs causing greater mistrust in the system. But it is also true of the media where 'fake news' is more difficult to rely on. Edelman reports that there are also widening divisions between the 'haves and have nots' due to increasing divergence of wealth and corruption scandals.

The upshot appears to be that people are becoming 'more local' in who they give their trust to. In particular the most trusted institution in the world is now 'my employer'.

And yet trust is one of the most critical elements of healthy relationships between friends, families, teams, organisations, communities and even countries. It is built and earned through actions meeting words. Remember no promise is ever too small and keeping your promises is fundamental to trust. Other factors that help build trust include:

- Feeling emotionally and physically safe
- Reciprocity of giving and receiving based on shared expectations and needs
- Confidence between the two parties based on reliability and truthfulness
- Open and honest communication based on listening, talking, sincerity, authenticity and feedback
- Acceptance of each others values and a non-judgmental approach
- Respectfulness. discretion and sensitivity
- Forgiveness
- Supportiveness in both good and bad times

These are all topics, we have, or will discuss throughout this book, so it is clear that a focus on wellbeing can also help us rebuild levels of trust. However Edelman goes on to recommend a four pronged approach to rebuilding trust that also aligns with building wellbeing:

1. Have a big idea and purpose to show how your organisation is making the world a better place
2. Communicate first with your people. Tell them a story
3. Support your community
4. Leaders to speak up for what your organisation believes in

Some key areas that this leads to include: fair pay, managing diversity, re-training due to automation and climate change, but I suggest we also look at the CANBE Model for answers to how we can begin to rebuild trust. One of those, which was outlined above, is to make sure our people are supported.

SUPPORT

Wellbeing Domains - 'Territories' - Interconnected areas of our lives

Wellbeing Dimensions 'Highways' Intertwined routes we use to navigate our lives	**Mental** Our thoughts	**Emotional** Our emotions	**Physical** Our actions	**Spiritual** Our spirit	**Social** Our communities	**Cultural** Our way	**Environmental** Our spaces	**Economic** Our trade
Creating meaning	Thinking	Feelings	Behaviour	Identity	Friendship	Way of life	Affinity	Needs
Achieving potential	Focus	Control	Mastery	Motivation	Teamwork	Governance	Cultivation	Impact
Nurturing relationships	Regard	Empathy	Interaction	Stories	Trust	Belonging	Cohesion	Fairness
Building resilience	Flexibility	Agility	Health	Growth	Support	Diversity	Adaptation	Integrity
Enriching lives	Imagination	Wisdom	Energy	Purpose	Empowerment	Integration	Renewal	Freedom

Wellbeing Factors - 'Signposts' - Interconnected things that can help us improve wellbeing

> "It is in the shelter of each other that the people live."
>
> IRISH PROVERB

Relationships help us develop and provide access to additional financial, emotional, physical, spiritual and mental resources. It is no wonder then that the strength of our support network is often seen as the most important aspect of managing stress, developing resilience, and even our wellbeing as a whole. Let's take a further look at how support plays a part in building our resilience so that we can adapt, reorganise, and grow in response to disruption and generate more than the sum of our parts.

Further research outlined in Shawn Achor's book, *The Happiness Advantage*[1], shows that employees who provide social support to their colleagues are 40% more likely to receive a promotion in the following year, report higher job satisfaction, and feel 10 times more engaged in their jobs than employees scoring in the lowest quartile.

The long and short of it is that we need other people, and they need us. No matter how 'self-made' we think we are, the fact is we're standing on the shoulders of many other people who have helped us get to where we are today. Just take some time to think about that. Who has helped you? Where would you be without their help? Who have you helped? Where would they be without your help?

BUILDING NETWORKS OF SUPPORT

Bottling things up and keeping them to yourself is not an effective strategy for dealing with stress and building resilience. Social support can be invaluable when you are feeling stressed. It can also help to improve your wellbeing. This is why groups of like-minded people, such as Weight Watchers or Alcoholics Anonymous, have been so effective in providing support to millions of people. Who do you already use as your support network? Is there anyone else that you could build connections with?

Some areas you might like to consider include your manager, your manager's manager, peer group, mentors, coaches, friends and family, members of hobby groups or community projects. Remember that, at work, you might also have more options for support, such as Occupational Health or Employee Assistance Programmes.

On the more positive side, forming groups during times of stability can help prepare for the future. As an example, Jim Collins describes in *Good To Great*[2] how many of the successful businesses he researched set up bodies, which he refers to as 'The Council', to debate existing and future challenges.

These bodies typically consisted of 5-12 people ranging in seniority and function meeting periodically to argue and debate issues that were then used to inform the Executive team. This type of idea can be used by any organisation to inform strategy. As an example, one topic of debate could be 'disruption'. With the growth in exponential technologies such as mobile, artificial intelligence, the internet, blockchain, and quantum computing, many business models will come under increasing pressure. Why not get a team of people together, if you haven't already, to discuss how your organisation could respond adaptively to unforeseen problems and challenges like these? Hopefully, it is clear from this that a strong approach to diversity will also help facilitate social resilience by providing access to a wider range of views and perspectives.

In the workplace, other recognised ways of providing support include schemes such as volunteering, buddying, mentoring and coaching. From a personal perspective, another way to think of this might be to consider ensuring you have support across each of the eight domains of wellbeing. Where can you get support to help your mental, emotional, physical, spiritual, social, cultural, environmental and economic wellbeing?

Social psychologists have found that we can effectively work to strengthen our support networks by both giving and receiving support. Often people are too proud to ask for and accept support, so the first step is opening up and allowing yourself to be vulnerable. Recognising your own limitations and feelings can be the most difficult part.

In terms of the type of support we provide and receive, here are some guiding principles.

BE PROACTIVE & RESPONSIVE

You can be proactive by simply noticing who might be in need of support around you. Showing you thought about someone and that you care about them may even be enough. Of course, if someone directly asks for your support, responding appropriately is key. If they are asking for feedback, then the enthusiastic and supportive, active, constructive approach we discussed under the section on communication in physical wellbeing is best. This is associated with increases in positive emotion, life satisfaction, and relationship satisfaction.

OFFER SUPPORT TO BOTH SUCCESSFUL AND STRUGGLING PEOPLE

Remember all people can benefit from support.

OFFER SUPPORT THAT IS BOTH INFORMAL AND FORMAL

Support can be offered by just being there for someone through to more formal processes.

RESPECT INDIVIDUALITY AND BE DISCRETE

It is often better to listen and ask than tell people what to do and provide advice. A simple question like: 'How can I best help you'? can reveal exactly the level of support that someone requires which you may not even have thought about. Of course, some people may feel embarrassed about receiving support, so discretion will help to build their trust.

ENCOURAGING COMPASSION AND KINDNESS

Compassion is deeply rooted in human nature and has a biological basis in the brain and body. It takes empathy one step further.

Whereas empathy is about sensing or understanding someone else's emotions, compassion is the feeling that arises when you witness suffering and want to do something to help relieve it. It has been proven to benefit sufferers, those who provide support, and even those who witness the support being provided.

An article produced by Kanov, Powley, and Walshe[3] reflects research showing that suffering is a 'pervasive, though often invisible aspect of organisational life' and that compassion is a 'healing force that is indispensable in organisations'. It goes on to reflect the 'psychological, physiological, relational and job performance benefits (for sufferers, compassion providers, and third parties who witness or learn about the compassion) and can thus mitigate the hundreds of billions of dollars in annual organisational losses associated with suffering.'

Suffering is a prime example of why a wellbeing approach should consider the whole person in the workplace. It seems inconceivable that we should expect a person going through divorce, financial difficulty, bereavement, serious illness or other traumatic life experiences, to keep their work and home lives separate and yet that is not an untypical experience. Whilst suffering can be caused by these types of experiences, the workplace itself can also be a cause through, bullying, harassment, workplace re-organisation and destructive relationships. With plenty of opportunities for suffering in our organisations, it seems clear that we also need more compassion.

It's sad but many people are kinder to others than they are to themselves. Self-compassion is, in a sense, taking on the attitude we have towards our friends when they share their failures with us. Rather than criticising and judging them, we (hopefully) listen with empathy and understanding. We encourage them to remember that mistakes are normal, and to move on or pick themselves up and try again.

With self-compassion, we view failure with greater calm and understanding and see it as an opportunity to grow. Just like on a plane when you put on your own oxygen mask before helping others, or in first aid training, where you are taught to ensure your own safety before treating the patient, self-compassion allows us to do better for those around us.

You can boost your own self-compassion by recognising those times when you're self-critical, writing down what your 'inner critic' is telling you, and then asking what a friend might be saying to you right now. Would they be saying what your 'inner critic' is telling you, or would they be more considerate and understanding? It's also worth remembering that suffering is something we all go through and that often external influences, not under our control, play a big part in this. Finally, taking a balanced approach to negative emotions, without exaggerating or suppressing them, ensures we keep things in perspective.

A lack of self-compassion shown by many is also perhaps reflected by the absence of compassion that is all too often experienced in the workplace. Whilst much of what you have just read may seem common sense, it is also a theme of this book that 'common sense isn't always common action'. It's the action part that's important and this can take a great deal of courage!

Although compassion is a fundamental and biological component of human nature, it won't always follow that suffering results in compassionate action, particularly in organisational contexts. Going back to the research mentioned earlier, Kanov, Powley, and Walshe describe how compassion is 'the exception rather than the norm' in many workplaces. This is due to its complexities and the uncertainty faced by both those suffering and their potential supporters. To bring this to life a little, perhaps you've experienced the anxiety of not knowing what to say or do when a colleague suffers a bereavement, or from the other perspective, you've kept a 'stiff upper lip' for fear of being ridiculed or seen in a negative light when suffering yourself.

These types of uncertainties for both sufferers and their potential supporters, combined with organisational cultures where showing emotion is perceived negatively, can all play their part in stifling compassion.

You can start to change culture and help your organisation become more compassionate by noticing, empathising, taking responsibility, and then acting to support the person who is suffering. This draws on many of the skills we've discussed around emotional intelligence. But how do we reduce the uncertainty that often acts as an obstacle to a more compassionate workplace. Whilst there is not one solution, and individuals will respond differently, it makes sense that improving communication will help. When people are left to fester, or feel like they are in a void, uncertainty is likely to increase. An environment of talking about and sharing feelings, in addition to activities, can open people up to more compassion. As a leader, we can help by honouring compassionate actions, reducing uncertainty where we find it, and role-modelling. A good place to start might be showing more self-compassion, if we're not already!

EMPOWERMENT

		Wellbeing Domains - 'Territories' - Interconnected areas of our lives							
		Mental Our thoughts	Emotional Our emotions	Physical Our actions	Spiritual Our spirit	Social Our communities	Cultural Our way	Environmental Our spaces	Economic Our trade
Wellbeing Dimensions 'Highways' Intertwined routes we use to navigate our lives	Creating meaning	Thinking	Feelings	Behaviour	Identity	Friendship	Way of life	Affinity	Needs
	Achieving potential	Focus	Control	Mastery	Motivation	Teamwork	Governance	Cultivation	Impact
	Nurturing relationships	Regard	Empathy	Interaction	Stories	Trust	Belonging	Cohesion	Fairness
	Building resilience	Flexibility	Agility	Health	Growth	Support	Diversity	Adaptation	Integrity
	Enriching lives	Imagination	Wisdom	Energy	Purpose	Empowerment	Integration	Renewal	Freedom
		Wellbeing Factors - 'Signposts' - Interconnected things that can help us improve wellbeing							

"A leader is best when people barely know he exists. When his work is done, his aim fulfilled, people will say 'we did it ourselves'."

LAO TZU, TAOISM

"Before you are a leader, success is all about growing yourself. When you become a leader, success is all about growing others."

JACK WELCH

In the Chapter on Spiritual Wellbeing we discussed the power of purpose and motivation to give people a reason why. Once people buy into 'why', they'll become more motivated. To really leverage this motivation your role as leader is to free people up and give them as much autonomy as possible. If people are constrained by unnecessary processes, policies, and procedures it will sap their energy. In fact, research shows it can even damage their health! Kuper and Marmot looked at a cohort of over 10,000 British civil servants[1]. The results revealed that factors in the job, such as low levels of control and autonomy, were associated with an increased risk of serious illness.

When people can deliver in their own unique way, they'll take greater pride in their work and gain confidence. There is an added benefit in that autonomy naturally facilitates creativity, meaning that the organisation as a whole will also benefit from greater innovation and original solutions. Obviously, there are instances where policies and processes need to be followed, and those rules exist for a reason. For example, Health and Safety or Quality Control. However, when people believe they are being constrained unnecessarily, it's time to question and challenge the existing systems.

Introducing policies like flexible working, helping managers with effective delegation, looking at your people structure, job design and quality, policy and procedural reviews are all examples of things that could help here. For example, John Lewis, the top UK retailer, teaches staff six clear principles of customer service and then steps back and lets them interpret this as they see fit. Giving staff this level of autonomy allows them to make customer service decisions on the spot, empowering employees and providing better service to customers.

Reflecting on the levels at which leaders must operate, this approach can also be applied externally with customers and suppliers. As an example, the introduction of apps to help customers self-serve, or put information at their fingertips, will provide greater autonomy and give them more control.

When people are disempowered and feel like they are "slaves to the system", the results will be reflective of that. Involving your people in decision-making, and giving them more of a say, provides them with greater ownership of results and outputs. A lot of organisations say they want their staff to take more responsibility and 'ownership' of their actions and decisions, yet do not provide them with the necessary powers to make executive decisions or take action immediately. It is a dangerously de-motivating paradox.

If people are given input into how a flexible working policy might be applied, then it will be in their best interest to make it work should it be introduced. Likewise, involving customers in the development of products will give them greater control and help them feel more connected to your organisation.

One of the key areas where employees become disenfranchised is with employee surveys that aren't acted upon. Why ask employees for feedback if you don't do anything with it? It is much better to involve employees as much as possible in the decisions that will impact their daily working lives.

Giving people freedom, flexibility, and involving them is really about movement. If you shackle people or box them in they will feel constrained. But you can also help people and yourself move through time. Yes, that's right you can be a time traveller. Not literally but metaphorically. If too much of our energy is focused on the past or we're overly worried about the future we can get stuck.

MOVING ON FROM THE PAST

In the Chapter on Mental Wellbeing we've already discussed the benefits of reflecting on and learning from the past. But there are other ways we can improve our wellbeing, and that of others, when it comes to the past.

FORGIVENESS

Forgiving helps us move on from the past and focus on the now. At a team and business level, developing a culture where employees are encouraged to make mistakes and learn from them creates greater innovation. If people can learn to forgive in the most challenging of circumstances, we must be able to forgive those around us in situations that, in comparison, pale into insignificance.

Paul Boese said, 'Forgiveness does not change the past, but it does enlarge the future'. I like this quote because it gives us space to remember but also challenges us to understand that we can't change the past. If we can't forgive, perhaps a certain part of us always remains in the past, pulling us backwards. Forgiveness then, enables us to move forward with more possibility.

How could we be more forgiving of ourselves, our partners, children, family members, team-mates, customers, suppliers or anyone else who could benefit from a more understanding approach?

5 STEPS TO HELP YOU FORGIVE

One of the best known models to help facilitate forgiveness is that of Psychologist Everett Worthington Jr., a pioneer researcher in the field. He constructed a 5-step model to facilitate the process as follows:

- **R**ecall what hurt you
- **E**mpathise with the other person's perspective
- **A**ccept that it is in your gift to forgive
- **C**ommit yourself to forgiving publicly
- **H**old onto forgiveness

So who can you REACH out to today with a little more forgiveness? Forgiveness assumes that we have done harm to ourselves or been harmed by others. But we can also benefit from being grateful for the good things that have happened to us.

GRATITUDE

Be more grateful and kind – from simple words of thanks to writing a more formal letter, taking time to demonstrate your appreciation is a simple yet powerful way to create a more positive atmosphere. How can you demonstrate your thanks to colleagues, bosses, customers, suppliers, partners, friends and anyone else you can think of?

LIVING IN THE PRESENT

We've explored the benefits of mindfulness and some of the 'pros and cons' of letting your mind wander in the chapter on Mental Wellbeing, but here are a few more ideas on mindfulness and how to make the most from the present for you and your people.

BE MORE MINDFUL

Mindfulness is about 'living in the moment'. This can be as simple as taking time out to enjoy and appreciate your lunch, slowing down from time to time to focus on your breathing, through to regular more focused meditation. As an individual, team, or business, where are you spending most of your energy: the past, the future or 'living in the moment'?

SAVOUR THE MOMENT

Regularly take time to share and celebrate individual, team, and organisational achievements. Take mental pictures of success, use pictures, collect souvenirs, trophies, awards. Maintain a 'victory log' of individual, team or business successes. Smile more.

INVEST MORE IN PERSONAL GROWTH AND DEVELOPMENT

Whether at individual, team, or business level, taking on new and interesting challenges that make use of virtues, skills, and character strengths creates greater positivity. We all like to accomplish new things. It makes us feel good and builds our confidence.

LOOKING FORWARD TO THE FUTURE

Again, we've explored the following topics elsewhere in the book but here are just a few more ideas to empower yourself and others for the future.

OPTIMISM AND CONFIDENCE

Spend time with and help others. Be inspired by and inspire others – watch inspiring videos, read inspiring stories. Get a coach or mentor.

KEEP PERSPECTIVE

Most challenges we face, whilst sometimes large and looming in our lives, are insignificant in comparison to the greater problems in the world. Keep perspective and know that 'this too will pass'.

CHAPTER SUMMARY

Social Wellbeing is about the relationships between people. There are growing divisions in societies across the world including the increase in poor mental health, divergences between those going hungry and those that are obese, increased isolation, political polarisation, environmental degradation and economic disparity.

Whether in schools, communities, business, politics, or any other organisation, leaders must take responsibility for repairing the 'social fabric' that binds together these relationships. This will enable us to overcome our problems and focus on opportunities to thrive. We can do this by creating more opportunities for quality connection through ***friendship***, ***teamwork***, ***trust***, ***support*** and ***empowerment***.

KEY CONCEPTS FOR IMPROVING SOCIAL WELLBEING

Create more friendships

- Be a good friend
- Create opportunities for people to make friends
- Befriend someone outside of your typical group
- Check on people that might be isolated

Improve teamwork

- Use the CANBE Model to find areas where you can improve

Build trust

- Do what you say you will
- Give and receive
- Be reliable, truthful, open, and honest
- Be respectful, non-judgmental, discrete, sensitive and forgiving

Give and receive support

- Ensure your support network covers the 8 domains of wellbeing
- Consider volunteering, buddying, mentoring and coaching
- Notice people around you who might need support
- Be more compassionate and kind, including to yourself

Empower yourself and others

- Be more forgiving
- Be more grateful
- Be more mindful
- Savour the moment
- Develop confidence and optimism
- Keep perspective

KEY BEHAVIOURS:

Where do you score on the following behaviours that can help develop greater Social Wellbeing?

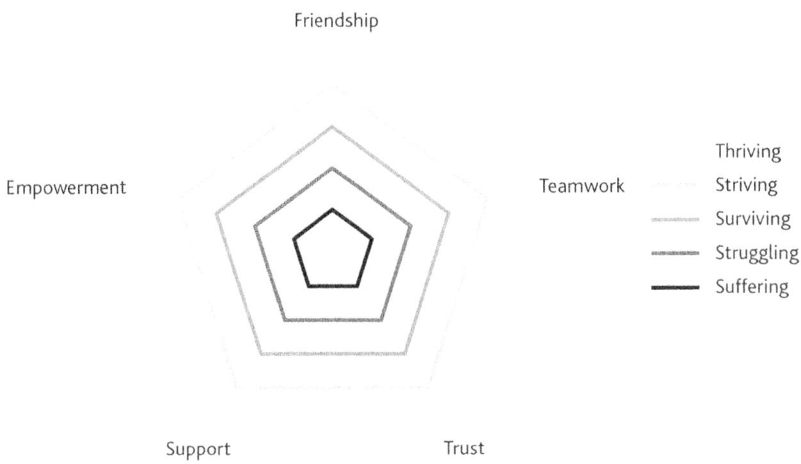

What would you like to do differently?

CHAPTER TEN

IMPROVING CULTURAL WELLBEING

		Wellbeing Domains - 'Territories' - Interconnected areas of our lives							
		Mental Our thoughts	**Emotional** Our emotions	**Physical** Our actions	**Spiritual** Our spirit	**Social** Our communities	**Cultural** Our way	**Environmental** Our spaces	**Economic** Our trade
Wellbeing Dimensions **'Highways'** **Intertwined routes we use to navigate our lives**	Creating meaning	Thinking	Feelings	Behaviour	Identity	Friendship	Way of life	Affinity	Needs
	Achieving potential	Focus	Control	Mastery	Motivation	Teamwork	Governance	Cultivation	Impact
	Nurturing relationships	Regard	Empathy	Interaction	Stories	Trust	Belonging	Cohesion	Fairness
	Building resilience	Flexibility	Agility	Health	Growth	Support	Diversity	Adaptation	Integrity
	Enriching lives	Imagination	Wisdom	Energy	Purpose	Empowerment	Integration	Renewal	Freedom
		Wellbeing Factors - 'Signposts' - Interconnected things that can help us improve wellbeing							

"A good cult delivers on its promises. A good cult nourishes the needs of its members, has transparency and integrity, and creates provisions for challenging its leadership openly. A good cult expands the freedoms and well-being of its members rather than limits them."

PHILIP ZIMBARDO

"The beauty of the world lies in the diversity of its people."

ANONYMOUS

The legendary Management Consultant and author Peter Drucker once said: "Culture eats strategy for breakfast." I would argue that wellbeing eats strategy *and* culture for breakfast. Culture or '***the way we do things***' is built on the norms, customs, traditions and values of a group of people. It includes tangible elements such as art, architecture, music, dance, ritual, religion, clothing and technologies as well as intangible aspects like beliefs, ***governance*** through leadership, political systems, and legal frameworks, as well as myths and philosophy. Culture is flexible and adapts over time to changing circumstances, influences, innovations and conditions.

With high levels of cultural wellbeing there are feelings of ***belonging*** and ***integration*** within and between different groups, whereas low levels are characterised by division and alienation. The worst levels of cultural wellbeing lead to ***conflict*** and war. The best lead to ***harmony***.

It's worth elaborating here on what we mean by conflict and harmony. Earlier, in the Chapter on Social Wellbeing we discussed how conflict, at its best, can be a useful sign that all is not well. At its worst it can lead to physical, mental, emotional, social, environmental and economic harm.

Harmony at its worst can lead to unwarranted agreeableness, stagnation, complacency, avoiding change or challenging the status quo. Two creatives who agree on everything will likely produce work that is so-so. It's creatives that disagree, and are prepared to explore their differences boldly, who create something truly new and exciting. At its best, harmony invokes open-mindedness, confronting the truth, highlighting problems, encouraging new and creative thinking, and builds understanding and respect for different points of view.

Good cultural wellbeing is about having the freedom to express our own culture, and still feel that we belong to the wider group. It helps us be who we are as individuals and comes from an appreciation for **diversity** of beliefs, history, and roots. But it also helps us realise that we have a responsibility as part of the wider group. After all, one person doesn't make a culture!

Peter Drucker said "culture eats strategy for breakfast" on the basis that the success of an organisation is inextricably linked to how its people deliver the strategy. If people are disengaged, stressed, and hindered by bureaucracy it doesn't matter how good your strategy is, it won't get delivered to full potential.

But what influences culture? I'd argue that the biggest influence is wellbeing. Our culture will depend on our collective mental, emotional, physical, spiritual, social, environmental and economic wellbeing. The same concepts apply whether we are talking about an organisation or a country. If we focus on improving these elements ,and being at our best personally and collectively, then our culture will have the best chance to thrive.

Although we are not always aware of it, culture influences the way we see the world and the actions we take to function as part of society. We can shape our culture but our culture also shapes us. There's a great example of this in a story my friend once told me. He was about to undertake a new business venture with a South African business partner, whom he had never met in person. The two agreed it would be best for them to meet face-to-face to conclude the final part of the deal. The South African business owner agreed to come to England. When he arrived for the business meeting, my friend was shocked: the South African business owner had a thick wad of cash stuffed into the top pocket of his shirt, for all to see! My friend discreetly inquired as to why he had the money there. The South African business owner replied that in South Africa, this was the cultural norm. When meeting a business partner for the first time, you proved that you weren't a fraud by demonstrating you had the funds to back up your promises. It was considered a gesture of transparency and trustworthiness!

As leaders, we need to be aware of this and where we see values, beliefs, habits, biases, convention or actions that are impinging on wellbeing, it is our responsibility to make change happen. My friend had the sensitivity not to immediately jump to conclusions based on a cultural practice he knew nothing about. But many people do.

Research on cultural wellbeing is growing but still inconclusive in many areas. My review of some recent studies[1, 2, 3, 4, 5] supports the key themes outlined in the CANBE Model. It is my contention, then, that leaders should focus on creating and managing experiences that seek to enhance all of the domains and dimensions of the CANBE Model to deliver better cultural wellbeing.

However, an element of caution also needs to be applied here. Culture is both multi-faceted and nuanced. The key message is to respect differences. For example, self-regard, positive emotions, and 'happiness' in general, whilst recognised as consistent contributors to wellbeing across nations, also vary greatly in their significance.

In individualistic cultures, where there is a greater emphasis on 'self-esteem', positive emotions, and even 'the pursuit of happiness' people tend to place greater emphasis on these elements as contributors to their overall wellbeing. However, in collectivist cultures 'how others see me', 'my contribution to society' and a more balanced view about positive and negative emotions are more important. I believe the CANBE Model, with its focus on wellbeing (not happiness) and promoting a 'Me, We, World' approach, caters for these different world views.

Another area of sensitivity is how generalist we tend to be in the use of the term culture. People often belong to more than one group, or culture. So often we tend to talk about organisational culture as if there is just *one*. Perhaps this is a mistake. Within a large group of people, an individual will identify with a variety of different values and influences and may belong to many different groups. Perhaps, then, we should appreciate our nations, organisations and communities as groups of 'cultures'. The leadership role is to bring these diverse groups and individuals together by managing conflicts and creating tolerance and harmony. My belief, as I'm sure you've come to expect, is that focusing on the domains and dimensions of wellbeing is the best way to achieve this.

WAY OF LIFE

		Wellbeing Domains - 'Territories' - Interconnected areas of our lives							
		Mental Our thoughts	Emotional Our emotions	Physical Our actions	Spiritual Our spirit	Social Our communities	Cultural Our way	Environmental Our spaces	Economic Our trade
Wellbeing Dimensions 'Highways' Intertwined routes we use to navigate our lives	Creating meaning	Thinking	Feelings	Behaviour	Identity	Friendship	Way of life	Affinity	Needs
	Achieving potential	Focus	Control	Mastery	Motivation	Teamwork	Governance	Cultivation	Impact
	Nurturing relationships	Regard	Empathy	Interaction	Stories	Trust	Belonging	Cohesion	Fairness
	Building resilience	Flexibility	Agility	Health	Growth	Support	Diversity	Adaptation	Integrity
	Enriching lives	Imagination	Wisdom	Energy	Purpose	Empowerment	Integration	Renewal	Freedom
		Wellbeing Factors - 'Signposts' - Interconnected things that can help us improve wellbeing							

"A nation's culture resides in the hearts and in the soul of its people."

MAHATMA GANDHI

Our 'day to day' activities or 'way of life' are influenced by, and impact on, our culture. Key elements of this, which we have already explored, include the way we think, feel, behave, who we are and the society we live in. Of course our environment and economic circumstances, which we'll come onto in the following two chapters, also play a huge part in influencing our cultural wellbeing.

If we live in a work culture of '9 to 5' then generally that is what we will do without any real thought as to whether this is the best way of approaching things. If we live in a culture where poor mental health is stigmatised and misunderstood or it is 'bad form' to share our emotions then we will keep them to ourselves or, even worse, subdue them. If the importance of a good diet, physical exercise and relaxation are underplayed then we are more likely to eat poorly, exercise less and get more stressed. When our leaders don't listen effectively, and all we see is them shouting each other down, we are more likely to have a divided society. You get the point!

But we aren't the victims of our culture, we are the creators. To create the culture we want, however, requires wellbeing. This is because only by changing our own thinking, along with the way we handle emotions, our physical health, spiritual awareness, social connections, environment and economic wellbeing, can we begin to shift culture and influence those around us positively.

The CANBE Model provides the 'signposts' to deliver a better level of cultural wellbeing but there are a few specific areas I'd like to focus on. Perhaps none more important than the following.

VALUES & BELIEFS

The work of Martin Seligman in developing character strengths, mentioned earlier in this book, is an example of *traits* that have been identified across cultures and time. We have also discussed Maslow's work on human *needs* and the Self Determination Theory of Deci and Ryan that describes universal human *motivation* for autonomy, competence and relatedness. Work by S.H. Schwartz, a social psychologist and cross cultural researcher, has also empirically identified a set of 56 specific *values*, and ten types of universal ones, in his

Theory of Basic Human Values. It's clear that people of the human race share more in common than we do in our differences.

The following table then, brings together the work by Schwartz (Theory of Human Values), Seligman et al, (Character strengths), Deci and Ryan, and Maslow (Hierarchy of Needs). The way I have brought the information together is unscientific, although the work it represents is, and is based on my own observations of how they 'fit' together. I've done this to demonstrate two things.

1. There are many universal values, traits and motivations binding the human race together. Leaders can tap into this to manage cultural conflict and develop greater harmony
2. Leaders, across the world, should work to repair the deepening rifts developing between **what** is important to us, **who** we are and **why** we do things.

Theory of Human values What is important to us			Character strengths Who we are (our virtues)	Self Determination Theory and Maslow's needs Why we do things
Value category	**Universal values**	**Behaviours associated with the values**		
Openness to change	• Self direction • Self enhancement	• Independent thought and action • Choosing, creating, exploring. • Excitement, novelty and challenge	• Bravery • Creativity • Curiosity • Love of learning • Zest	• Autonomy
Self transcendence	• Benevolence • Universalism	• Preserving and enhancing the welfare of frequent personal contacts (the 'in-group'). • Understanding, appreciation, tolerance, protection and welfare of all people and nature.	• Appreciation of beauty and excellence • Fairness • Forgiveness • Gratitude • Honesty • Hope • Humility • Humour • Kindness • Love • Perspective	• Transcendence
Conservation	• Security • Conformity • Tradition	• Safety, harmony & stability of society, relationships and self. • Restraint of actions likely to upset or harm others and violate social norms. • Respect, commitment and acceptance of cultural customs and ideas	• Judgment • Prudence • Self regulation • Social intelligence • Teamwork	• Basic survival • Safety • Relatedness • Belonging
Self-enhancement	• Hedonism • Achievement • Power	• Pleasure or sensuous gratification for self. • Personal success through demonstrating socially accepted competence • Social status & prestige, control or dominance over people and resources.	• Leadership • Perseverance • Spirituality	• Competence • Self esteem

If what we value and why we do things isn't aligned with who we are it can create tension and anxiety in our lives. Well this is exactly what is happening at a global level.

Our basic survival needs, environment and nature are being threatened by our focus on materialism and consumerism. We are demonstrating a lack of judgement, prudence, and self-regulation, reflected by our continued focus on quantity over quality. We measure economic productivity (GDP) as opposed to quality, we eat more than we need, we buy one, we get one free, and so on.

We value people with wealth, celebrity status or fame as successful by our social standards rather than everyday heroes who surround us. We trust 'influencers' on social media rather than ourselves.

There was a young man I knew who wanted nothing more than to be a YouTuber. YouTube, it must be said, is something of a culture in and of itself! The young man wanted to play video-games, run commentary, and become a celebrity. He saw this as an escape from the drudgery of his job, which made him very unhappy - suffice to say his emotional and mental wellbeing was in survival mode. Every week, he wrote messages to his favourite YouTuber, someone with millions of followers apparently making a very comfortable living playing games, asking for advice on how to do it. One day, he received a response: "Only make YouTube videos if it brings you joy. Dude, I have a day job." It turned out that the YouTuber, who seemed to be a wealthy and successful influencer with a dream lifestyle, was in fact working 9 - 5 just like everyone else. He made videos in his spare time because it was what he enjoyed doing. Appearances can be incredibly deceiving, and we must question what we truly value. When our culture pushes us to pursue goals that are not truly tangible (the image of a lifestyle that doesn't exist), we must question our culture and take the reins. The young man I knew experienced a "dream shattered" moment. But it was also transformative, because it helped him realise what he truly wanted: a change in lifestyle and culture, from surviving to something more like thriving.

The hedonism and power that wealth brings is increasingly polarised with the few, challenging our views on fairness and threatening to destabilise society.

An unbalanced focus on individualism, and competition prioritised over interdependence and co-operation, destabilises our motivation for relatedness, belonging, and transcendence. We value things over experiences and rights over responsibilities.

These imbalances, threats, and mis-directions have been described as "cultural fraud"[1] in that they promote lives that serve the economy, but do not meet our real needs. For some time, they have flown beneath the radar, but are increasingly rising in the public consciousness. We must increasingly focus on the aspects of life that really matter - health, friendship, accomplishment, financial and environmental security, kindness and caring. In essence we must focus on wellbeing. One way of doing this is to begin using a common language. This is one of the reasons for the CANBE Model. It provides a language around wellbeing that I hope everyone can understand and bridges the gaps between the different models currently used at international, regional, organisational and individual levels. Let's take a more detailed look at the role of language in culture.

LANGUAGE

At the very basic level being able to speak the language of the people with whom you live improves wellbeing. Technology can have a big impact here. The introduction of Google translation and developments in smartphone technology mean we can speak with people from other nations in our own language and still be understood right then and there.

Understanding each other is the starting point and sensitivity towards the protection of local dialects, as an important part of diverse culture, is also key in protecting the identity and wellbeing of groups across the world. Of course, learning a new language can also be a fantastic way of helping improve wellbeing in respect to the mental challenge and opportunities it creates to build relationships. With improvements to technological developments in immediate translation, we can achieve the best of both.

But away from this very basic level, language plays a more nuanced role in our cultural wellbeing. We've already touched on the use of questions to tackle limiting beliefs, and the importance of tone and body language in conversations. The words we use and the way we use them can also have a powerful impact. Which of the following words do you hear most from people around you? Me, I, mine, or we, us, ours. In this instance, by using we, us, ours more, we can change the mind-set of people around us to think more in respect to the team than individual requirements.

To provide examples of how language might work culturally at a national level, what differences would you perceive if the language of success became more about wellbeing, spirituality, connection, harmony, flourishing and prosperity, rather than growth, competitiveness, income, wealth?

Only the other day I was talking to the wellbeing manager at a multi-national construction business which is making great strides in developing a wellbeing strategy. Having done a little research beforehand, I pointed out that they still refer to a Director of 'Human Capital'. The manager had to admit that they had more work to do in respect to culture and that their use of language was an important part of this!

What language would you like to see change in your culture(s)? Which words that you currently use would you like to change?

FOOD

We explored diet in the earlier chapter on Physical Wellbeing. But food is also linked closely to our cultural wellbeing, values & beliefs. Most of us have been brought up on particular diets and have been accustomed to eating certain foods. However, this is a key area where we need to challenge our thinking. Most of us, including me, are sleep walking. Being more *mindful* is probably a good starting place. Understanding *how much* we are eating, and the *quality* of what we eat, will help inform any actions we need to take. Of course being mindful will also help us enjoy food more as it plays a big part in our *emotional wellbeing*.

In their excellent article "The Effects of Plant-Based Diets on Body and Brain"[2] Medawar, Huhn, Villringer, et al describe a spectrum of diets ranging from animal based to plant based. This ranges from omnivore (meat eaters), through pescatarian (fish eaters), to ovo-lacto vegetarian (dairy), and finally vegan (plant-based).

The article, which systematically reviewed 32 studies, demonstrates their finding that there is "robust evidence for short- to moderate-term beneficial effects of plant-based diets versus conventional diets (duration ≤ 24 months) on weight status, energy metabolism and systemic inflammation in healthy participants, obese and type-2 diabetes patients."

Whilst it appears that there are some strong arguments emerging for the benefits of plant-based diets on our Physical Wellbeing, there is no proof that people actually live longer as a result and there needs to be further research on the long term effects.

From a Mental Wellbeing perspective, the article is less conclusive and "a causal impact of plant-based diets on cognitive functions, mental and neurological health and respective underlying mechanisms has yet to be demonstrated."

In researching the topic of nutrition and diet it is clear that there is much confusion. The picture on whether a plant or meat based diet is best for our wellbeing remains cloudy. Plant-based supporters will argue that we can get all our nutrients (excluding vitamin B12) from a plant-based diet, and that meat eating is contributing to environmental damage and causes unnecessary harm to animals. Omnivores put forward that meat is the most nutritionally optimum grade of food, and that the environmental damage caused is less than many other industries.

However, what is clear from the high levels of obesity and hunger and diseases linked to certain food types is:

1. Some people are eating too much
2. Some people are eating too little
3. There's room for improvement in all of our diets and the way food is produced

From an individual perspective then, for those with adequate access to food, perhaps the best advice is to start taking more responsibility for how much you eat and what you eat. You have a right to good food but you also have a responsibility to eat a healthy diet. The costs of unhealthy eating are not just born by individuals. If unhealthy eating and drinking leads to disease or illness requiring medical attention then the costs are borne by all of society.

In terms of how many calories you require, type in 'Basal Metabolic Rate (BMR) Calculator' into your search engine and calculate your BMR and calorie requirements. Other food/diet based websites and your doctor may also be able to provide advice here.

In respect to the quality of your food, 'eating the rainbow', a diet with many colours of food in, is good advice, as is eating a balanced diet with reduced processed foods. Of course, the cultural aspect of food is only one element we should consider. There are also environmental factors which we should think about and I'll come onto these in the next chapter.

Unfortunately, there are still many people without adequate access to food and water. The UN states that 'latest available estimates indicate that about 821 million people in the world were undernourished in 2018. That means one in nine people do not get enough food to be healthy and lead an active life. Hunger and malnutrition are in fact the number one risk to health worldwide – greater than AIDS, malaria and tuberculosis combined'. It is fair to say that the majority of problems are in developing nations with two thirds of the undernourished living in Sub-Saharan Africa or Southern Asia. However, there are also too many people in developed nations without access to food, or consuming too much of the wrong things.

As leaders we can help change our food culture(s) to increase wellbeing across the world. This could include:

- Eating less and being less wasteful
- Reviewing what we eat and focusing on quality
- Education and research to improve our diets

- Sharing food with others
- Producing and growing food sustainably and reducing our carbon footprint
- Using more local producers, where possible
- Adapting to the impacts of extreme weather on our food supply
- Ensuring markets provide opportunities for all to access food through removing trade restrictions, market distortions and extreme food price volatility

Of course technology will be one contributor to the improvement of food production and consumption across the world.

TECHNOLOGY

Technology is undoubtedly transforming our culture. Technology in our modern world offers us great potential across all the domains and dimensions of wellbeing, but also raises many concerns.

On the plus side, technology can help us find answers and get support even to the extent that 'self management' is now possible for many situations. It can connect us to others around the world, socially or in a business context. We can have access to emotional support from counselling, coaching and other therapy or apps and information to improve memory, thinking, physical health and just about anything you can think of at our fingertips.

Technology can help us save time, money and even CO_2 emissions from reduced travel. The reduced cost of providing services online has also opened up access, and in many cases meant that services can be provided for free. In addition, the increased access to data is providing professionals with richer information to help improve all areas of our lives. The development of blockchain, quantum computing, and AI are accelerating the opportunities for us to solve some of the greatest problems we face. I am extremely optimistic about the contributions technology can make to help us on our journey towards thriving. However, I also recognise its drawbacks.

The phone beeped and Tony, without thinking, picked it up to see what it was. It was only a message about the latest offer to an online store he had an account with. Tony immediately put his phone back down and resumed his conversation with Sue, unaware of the 'hurt' she was feeling that he could be so easily distracted. This often happened in her conversations with Tony, and Sue was beginning to think that their relationship was heading nowhere.

We see this type of activity day in day out. Technology used inappropriately can lead to distraction, reduced social skills, heightened isolation and even depression. The beep we hear on our phones, alerting us to a new message, gives us a 'dopamine hit' and triggers the reward circuitry in our brains. Without thinking we pick it up unaware of the harm we are doing to our personal and professional relationships.

But technology can also have a bad impact on our physical health. Screen glare and small type, poor lighting, incorrect viewing distances and posture can lead to eye strain, poor sleep, neck and back problems. An over sedentary lifestyle is also a major contributor to the high levels of obesity we see in the world today. 'Sitting is often referred to as the new smoking'.

Socially, harmful tweets, incriminating photos and damaging Facebook posts are part of an increasingly worrying trend in 'cyber bullying' and 'trolling' that, in their worst cases, have led to tragic suicides.

With increasing developments in the internet, artificial intelligence, automation, quantum computing, blockchain and other technology it is important that leaders make the most of the opportunities whilst limiting the downsides.

ARTS & LEISURE

A growing number of studies support the belief that cultural participation in things like the arts and leisure are good for our health and wellbeing. They help us feel emotions such as joy and happiness, but also help us create meaning in our lives. Cultural activities can also help relieve stress, which in turn can help protect us from certain diseases, and build mental health through exposure to new ideas and ways of thinking.

GOVERNANCE

		Wellbeing Domains - 'Territories' - Interconnected areas of our lives							
		Mental Our thoughts	**Emotional** Our emotions	**Physical** Our actions	**Spiritual** Our spirit	**Social** Our communities	**Cultural** Our way	**Environmental** Our spaces	**Economic** Our trade
Wellbeing Dimensions 'Highways' Intertwined routes we use to navigate our lives	**Creating meaning**	Thinking	Feelings	Behaviour	Identity	Friendship	Way of life	Affinity	Needs
	Achieving potential	Focus	Control	Mastery	Motivation	Teamwork	Governance	Cultivation	Impact
	Nurturing relationships	Regard	Empathy	Interaction	Stories	Trust	Belonging	Cohesion	Fairness
	Building resilience	Flexibility	Agility	Health	Growth	Support	Diversity	Adaptation	Integrity
	Enriching lives	Imagination	Wisdom	Energy	Purpose	Empowerment	Integration	Renewal	Freedom
		Wellbeing Factors - 'Signposts' - Interconnected things that can help us improve wellbeing							

"A leader is a dealer in hope."

NAPOLEON BONAPARTE

"Leaders aren't born, they are made. And they are made just like anything else, through hard work."

VINCE LOMBARDI

> "Every man's ability may be strengthened or increased by culture."
>
> JOHN ABBOT

The link between wellbeing and governance is bi-directional. Governance influences our wellbeing but is also a reflection of the people being governed. In fact, I would argue that the whole purpose of governance should be about creating wellbeing for the people. Good governance creates tolerance and harmony and enables people to achieve their potential. Bad governance creates conflict and barriers that stop people achieving their potential. When it ceases to reflect the people, sooner or later, it will be replaced.

Governance comprises all of the processes of government, a state, market or network over society including systems, leadership, law, technology and economy. We've already covered technology and will discuss the economy in the chapter after next. For now, let's take a look at the other three.

SYSTEMS

We are all part of many different systems that impact on our wellbeing and culture but over which, individually, we have very little impact. These systems include:

- The Universe, the Earth, marine and land ecosystems.
- Communication and social systems like nation, monarchy, republic, capitalism, communism, democracy, autocracy, community, workplace and family.
- Technological systems include things like our infrastructure, the internet and energy.

For individuals the best we can hope for is to focus on what we can control, and to work collectively to change those things we can't influence on our own. But this is also why we require stronger, braver leadership. The CANBE Model inspires a 'systems thinking approach' and it also provides leaders with some direction as to what our systems should be achieving. The best systems in the world aren't really very effective if they deliver the wrong things. As we know from the key problems outlined in this book, many of our systems aren't anywhere near as effective as they need to be!

Is one system better than another for wellbeing? At this present point I think this is a largely unanswered question although the UN pushes for greater democracy. But democracies are not infallible. The centralisation of wealth and power mean many are open to criticism due to an imbalance of influence. In fact the UN itself is perceived as undemocratic by some nations, as a few powerful states, in particular the USA and China, seem to have greater control over the international system. An autocrat with the best will of the people at heart may be better than a self centred democrat.

Perhaps we should focus less on pushing our 'systems' as the best and more on what our systems are delivering. If they aren't delivering greater wellbeing then they are broken and need fixing. Whatever system we look at, whether it be our workplace or our country it should be designed to deliver greater mental creativity, emotional balance, physical vitality, spiritual fulfilment, social connection, cultural harmony, a flourishing environment and economic prosperity. So whichever systems you are influenced by ask yourself whether they are delivering the right things. If they don't, do what you can to change them.

One principle that is aligned with delivering greater wellbeing is subsidiarity. This is the principle, adopted by the United Nations and European Union amongst others, that central authorities will only perform those tasks which cannot be performed effectively at a more immediate or local level. Central authorities only get involved if they can add additional value, scale, expertise, knowledge or competencies, unavailable to the people or states affected.

This obviously has implications at a global, national, and local level, but overall aims to put power in the hands of the people that need it the most. I believe it aligns with wellbeing as it serves to deliver greater autonomy and freedom. But it is also based on using and developing competencies. When nation states, organisations or individuals use their strengths to accomplish things it helps build wellbeing.

However as we've seen above, in respect to the perception of the UN as being undemocratic by some nations, whilst the intention is good the reality and perception can be different. Nation states are also at different levels of capability and maturity, particularly economically. This can lead to greater emphasis on sovereignty rather than support for international goals. We can see this in the resistance of The Association of Southeast Asian Nations (ASEAN) states to the calls for greater democracy and human rights by some western states.

So whilst giving power to people is a good principle it may need to be backed up with varying levels of support and assistance. For example, certain developing nations have fewer resources and competencies and so may require greater assistance from the UN. This may also be true of business units and individuals in your organisation.

Leaders must help create and implement systems which deliver greater wellbeing.

LEADERSHIP STYLE

As a leader, you will influence culture and the wellbeing of the people you lead through your leadership style. There is no right or wrong style. Various models, including Blanchard (Situational Leadership), Goleman (Emotional Intelligence Derived Leadership) and others, have been developed over the years which, between them, reflect the need to adapt your style in relation to various criteria including:

- **The situation** – If you are in a crisis situation you

might be much more likely to use a directive 'tell' style of leadership. In extreme situations, such as a battlefield, this might mean 'barking orders' that your people are expected to follow without question. All of us have experienced this most recently with the outbreak of Coronavirus. Governments across the world have taken much more control and been more directive by 'locking down' many of our freedoms and asking us to stay at home. In the circumstances this style of leadership is totally appropriate.

- In the modern office environment however, a 'coaching' approach, where you help build awareness and responsibility through active listening and asking questions, is much more suitable. However, even here, in a crisis situation, your people may want a more directive approach. 'Just tell me what to do and I'll do it!' I think this is relevant to many of the situations we are now facing. People don't always know which are the most sustainably developed products. Due to poor labelling they don't always know which packaging can or can't be recycled. Which diet is the best? Most people don't know what their environmental impact is and the best ways to reduce it. These are all examples where we need stronger leadership to provide greater education, improved incentives, stronger regulation and more honest, transparent communication.

- **The organisation** - An operational environment where things are running smoothly will require a different leadership style to a more strategic environment where there is a need for change in order to succeed. The size and levels of hierarchy in your organisation will also have an impact. Lots of layers will slow decision-making and may require a more collaborative, influencing approach to leadership. Fewer layers will require a more dynamic, accountable approach. In our modern world, with the increasing pace of change, there is a trend towards this latter approach to enable quicker decision making, action and provide greater autonomy, agility and creativity.

- **The objective** – Leading a manufacturing unit, focused on delivering x amounts of units per week, will have a different emphasis to leading a design function with the aim of coming up with the next new widget to light up the marketplace. Whilst both need people and process leadership, the focus in each will typically be skewed and require an adaptation of approach. However, by using the CANBE Model a leader can ensure that there is a good balance given to both people and process.

- **The people** – New teams or employees are much more likely to require additional support and a more directive approach. Of course, this will also vary by individual. As individuals and teams become more confident they will require less direction and support, and you may be able to delegate with very little intervention. Of course, each country has its own unique culture (cultures, in fact), and this will create unique requirements. Whilst one country's workplace culture might be generalised as formal, hierarchical, and sincere; another might be seen as de-centralised, democratic, and traditional. These varying hierarchies will require an adapted approach.

- **You** – Your values, beliefs, character, personality and experience will all influence your leadership style. Based on the complexities of your personal focus on people,

> task, extroversion and introversion, you will be inclined to lead others in a certain way. Understanding this through things like DISC Personality Profiling and your character strengths can help you adapt. Your own values and beliefs will also influence your approach. Understanding strengths and weaknesses and that your values and beliefs are no less or more important than anyone else's will help you look at things from others' perspectives. Personal experience and authority also play a part. For example, a new leader may feel the need to establish their authority and, in so doing, come across as more directive.

While these models are useful they can never reflect the full range of complexities and permutations that leaders must adapt to. In this respect, you will need to adopt different styles for short term situations, and these could even change during the course of one day! However, over the longer term you might show preference for one particular style. This is where most modern books and experts are reflecting preference for a 'coaching style' of leadership, the benefits of which were highlighted earlier in the book. This coaching style of leadership can also play a big part in how language affects cultural wellbeing through asking better questions and talking less!

LAW, POLICIES AND PROCEDURES

Procedures and policies will also influence culture and as a leader you may be in a position to influence these. We mentioned previously the importance of habits. Have some of these policies existed for some time without any review or challenges? Have they just become bad habits?

You can ask people which policies and procedures are causing them the most frustration and see what can be done to make them easier to navigate. How do your laws, policies and procedures either detract from, or add to, the culture you would like?

Examples of some policies and procedures in the workplace that can either hinder or support employee wellbeing include, but are not limited to, flexible working, manager and supervisor support, child and elderly care and the use of technology.

A study by Beauregard at the London School of Economics investigated the link between organisational work-home culture and employee wellbeing[1]. It found that, "the degree to which organisational norms demand that employees subjugate their personal lives to their work responsibilities influenced the amount of work interference with home experienced, which in turn predicted increased levels of psychosomatic symptoms such as anxiety, fatigue, and depression."

What is clear from this research is that when implementing policies and procedures people need to be treated as individuals. Different societal expectations of gender, support from a partner, skills in self-control are all cited as having an impact on whether, or how much, individuals' wellbeing suffers if demands from work impact on the work-home dynamic.

Another key point is that it is not just through offering flexible working and other benefits that wellbeing can be enhanced. As outlined previously in the section on energy, as so often with actions, it is the intent, commitment and culture that supports the action that is important. If employees see that flexible working is viewed with derision, then the impact on improving their wellbeing will be diminished or negated.

BELONGING

		Mental Our thoughts	Emotional Our emotions	Physical Our actions	Spiritual Our spirit	Social Our communities	Cultural Our way	Environmental Our spaces	Economic Our trade
		Wellbeing Domains - 'Territories' - Interconnected areas of our lives							
Wellbeing Dimensions 'Highways' Intertwined routes we use to navigate our lives	Creating meaning	Thinking	Feelings	Behaviour	Identity	Friendship	Way of life	Affinity	Needs
	Achieving potential	Focus	Control	Mastery	Motivation	Teamwork	Governance	Cultivation	Impact
	Nurturing relationships	Regard	Empathy	Interaction	Stories	Trust	Belonging	Cohesion	Fairness
	Building resilience	Flexibility	Agility	Health	Growth	Support	Diversity	Adaptation	Integrity
	Enriching lives	Imagination	Wisdom	Energy	Purpose	Empowerment	Integration	Renewal	Freedom
		Wellbeing Factors - 'Signposts' - Interconnected things that can help us improve wellbeing							

"To say goodbye is to die a little."

RAYMOND CHANDLER, *THE LONG GOODBYE*

Belonging is a relationship and powerful human motivation determined by our need to give and receive attention to and from others. It describes mutual concern for one another and, as outlined previously, is a common need across cultures and different people. When individuals are accepted, welcomed and included it leads to feelings of positive emotions such as happiness, elation, calm, and satisfaction.

However, when individuals are rejected or excluded, they feel strong negative emotions such as anxiety, jealousy, sadness, depression and even grief. In fact, the psychological pain caused by social rejection is so intense that it involves the same brain regions involved in the experience of physical pain. In a similar vein breaking off an attachment, even in situations where the relationship is abusive or harmful, can cause pain that is deeply rooted in the need to belong.

We can find belonging in many places including spiritual groups, with friends, family, social media, clubs, in our community and workplaces. As with anything valuable and durable, belonging takes time and investment. It is facilitated and developed by all of the things we've discussed so far in this book. But what else can we do to help develop cultures where people feel like they belong?

Starting at the beginning we can look for people who might want to belong to our group. People who share our values, traditions, interests and can care and be cared for. But we also want to look out for people who can help us grow. People we can help, and they can help us. Just focusing on being with people the same as us will lead to a lack of ideas, narrow perspectives and stagnation.

This is where acceptance and letting go of judgement is so important. It's fine to have values and a sense of identity, but if we are too 'hard' and 'fixed' there is a danger that no one will want to join with us. We need to be more 'soft' and 'fluid'.

Once we've found people who want to belong, a personal invitation and warm welcome can either ignite or extinguish a sense of belonging. This might seem obvious but I've heard countless stories of new starters in companies who arrive on their first day only to find a lack of training, no thought into what they will be doing, and a general lack of preparedness.

Of course, on a macro level, we will see this increasingly in respect to the higher levels of migration. Migration will not go away. Climate change, decreasing biodiversity, urbanisation, conflict and a

BELONGING

		Wellbeing Domains - 'Territories' - Interconnected areas of our lives							
		Mental Our thoughts	Emotional Our emotions	Physical Our actions	Spiritual Our spirit	Social Our communities	Cultural Our way	Environmental Our spaces	Economic Our trade
Wellbeing Dimensions 'Highways' Intertwined routes we use to navigate our lives	Creating meaning	Thinking	Feelings	Behaviour	Identity	Friendship	Way of life	Affinity	Needs
	Achieving potential	Focus	Control	Mastery	Motivation	Teamwork	Governance	Cultivation	Impact
	Nurturing relationships	Regard	Empathy	Interaction	Stories	Trust	Belonging	Cohesion	Fairness
	Building resilience	Flexibility	Agility	Health	Growth	Support	Diversity	Adaptation	Integrity
	Enriching lives	Imagination	Wisdom	Energy	Purpose	Empowerment	Integration	Renewal	Freedom
		Wellbeing Factors - 'Signposts' - Interconnected things that can help us improve wellbeing							

"To say goodbye is to die a little."

RAYMOND CHANDLER, *THE LONG GOODBYE*

Belonging is a relationship and powerful human motivation determined by our need to give and receive attention to and from others. It describes mutual concern for one another and, as outlined previously, is a common need across cultures and different people. When individuals are accepted, welcomed and included it leads to feelings of positive emotions such as happiness, elation, calm, and satisfaction.

However, when individuals are rejected or excluded, they feel strong negative emotions such as anxiety, jealousy, sadness, depression and even grief. In fact, the psychological pain caused by social rejection is so intense that it involves the same brain regions involved in the experience of physical pain. In a similar vein breaking off an attachment, even in situations where the relationship is abusive or harmful, can cause pain that is deeply rooted in the need to belong.

We can find belonging in many places including spiritual groups, with friends, family, social media, clubs, in our community and workplaces. As with anything valuable and durable, belonging takes time and investment. It is facilitated and developed by all of the things we've discussed so far in this book. But what else can we do to help develop cultures where people feel like they belong?

Starting at the beginning we can look for people who might want to belong to our group. People who share our values, traditions, interests and can care and be cared for. But we also want to look out for people who can help us grow. People we can help, and they can help us. Just focusing on being with people the same as us will lead to a lack of ideas, narrow perspectives and stagnation.

This is where acceptance and letting go of judgement is so important. It's fine to have values and a sense of identity, but if we are too 'hard' and 'fixed' there is a danger that no one will want to join with us. We need to be more 'soft' and 'fluid'.

Once we've found people who want to belong, a personal invitation and warm welcome can either ignite or extinguish a sense of belonging. This might seem obvious but I've heard countless stories of new starters in companies who arrive on their first day only to find a lack of training, no thought into what they will be doing, and a general lack of preparedness.

Of course, on a macro level, we will see this increasingly in respect to the higher levels of migration. Migration will not go away. Climate change, decreasing biodiversity, urbanisation, conflict and a growing population will all lead to increasing levels of population mobility across the globe. We can either welcome it or resist it. Resisting it seems a little short sighted as it isn't going to go away. When different people come together there are typically short term periods of wariness, confusion, misunderstanding and even conflict. This is to be expected. After all, these people don't really know each other yet!

The easy thing to do in this situation is to decide that it just doesn't work, to resort to segmentation, or stop people from joining us altogether. Because it is easy, this is typically what tends to happen. We take the path of least resistance. But leadership isn't always about taking the easy path. Sometimes we need to show people that there is a better way, even if along the route there may be complications, obstacles and even set backs.

After all, this is the story of human history. Throughout time different races have travelled, settled, and bred to create the diverse population we see today. As outlined earlier, our different cultures share more values, needs, wants, desires and characteristics than we do differences. Isn't it about time we were more welcoming of our fellow humans in all groups, organisations, communities and countries across the globe? Greater diversity will lead to more benefits and increased resilience over time than the short term difficulties we may encounter.

These similarities mentioned above are a great platform for creating belonging. Focusing on similarities first can help people feel safer and create connections. Accepting differences, without judgement, naturally follows on from this. By creating these 'safer spaces' people will be more open to being themselves, sharing their passions, beliefs and vulnerabilities.

Of course, whilst we have a right to inclusion and belonging, we also have a responsibility to get involved. We can learn to say yes to opportunities presented, and get involved in helping others where we can. Who knows what might happen? We might even begin to feel like we belong!

DIVERSITY

		Wellbeing Domains - 'Territories' - Interconnected areas of our lives							
		Mental Our thoughts	**Emotional** Our emotions	**Physical** Our actions	**Spiritual** Our spirit	**Social** Our communities	**Cultural** Our way	**Environmental** Our spaces	**Economic** Our trade
Wellbeing Dimensions 'Highways' Intertwined routes we use to navigate our lives	Creating meaning	Thinking	Feelings	Behaviour	Identity	Friendship	Way of life	Affinity	Needs
	Achieving potential	Focus	Control	Mastery	Motivation	Teamwork	Governance	Cultivation	Impact
	Nurturing relationships	Regard	Empathy	Interaction	Stories	Trust	Belonging	Cohesion	Fairness
	Building resilience	Flexibility	Agility	Health	Growth	Support	Diversity	Adaptation	Integrity
	Enriching lives	Imagination	Wisdom	Energy	Purpose	Empowerment	Integration	Renewal	Freedom
		Wellbeing Factors - 'Signposts' - Interconnected things that can help us improve wellbeing							

"You have your way. I have my way. As for the right way, the correct way, and the only way, it does not exist."

FRIEDRICH NIETZSCHE

"Strength lies in differences, not in similarities."

STEPHEN COVEY

The human race is diverse, and this is part of its strength and resilience. However, as globalisation continues, cultural diversity, such as languages and indigenous knowledge, is increasingly under threat. Many of the estimated 6000 languages still spoken across the world are rapidly disappearing, and we are in danger of losing local knowledge about the natural world. A reduction in our diversity will lead to lower levels of resilience at a time when we could really do with more.

So we need to protect and nourish diversity but we naturally align with people that are like us. We are all unconsciously biased. Think of all the different types of people that could work in your organisation. Write down a list.

Now review it against this list:

- Demographic diversity: gender, sexual orientation, race, ethnicity, age, ability/disability, socioeconomic status
- Experiential diversity: affinities, hobbies & abilities, religion, politics, educational attainment
- Cognitive diversity: personality and thinking style

What do the differences in your list and the one above tell you about your own biases?

The focus in the media, at least in the UK, tends to be very much on diversity in respect to gender, sexual orientation and race. This misses the point of diversity in the first place. A diverse workplace should include a unique mix of people from across these categories relevant to the specific organisational context. We need to focus on the issue as a whole, not on a specific category.

Rather ironically, and reflecting the point made above, the McKinsey & Company 2015 report "Diversity Matters"[1] looked at the leadership and executive team composition of women and ethnic/racial groups in large companies in the United Kingdom, Canada, Latin America, and the United States.

The results varied by country and industry but found a statistically significant relationship between a more diverse leadership team and better financial performance.

Many people now support the advantages of diversity. The inference from the McKinsey Report is that an organisation that is more reflective of the society in which it operates will benefit from attracting new talent, a strengthening of customer focus, increased employee satisfaction, improved decision making and a better company image.

When we look at it from the perspective of some of the top challenges we face in the world today including: accelerating change, migration, inequality, distribution of wealth, climate change and scarce resources, the increased creativity, experience and empathy that diversity can bring are also hopefully clear. Other benefits can include increased learning and knowledge sharing, the reduction of risk, and a richer organisational culture.

But, of course, diversity can also create challenges as we explored in the Chapter 'Course Correction'. Diversity can be bad for our short term wellbeing if it causes conflict. The challenge for leaders is to manage diversity well, knowing that over the longer term it is good for our resilience as groups, organisations, communities and nations.

So what can you do as a leader to improve the diversity and inclusion within your organisation? Firstly, by understanding yourself better, including your biases, you will be more open to understanding others. Introducing training that looks at building people's understanding of diversity and increasing empathy can also help.

Freeing people up through practices like flexible working, job sharing, and working from home can also encourage new and different people to apply for jobs in your organisation.

Just by helping people to be themselves through understanding values, beliefs, personality, and character, we can liberate them to share views and opinions without fear or recrimination. Thinking about diversity at all levels of your organisation is also important. Whilst we might have a diverse management group, what does it say if the executive team is still constituted by a majority?

Including and empowering people in the decision making process, particularly with decisions that will impact on them, is also a great way to encourage diverse thinking and approaches. As explained earlier, diversity is not without its pitfalls and in order to benefit from the upside we need to ensure effective integration of different groups.

INTEGRATION

		Wellbeing Domains - 'Territories' - Interconnected areas of our lives							
		Mental Our thoughts	Emotional Our emotions	Physical Our actions	Spiritual Our spirit	Social Our communities	Cultural Our way	Environmental Our spaces	Economic Our trade
Wellbeing Dimensions 'Highways' Intertwined routes we use to navigate our lives	Creating meaning	Thinking	Feelings	Behaviour	Identity	Friendship	Way of life	Affinity	Needs
	Achieving potential	Focus	Control	Mastery	Motivation	Teamwork	Governance	Cultivation	Impact
	Nurturing relationships	Regard	Empathy	Interaction	Stories	Trust	Belonging	Cohesion	Fairness
	Building resilience	Flexibility	Agility	Health	Growth	Support	Diversity	Adaptation	Integrity
	Enriching lives	Imagination	Wisdom	Energy	Purpose	Empowerment	Integration	Renewal	Freedom
		Wellbeing Factors - 'Signposts' - Interconnected things that can help us improve wellbeing							

"We may have different religions, different languages, different colored skin, but we all belong to one human race."

KOFI ANNAN

What is clear from research is that cultural integration is extremely complex. For example, it is not new news that between 50-90% of culture/change/transformation programmes in companies are deemed as unsuccessful. Many mergers and acquisitions fail to realise their true potential. And when we look at the stories of many indigenous peoples and immigrants across the world, it is clear that failures abound here too.

Reading through reports and articles on the subject, many reasons are given for this high failure rate including: not understanding culture, not focusing on people, a clash of cultures, lack of planning, prohibitive policies, governance and social structures and poor execution. What is particularly interesting is that many of these research papers focus on how the 'minority' either aligns with, or separates itself from, the 'majority'. They focus on how we approach cultural integration now. What they don't tend to do is focus on how we could do much better. How we could create even better cultures.

It doesn't take research or science to know that the best partnerships or relationships occur when each individual party brings out the best in the other. This doesn't happen through dominating, coercing, or subjugating the other, but through open discussion and understanding of strengths and weaknesses. At its best, successful integration is the action or process of combining, amalgamating, fusing, and blending to achieve something greater than the sum of its parts. It's a **'best of both approach'** or where more parties are involved a **'best of the bunch approach'**.

However, in reality there are often weaknesses in the approach of both parties. Perhaps one party isn't contributing enough or adding enough value? Perhaps the dominant party is subjugating the minor? Successful integrations require the full participation of both parties.

In this regard perhaps we should be more imaginative, exploratory and open? How could we learn more effectively from new people joining our dominant group? What if, rather than trying to educate them in 'our ways', we were more open to shared dialogue so we could both learn together and create the best of both?

Practically what might this look like? Well, in an organisation, what if we asked the new joiner to deliver a presentation/talk about their previous organisation, group or country culture? In this way we get to know more about them and listen to any good ideas they might have for working more effectively. In a merger and acquisition scenario this would be the equivalent of a collaborative leadership team building a new vision of a merged entity taking the best practices from each of the companies involved.

Ultimately leaders must seek to protect and enhance the way of life for all people. This involves giving them autonomy, choices and responsibilities. Some will choose to adopt the new culture. Some will choose to remain true to their existing culture. And then there's everything else in between.

CHAPTER SUMMARY

There is an irony that whilst there is growing recognition of the importance of diversity, in many ways, the world is becoming less diverse. It is a much smaller place now than it was even 50 years ago. Globalisation, technology, migration, urbanisation, climate change, a growing population, amongst many other factors, are converging to bring us all closer together. This 'coming together' is presenting us with opportunities and problems. On the one hand we benefit from increased sharing of knowledge. On the other hand, differences can lead to conflict.

These conflicts are often based on different values and beliefs. As evidenced by increased mental health issues, materialism, consumerism, falling levels of trust, climate change and growing inequalities, many of our beliefs and values have become distorted and misplaced.

We need a new vision and set of values of how to get along better. As already explored the UN Sustainable Development Goals take us some way towards this. However they are too problem focused. We need a new 'solution focused' approach.

I believe wellbeing can be the key driver here. There is a growing collective understanding of what wellbeing constitutes across the world, which is reflected by the domains, dimensions, and 'signposts' in the CANBE Model. Whilst this knowledge and understanding is still growing the model does provide us with a framework to develop greater wellbeing within and between different cultures. The domains, dimensions and 'signposts' provide enough flexibility for interpretation at local cultural levels for individuals, groups, organisations and countries. In order to use the framework effectively we should, however, steer clear of broad stereotypical formulas and treat people as individuals.

The importance of agency and autonomy, balanced with responsibilities to self and others, cannot be underestimated. People's lives are often influenced by social or cultural constructs they are unable to affect such as class, status, sex, ethnic group, age, and gender preference. Where people, or even whole countries, lack the power, resources or ability to change it can lead to feelings of futility.

Leaders need to be diligent in recognising any discriminatory practices and instigating positive change. As leaders we should start to think less about 'majorities' subjugating 'minorities' and more about how we can learn from both to create something 'greater than the sum of its parts'. 'Outliers' and 'anomalies' should be treated with curiosity.

KEY CONCEPTS TO IMPROVE CULTURAL WELLBEING:

Improving 'Way of life'

- Accepting the different 'ways of living' that people have
- Using language to positively change culture
- Using technology to improve wellbeing
- Managing the downsides of technology
- Improving diet
- Engaging in artistic, leisure and other cultural activities

Improving governance

- Designing systems to deliver wellbeing
- Changing leadership style to reflect the situation, objective, people and your own values and beliefs
- Reviewing laws, policies and procedures to check that they support wellbeing
- Freeing people up. Giving them more autonomy

Helping people feel like they belong

- Let go of judgements
- Be more welcoming
- Focus on similarities and accept differences
- Persevere

Encouraging diversity and inclusion

- Think more broadly about diversity. It is more than gender, race and sexual orientation.
- Understand biases
- Introduce training
- Review policies to ensure they support a diversity
- Be prepared to managed conflict
- Involve people in decision making

KEY BEHAVIOURS:

Where do you score on the following attributes that can help develop greater Cultural Wellbeing?

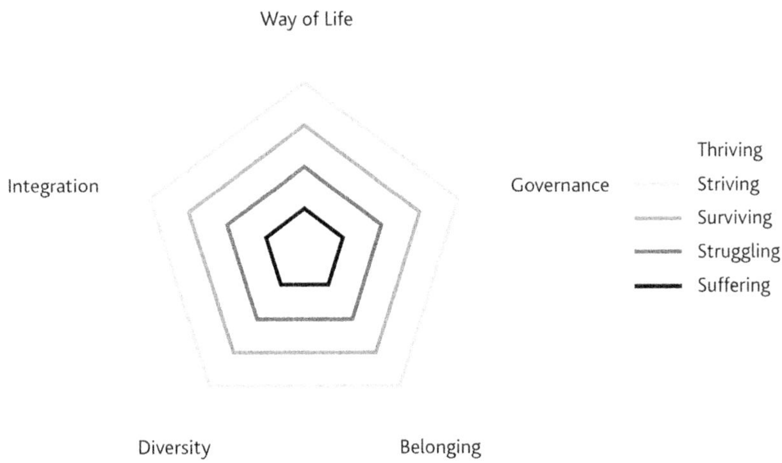

What would you like to do differently?

CHAPTER ELEVEN

IMPROVING ENVIRONMENTAL WELLBEING

Wellbeing Domains - 'Territories' - Interconnected areas of our lives

Wellbeing Dimensions 'Highways' Intertwined routes we use to navigate our lives	Mental Our thoughts	Emotional Our emotions	Physical Our actions	Spiritual Our spirit	Social Our communities	Cultural Our way	Environmental Our spaces	Economic Our trade
Creating meaning	Thinking	Feelings	Behaviour	Identity	Friendship	Way of life	Affinity	Needs
Achieving potential	Focus	Control	Mastery	Motivation	Teamwork	Governance	Cultivation	Impact
Nurturing relationships	Regard	Empathy	Interaction	Stories	Trust	Belonging	Cohesion	Fairness
Building resilience	Flexibility	Agility	Health	Growth	Support	Diversity	Adaptation	Integrity
Enriching lives	Imagination	Wisdom	Energy	Purpose	Empowerment	Integration	Renewal	Freedom

Wellbeing Factors - 'Signposts' - Interconnected things that can help us improve wellbeing

---

"What is the use of a house if you haven't got a tolerable planet to put it on?"

HENRY DAVID THOREAU

As Sir David Attenborough told the UN climate change conference in Poland, "the collapse of our civilisations and the extinction of much of the natural world is on the horizon."

I think we are all becoming more aware of the challenges at this global level, and it is clear that we need to take more positive actions. However, when I refer to environmental wellbeing I am including all of our spaces, places and planet earth because they are all connected. Just think about your immediate environment now. Where are you reading this? Look around.

- What do you see?
- What do you feel?
- What do you hear?
- What are you touching?

All of these things will be affecting your wellbeing. The air that you are breathing, the temperature, water, light, the physical environment, messages, pictures, or other information, music and loud or other background noises.

Environmental Wellbeing is about living a lifestyle that is respectful and in harmony with our surroundings, nature, planet earth and all species living in it. It is the bi-directional impact between us and our environment whether built, natural, physical or virtual and includes our home, neighbourhood, workplace, community, country, planet and even the universe (think space junk!). When referring to 'creating the right environment' many people include social and cultural aspects. I've covered those in separate chapters so here I focus more on the physical aspects.

With high levels of Environmental Wellbeing we feel an ***affinity*** or connection with the place we are in. We may describe this as 'feeling at home'. To achieve what we want, we need to ***cultivate***, give to, and take from our environment. At the basic level this includes quality of air, noise, temperature, light and cleanliness, to the security of our neighbourhoods, communities, and countries. Cultivation can also include organising our office space or home, growing food, managing livestock, building houses or mining resources.

Our environments must also satisfy our social needs to collaborate and promote ***cohesion*** through things like infrastructure, enabling us to move freely between places, to access amenities, and promote togetherness. Environments are dynamic, whether that be moving to a new house, changing seasons or, on a wider scale, climate change. So, in order to maintain wellbeing we must ***adapt*** to our environment.

Finally our environment also provides opportunities for ***renewal***. We must give to our environment and steward it for future generations, but in return we receive the benefits already outlined, as well as being able to enjoy its beauty, freedom, and growth.

If we can achieve these things then we will ***flourish*** along with our environment. If not our environment will **degrade**, with obvious implications for us!

Climate change, the threat to biodiversity, deteriorating mental health, finite and scarce resources, population growth, migration and urbanisation are all challenges linked to our environment. Recognising these challenges, the concept of 'liveability' has grown increasingly important in developing policy and planning our environments. This is a broad concept that includes many complex characteristics such as sustainability, character and identity of a place, health, food, security, cultural expression and a sense of belonging. The Global Liveability Index[1], produced by The Economist Intelligence Unit, is one such example.

The CANBE Model is an excellent proxy for 'Liveability' and I believe it can be used by anyone to help design an environment that supports wellbeing, but in a way that is also mindful of our planet's boundaries. After all, the places we occupy should support our mental, emotional, physical, spiritual, social, cultural and economic wellbeing. Our places / spaces should also feel like home (meaningfulness), help us achieve what we want (potential), provide opportunities for togetherness (relationships), support change (resilience) and help us and future generations feel good (enrich lives). Here are a few example questions in each of the domains to help you think about your environments.

- Mental - How will this help us think better and be more creative?
- Emotional - How will this help us feel better?
- Physical - How will this help us do better things, feel healthy and communicate effectively?
- Spiritual - How will this reflect us, tell our story, motivate us, help us grow and serve others?
- Social - How will this empower us to build friendships, trust, connect and work together?
- Cultural - How will this reflect the way we do things, improve governance, belonging, diversity and integration?
- Environment - How will this help us feel at home, collaborate, adapt and renew?
- Economic - How will this meet our needs, achieve our potential, encourage fairness, integrity and progress?

So whether we are viewing this from the perspective of our home, workplace, community, country or even our planet, we can use the CANBE Model to help preserve, protect and enhance our wellbeing and that of our environment.

Following the common theme throughout this book, environmental wellbeing is linked to all other domains of wellbeing. Our environment can have a significant impact on our **Emotional** and **Mental** Wellbeing. Noise, overcrowding and distractions can all impact negatively on the quality of our thinking and how we feel. On the flip side, calm, creative spaces can stimulate our imagination.

Physically, characteristics such as air quality, temperature or natural light can impact significantly on our health. Just recently we've seen examples of this with air pollution in Beijing. At its worst, an environment that we neglect or harm can actually take lives, as we've seen with the fires in Australia.

Large differences in the livability of cities and suburbs can create deep dissatisfaction and **social** unrest threatening the fabric of communities. But well planned and distributed amenities can create opportunities for social togetherness and cohesion.

Natural environments offer many characteristics that have the potential to reduce risk factors associated with the non-communicable diseases we mentioned earlier in the book. In an increasingly urbanised world, nature, including forests, woodlands, parks, lakes and waterways, play an important tangible and intangible role in human wellbeing. This includes everything from the air we breathe, our food supply, the natural resources we use for our **economy** through to opportunities to relax and de-stress.

Our environment also plays an important part in our **cultural** wellbeing. Studies have shown that market towns in the UK are regularly voted as the "happiest" places for people to live. Market towns are often defined by their links to culture: older buildings and architecture, historical landmarks, traditional markets, local businesses that have been alive for hundreds of years. Of course, culture is not always about antiquity. For some, the lightspeed buzz of a modern city such as New York might well be a better fit for their needs. However, it is surely no coincidence that culture correlates with wellbeing, and a large part of this is environmental. From the roads and infrastructure to the built environment, all play a part in the quality of our lives.

A good starting place for environmental wellbeing is to make sure we are in places that we actually want to be in. This is the subject of affinity.

AFFINITY

		Wellbeing Domains - 'Territories' - Interconnected areas of our lives							
		Mental Our thoughts	Emotional Our emotions	Physical Our actions	Spiritual Our spirit	Social Our communities	Cultural Our way	Environmental Our spaces	Economic Our trade
Wellbeing Dimensions 'Highways' Intertwined routes we use to navigate our lives	Creating meaning	Thinking	Feelings	Behaviour	Identity	Friendship	Way of life	Affinity	Needs
	Achieving potential	Focus	Control	Mastery	Motivation	Teamwork	Governance	Cultivation	Impact
	Nurturing relationships	Regard	Empathy	Interaction	Stories	Trust	Belonging	Cohesion	Fairness
	Building resilience	Flexibility	Agility	Health	Growth	Support	Diversity	Adaptation	Integrity
	Enriching lives	Imagination	Wisdom	Energy	Purpose	Empowerment	Integration	Renewal	Freedom
		Wellbeing Factors - 'Signposts' - Interconnected things that can help us improve wellbeing							

"There's no place like home."

L. FRANK BAUM

"The ache for home lives in all of us."

MAYA ANGELOU

> "Perhaps home is not a place but simply an irrevocable condition."
>
> JAMES BALDWIN

Whilst research supports the beneficial effects of our affinity with nature, and we intuitively recognise this anyway, over the 19th and 20th Centuries we have become increasingly separated from the natural world with the advent of technological developments and increasing urbanisation. American biologist, Edward O. Wilson, and others have argued that such declines could have resulted in a loss of respect for, and desire to interact with, nature. Subsequently, this loss of connection has been cited as a potential factor contributing to environmental destruction and species extinction.

Some research[1] shows that by growing our appreciation and falling back in love with nature, we will automatically develop more environmentally friendly behaviour. As we'll see, from the benefits we receive from nature, this is a win, win, win situation. We get to relax and rejuvenate which helps our wellbeing, this stimulates more pro-environmental behaviour to protect the planet, which in turn results in better health for us. Watching films and videos, growing things in the garden, visiting and enjoying green spaces with family, friends, and colleagues are obvious examples of building this affinity. In the workplace ,we can bring nature into our buildings, encourage our people to take walks during their breaks, and even volunteer in local community projects.

Conservationists, particularly, recognise the importance of reconnecting us with nature. David Attenborough's *Blue Planet* is probably a prime example of this. So we need to rekindle our affinity with nature and the planet on which we live, but this can also work on a smaller scale in our other places.

If we have an affinity with our home, workplace, community or even country we might describe ourselves as 'feeling at home'. This feeling might allude to a natural attraction, liking, comfort, familiarity, attachment, or belonging to the places we are in, and is often tied to the people we share these places with. A large part of this 'affinity' is the meaning we attach to our places.

This will obviously be individual for all of us. Whilst one person may prefer the close proximity of a city for the benefits of employment and busy social life, another might be more comfortable living near the coast for the peace and creativity it provides.

The key question to ask is whether we are sacrificing our overall wellbeing to be where we are. When we feel out of place, we intuitively describe ourselves as like a 'fish out of water'. Feeling like we don't belong with the people or place we are in is a warning sign.

Once we understand this, there are some obvious options. The first is to move to a place which will be better for our wellbeing. Whilst this might sound quite drastic, we should remember that this is just what nomadic tribes continue to do, and have done throughout history. This is often linked to the seasons, or availability of important resources such as food and water.

Countries, communities and organisations are increasingly recognising the benefits of providing for the wellbeing of their people, so if you are thinking of moving, research the place you would like to move to thoroughly. You can even use the CANBE Model as a checklist for doing this. Use some of the questions outlined in the chapter introduction to help you think more specifically about your personal wellbeing needs.

If you'd like further help, many countries, communities, towns and cities are now publishing information on their approach to wellbeing so you can research where you would like to live. In the UK the Thriving Places Index[2] is an example of this, but there are others across the world.

Many countries and international bodies are also now publishing statistics on wellbeing and even adopting it as a policy making approach to varying degrees. Notable examples include, but are not limited to, the following:

- OECD - Better Life Index[3]
- Bhutan - Gross National Happiness Survey[4]
- UK - ONS Measuring National Wellbeing[5]
- New Zealand - The New Zealand Wellbeing Budget[6]
- Canada - The Canadian Index of Wellbeing[7]

Of course it may not always be possible or even desirable to move, so the second option for improving our environmental wellbeing is the subject of the next section. This is to cultivate the places we are in.

CULTIVATION

		Wellbeing Domains - 'Territories' - Interconnected areas of our lives							
		Mental Our thoughts	Emotional Our emotions	Physical Our actions	Spiritual Our spirit	Social Our communities	Cultural Our way	Environmental Our spaces	Economic Our trade
Wellbeing Dimensions 'Highways' Intertwined routes we use to navigate our lives	Creating meaning	Thinking	Feelings	Behaviour	Identity	Friendship	Way of life	Affinity	Needs
	Achieving potential	Focus	Control	Mastery	Motivation	Teamwork	Governance	Cultivation	Impact
	Nurturing relationships	Regard	Empathy	Interaction	Stories	Trust	Belonging	Cohesion	Fairness
	Building resilience	Flexibility	Agility	Health	Growth	Support	Diversity	Adaptation	Integrity
	Enriching lives	Imagination	Wisdom	Energy	Purpose	Empowerment	Integration	Renewal	Freedom
		Wellbeing Factors - 'Signposts' - Interconnected things that can help us improve wellbeing							

"But if each man could have his own house, a large garden to cultivate and healthy surroundings - then, I thought, there will be for them a better opportunity of a happy family life."

GEORGE CADBURY

"I think the Internet is comparable to the Homestead Act: Here's a parcel of land. Sign up, cultivate it, it's yours."

DAN ABRAMS

Cultivation is to grow, raise, farm, plant and improve. Throughout time we have always cultivated our environment to better meet our changing needs. Unfortunately some of our more recent cultivation is damaging the very thing we need to support us: Planet Earth.

To achieve our potential, we need the places we are in to support our wellbeing. But we must do this in a way that is also sustainable for our planet.

As leaders, we are responsible for our own wellbeing, but also for creating environments that help build the wellbeing of our colleagues. Whilst you may not be an expert in this area, you can still set the agenda. What I cover in the following section is an overview of the things to consider when thinking about how to cultivate environmental wellbeing for you, your colleagues, and communities.

In this respect, the International Wellbuilding Institute™ (IWBI™) is an excellent resource. The focus of this organisation is to 'transform buildings and communities in ways that help people thrive'.

There are eleven concepts on which design is centred, but these can be applied equally, with some creative thinking, as an individual in your own home, in the workplace, a community, or even a country. I'll cover these eleven concepts in more detail over the following sections within this chapter.

1. AIR

Exposure to air pollutants can lead to a variety of poor health conditions. 7 million premature deaths annually are linked to air pollution[1]. Obvious pollutants here include smoke and carbon monoxide. Education and policies to prohibit smoking, and installing detectors for smoke and carbon monoxide, are basic and simple solutions. Perhaps less obvious is just simple ventilation of premises and access to fresh air through windows that operate effectively, HVAC systems, and management of mould and bacteria build up. During COVID-19 the importance of air quality has been emphasised strongly when the British Lung Foundation reported that "two million people with lung conditions have experienced improved symptoms as a result of reduced air pollution during lockdown"[2].

2. WATER

Many people are inadequately hydrated due, in part, to the accessibility and quality of drinking water. Water is also used in other applications and systems including heating, cooling and irrigation which can lead to contamination. Provision of clean, quality water is a basic requirement. Having a plan to manage risks and potential break-outs of waterborne diseases is key.

3. NOURISHMENT

As we've already explored 'we are what we eat' and poor nourishment is a leading cause of non-communicable diseases across the world. Inspiring people to make healthier food choices through removing environmental barriers and providing greater access, availability, and opportunity are ways leadership can help. Cafeterias and vending machines with healthy food choices are examples of positive action here in the workplace. Of course food choices are not just impacted by environmental considerations. Personal attitudes towards food, what our friends eat, the information available to us (through marketing and education) and government policy all play a part.

4. LIGHT

Good lighting conditions are required for our optimal health. As outlined earlier in the section on sleep, light is a key driver of our circadian rhythm, and when this is disrupted our health can be negatively affected. As humans we are diurnal which means we need periods of both light (wakefulness) and dark (sleep). Studies have shown that light exposure is linked to our mood, stress, depression and overall health and recovery when we are ill. In the workplace, studies[3] also link improved performance with better views and lighting conditions.

5. MOVEMENT

Sitting is the new smoking and sedentary behaviour has been linked with many health issues including cardiovascular disease, depression, type 2 diabetes, stroke, dementia and some cancers. Environments and policies that encourage movement and physical activity can be put in place to counter this. Examples include cycle to work schemes, hot desking, rooms for physical activity such as yoga in the workplace, encouraging the use of stairs, desk based stretching, exercising and more. Worldwide it is estimated that one million deaths per year could be averted if physical inactivity were reduced by 25%[4].

6. THERMAL COMFORT

Not too hot and not too cold. As humans our optimal body temperature is between 36-38 °C [97-100 °F]. When the external temperature becomes too hot or too cold it can impact on our health and performance. Research by Seppanen O, Fisk WJ, Faulkner D reveals that "results of multiple studies are relatively consistent and show an average relationship of 2% decrement in work performance per ^{0}C when the temperature is above 25^{0}C."[5] Studies also show impaired performance due to lower temperatures. Obviously the use of workplace HVAC systems can help with this, and enabling people to control the temperature in their immediate workspace, independent of other zones, is also now possible.

7. SOUND

It should come as no surprise that exposure to sound sources such as traffic, transportation, ambient and background noise has been shown to have an impact on many aspects of our wellbeing. Just think of the distraction caused when someone near you is talking very loudly as you are trying to have a conversation. Policies on the use of mobile phones and technology, as well as acoustical building design including noise reducing facades, noise absorbing materials, door and window sealing, glazing, partitioning and barriers can all be used to manage sound levels more effectively.

8. MATERIALS

It is astounding that an estimated 95% of chemicals used in construction lack sufficient data on health impacts[6]. Today, whilst lead, asbestos and mercury are largely restricted in manufacturing use, they still pose a risk through their existence in older structures and environmental contamination. Hazardous waste, land contamination from chemicals and pesticides and effective cleaning practices are all other areas of focus that the IWBI™ recommends.

As an individual you can take more responsibility for being aware of the places you live in and challenging inappropriate or unlawful use of materials. As leaders, particularly those in construction, I urge you to follow the lead set by the IWBI™ to help create environments where people can thrive. Whilst this might seem obvious we only need to look back to 2017 when, in the UK, the tragedy of the Grenfell Tower fire claimed the lives of 72 people. As I write this the Royal Borough of Kensington and Chelsea has admitted its failings in signing off on the highly combustible cladding used on the exterior of the building. However representatives from other organisations including cladding company Harley Facades, building contractor Rydon, and the Kensington and Chelsea Tenant Management Organisation, have applied to the Attorney General for a guarantee that anything they say in the hearings will not be able to be used against them in prosecution. It appears they are failing to take responsibility at this time.

9. MIND

As we've already outlined the mind and body are connected so it is reasonable to assume, and indeed there is growing research to support, that the things we've already discussed such as air quality, food, water, light, temperature, sound, movement and even materials also have an impact on our mental wellbeing. But, as the IWBI™ explains, our environments are also a great place to promote, support and educate people on mental wellbeing through posters, other communications and rooms where we can meet to discuss and share our concerns and problems.

10. COMMUNITY

It is hopefully clear that our spaces can either bring people together or create divisions. I write more widely about communities in the Chapter 'Vision for the Future' but the design of our built environment can also have a big influence. At a very simple level just think of cubicles versus open plan. One boxes people in, the other opens people up to each other. Of course, office design does need to cater for the requirements of work and so spaces which minimise noise distraction are required, but you understand the point being made. Environment can also have an influence on the power dynamics within communities through access to resources and the way spaces are organised. Spaces that inspire our emotions, are inclusive, support diversity, provide fair access, encourage participation and promote healthy lifestyles help to build communities that thrive.

11. INNOVATION

There are different ways of looking at this. One way is to be innovative with our environments which is more of the approach taken by the IWBI™. Here they focus on innovative features that will help promote greater wellbeing. Another way is to understand how our environments help us to be more innovative. In this respect, our environments can helps us be more imaginative and innovative in a number of ways:

1. Bringing resources together that help us think better. This could include things like physical space, knowledge, or tools required to help inform thinking and develop ideas.
2. Encouraging people to collaborate and communicate. Innovation often benefits from a range of inputs and ideas from different people. Enabling people to connect in different ways and communicate effectively, whether that be face to face, virtually, indoors or outdoors, aids innovation.
3. Spaces can literally inspire us. Biomimicry is one example, where we take design from nature. But by stimulating our senses we can also be inspired by the spaces we are in. Visually we can be moved by colour, artwork, meaningful objects and lighting. Audibly things such as music, sounds of nature, and water can all enhance our mood. Different materials can help us feel through touch. Finally our sense of smell is increasingly thought of as a way to connect us with our environment.
4. Physical characteristics. Feeling safe, calm and open are often better for innovation than feeling unsafe, chaotic and closed. This won't always be true, but even the basic functions we described above like access to water, room

temperature, air quality and lighting will all have an impact.

Another example of cultivating our environment to improve wellbeing is the 5S or 6S philosophy, which was originally developed in Japan. The five S's stand for Sort, Set in order, Shine, Standardise and Sustain and are an organisational method used in many workplaces across industries. The sixth S, sometimes used, refers to Safety. I'd argue that they can all be equally applicable to individuals in the home environment.

- Sort means to remove unnecessary items or clutter
- Set in order means to put these remaining items in the most effective places to fulfil their function
- Shine means to keep clean or order
- Standardise means to systemise the above three points so that they are consistently reviewed over time
- Sustain refers to ensuring that the approach is followed, but I believe could equally be expanded to ensure that actions are 'environmentally friendly'.
- Safety is self-explanatory and within your jurisdiction there are most probably rules and regulations, such as set by the Health & Safety Executive in the UK, that outline what must be done to comply.

By cultivating our environment in certain ways, we are primed to engage in either positive or negative behaviours. Thinking back to the section on habits, by eliminating junk food from our environment and making vegetables and fruits more readily available we can encourage healthy eating behaviour. This is a very simple way that our environment is linked to our wellbeing.

However another key outcome of cultivation is to help us all collaborate more effectively whether that be in the home, workplace, community or even across the globe.

COHESION

		Wellbeing Domains - 'Territories' - Interconnected areas of our lives							
		Mental Our thoughts	Emotional Our emotions	Physical Our actions	Spiritual Our spirit	Social Our communities	Cultural Our way	Environmental Our spaces	Economic Our trade
Wellbeing Dimensions 'Highways' Intertwined routes we use to navigate our lives	Creating meaning	Thinking	Feelings	Behaviour	Identity	Friendship	Way of life	Affinity	Needs
	Achieving potential	Focus	Control	Mastery	Motivation	Teamwork	Governance	Cultivation	Impact
	Nurturing relationships	Regard	Empathy	Interaction	Stories	Trust	Belonging	Cohesion	Fairness
	Building resilience	Flexibility	Agility	Health	Growth	Support	Diversity	Adaptation	Integrity
	Enriching lives	Imagination	Wisdom	Energy	Purpose	Empowerment	Integration	Renewal	Freedom
		Wellbeing Factors - 'Signposts' - Interconnected things that can help us improve wellbeing							

"It is the long history of humankind (and animal kind, too) that those who learned to collaborate and improvise most effectively have prevailed."

CHARLES DARWIN

"Coming together is a beginning, staying together is progress, and working together is success."

HENRY FORD

Our environments can help to build or destroy relationships. With economic, political and social divisions growing, we need environments that help facilitate integration and social cohesion for the benefit of our collective and personal wellbeing.

Of the top ten risks to the economy, as identified by the World Economic Forum in its Global Risks Report 2020[1], at least six can be strongly linked to our physical or virtual environment. These include cyberattacks, energy price shock, profound social instability, data fraud or theft, interstate conflict and failure of critical infrastructure. I'll talk more about digital and infrastructure later in this chapter, but in this section we'll focus on social stability and cohesion.

Historical research has often found that diverse neighbourhoods suffer from lower social capital and trust. However, more recent research[2] shows that 'segregation plays a critical role in the neighbourhood diversity/trust relationship, and that its absence from the literature biases our understanding of how ethnic diversity affects social cohesion'.

In essence, a well integrated diverse community is just as likely to have high levels of trust as a non-diverse one.

Of course our attitudes, discrimination, harassment, prejudice and socio-economic inequalities can all lead to higher levels of segregation which further reinforces levels of distrust. As presented throughout this book, 'systemic' actions will be required at many different levels, but the implications for planners are to work towards less dividing walls, signs that exclude, or communities that 'gate' themselves away from others.

"Birds of a feather flock together" expresses a natural human trait to associate with people like ourselves, and whilst I'm in no way suggesting that people should be forced together, it is also clear that they shouldn't be forced apart.

The RICS® World Built Environment Forum[3] suggests that

planners and designers should "ensure that housing/jobs, common public transport links and town centres are equally accessible both spatially and affordably, and that place based programs focus on strong unique identities that offer universally loved activities."

Building on further research into this area it also suggests the following:

- Locating public spaces centrally to indicate they are valued and encourage natural flow through the site
- Clear visibility into these spaces and layers of openness and enclosure once inside so that people can choose their level of public exposure
- Being aware of and adjusting design to be representative of local communities
- Designing for spontaneous interactions in spaces which may be slightly congested, intensely used and overlap novel activities. Markets are one such example, and this of course links very much with buying more local produce mentioned in many other sections of the book
- Increasing the quality of the built environment
- Building unique, expressive environments with strong identities that encourage exploration, excitement and attachment
- Involving representative groups of users in design to ensure inclusivity

It finishes the article with the following: "With increasing social tension in our society, it is important now, more than ever, to ensure that we create environments where everyone feels welcome, that celebrate multiple, fusion identities and allow different groups to enjoy sharing the same space."

I'd argue that if anyone who is responsible for designing, developing, building or maintaining an environment were to use the CANBE

Model to inform their thinking, then they would design an environment with social cohesion and more.

In short, design, develop and maintain environments for greater wellbeing.

However, we can't stand still and our environment is constantly changing, so to be more resilient we must anticipate and plan to adapt.

ADAPTATION

		Wellbeing Domains - 'Territories' - Interconnected areas of our lives							
		Mental Our thoughts	Emotional Our emotions	Physical Our actions	Spiritual Our spirit	Social Our communities	Cultural Our way	Environmental Our spaces	Economic Our trade
Wellbeing Dimensions 'Highways' Intertwined routes we use to navigate our lives	Creating meaning	Thinking	Feelings	Behaviour	Identity	Friendship	Way of life	Affinity	Needs
	Achieving potential	Focus	Control	Mastery	Motivation	Teamwork	Governance	Cultivation	Impact
	Nurturing relationships	Regard	Empathy	Interaction	Stories	Trust	Belonging	Cohesion	Fairness
	Building resilience	Flexibility	Agility	Health	Growth	Support	Diversity	Adaptation	Integrity
	Enriching lives	Imagination	Wisdom	Energy	Purpose	Empowerment	Integration	Renewal	Freedom
		Wellbeing Factors - 'Signposts' - Interconnected things that can help us improve wellbeing							

> "We talk of our mastery of nature, which sounds very grand; but the fact is we respectfully adapt ourselves, first, to her ways."
>
> CLARENCE DAY

Although resilience is impacted by individual personality attributes and skills we should remember that when it comes to our environment we are both the master and servant. As has been demonstrated we can cultivate our immediate environment to improve wellbeing, but we must also adapt to nature's ways to foster resilience in the face of the adversity we currently face.

Unfortunately, in respect to our adaptation, there is some apathy I think, largely due to debates about how much impact we can have as individuals towards being 'environmentally friendly'. However, research[1] shows policies that encourage considerate behaviours can make substantial contributions. Regardless of this, if we are confident that our activities are doing no extra harm, surely it is our responsibility to act.

If we want the right to clean, healthy, safe, beautiful environments, then we have a responsibility to help keep them that way. In addition, we must remember that, even without environmental considerations, there are still good reasons for undertaking the following actions as they will help improve other domains of our wellbeing. My point is, whether you believe in climate change or not, these things are still worth doing!

Let's take a look at some of the things we can do as individuals and within organisations.

REVIEWING ACTIVITIES

A good starting place for adapting is to understand the impact of our activities right now. The two key areas which have the biggest impact on our environment are our consumption and transport activities. We'll come to these in a moment when we look at reducing our use in both areas. For now though, let's take a look at how we consume, in particular our use of online versus offline shopping habits.

Which do you believe is most beneficial for the environment - online or offline shopping?

It is tempting to jump to the conclusion that online is much better. However the answer is not quite as simple as it appears. Frequency of purchase, number of items purchased, the item itself, distance of local store compared to online distribution, storage, method of transportation, speed of delivery, and packaging are all factors that contribute to the difference in comparative emission levels.

Walmart stated in a 2017 company report titled "The Emissions Implications of Modern Retailing: Omnichannel vs. Stores and Online Pure-Plays"[2], that perhaps the best way to look at this is to ask the question, "When is each channel most efficient in terms of emissions?"

Walmart found "it holds generally true, regardless of where customers live, that store trips are more emissions efficient if the trip is chained or the basket is large, and ship to home is more emissions efficient for small baskets when the customer would otherwise make a dedicated trip."

Another key conclusion, perhaps unsurprisingly as it is Walmart's model, but also intuitively sensible, is that a combination of multi-channel (physical stores, brick & click and online only) "retailing provides the best opportunity to serve the customer efficiently today and looking forward when it comes to emissions."

Of course as vehicles become more emissions efficient, and with the increase in electric, these dynamics are expected to change and emissions overall reduce, but the general principles still hold true.

Based on this some general good advice for individuals is as follows:

- Online, if you don't need something immediately, then refrain from using next day delivery. This will help avoid the additional emissions typically caused through the reduced effectiveness of speedy delivery
- Try to make trips to local stores part of a 'chained' trip i.e. on the way home from work or school, rather than a 'dedicated' one. Single trips to stores obviously create greater emissions
- Use local stores where you are purchasing 4 or more items and try to aggregate your purchases together

However, what is abundantly clear from the complexity of decision making required is that a greater level of responsibility lies firmly at the door of the retailers. I believe Walmart acknowledges this by arguing that retailers have "many opportunities to make their operations even more sustainable, across channels." Suggestions include encouraging consumers to adopt lower carbon shopping behaviours, making operations as sustainable as possible, helping customers consolidate trips and purchases by providing multiple products and services in one location, bundling products for shipping together, minimising packaging and required distances for distribution and customer journeys.

Of course Walmart, and many other studies in this area, have really only considered the emissions and sustainability perspective. In terms of our shopping habits, and their benefits to wellbeing, we also have to consider mental, emotional, physical, spiritual, social, cultural and economic factors.

For example it is more beneficial for our physical wellbeing to walk to local shops than it is to order online. Whilst at these local shops or markets we may also come across people we know or even make new acquaintances, which will benefit our social wellbeing. At the same time shopping locally may immerse us in local culture, get us out into nature and support the local economy. These are all benefits that online shopping does not really provide. Hopefully this is also another key practical demonstration of why we should switch our focus from sustainability to wellbeing!

So I urge leaders in retail, planning and local government to consider all of these issues when thinking about retail needs and distribution. My intuition tells me that what we really need to do is get more efficient, as consumers and retailers, at buying local where we can, minimising miles travelled, whilst recognising that there is still a role for global distribution of goods and services to meet our needs. This is where the sweet spot will be.

As organisations we can also review our supply chains to ensure they are operating sustainably and be more responsible about our own production of goods and services. Is it your job to encourage people to consume more and more of your products and services, even if you know that might not be the best thing for their wellbeing?

Obviously people also need to take personal responsibility for their own decisions, but organisations must play a stronger role. Planned obsolescence is a prime example. Producing goods that only have a certain lifespan is unethical if those goods cannot be efficiently recycled. Different models are emerging, such as goods-as-a-service which follows the software-as-a-service (SaaS) approach. In this manufacturers produce, own and service the product whilst leasing out or charging subscriptions for an associated menu of services.

Examples include Rolls-Royce 'power-by-the-hour' where the company charges customers fees for ongoing use of its engines whilst continuing to maintain and service them. Philip's offers a 'Lighting-as-a-service' model where customers continuously pay for the light consumed without any upfront costs. Philips' own the lamps and services and maintain them as part of the package.

These types of models encourage the manufacturer to produce better, longer lasting, quality products that are likely to require less maintenance. In doing so they receive ongoing recurring revenue, greater overall profits, develop deeper customer relationships, and all in a way that is better for the environment.

Other factors that manufacturers might like to consider include products that are designed to be cleaned, repaired, upgraded or recycled more easily.

One of the best ways we can achieve greater wellbeing and reduce our impact on the environment is to consume less things, or even some things not at all.

REDUCING USE

In the chapter on economics, I write about thrift. This is much different to austerity. Austerity means severe or difficult economic conditions, implying that not everyone's needs are being met.

Thrift is clever thinking and discerning use where people's needs are met and they are able to thrive. Thrift is understanding the difference between wants and needs and knowing what is good for us.

The reality for many, in the developed world at least, is that we have more than we need. This will obviously vary by individual, due to the unfair distribution of wellbeing and wealth, but I believe it to hold true generally. So by being thrifty we can reduce our use of certain things whilst making sure we're investing in those things that are good for our wellbeing. Let's take a look at where we can reduce our use without impacting on our wellbeing.

Food and drink is probably the best example. How many of us eat and drink too much? There are online tools, shared earlier in the section on physical wellbeing, that help us understand how many calories we need each day and guidance from health services on alcohol limits. If we were to reduce our food and drink intake to the recommended levels we would actually improve our physical and financial wellbeing and feel no worse, even better. Ok, we might have cravings for a while and it might be difficult, but in the long term it would be better for us and the planet.

Now think about the products and services you consume. Look around your home at clothes, cosmetics, electrical goods, furnishings, cars, TV packages and so on. What would happen if you had less of these? Would it seriously detract from your wellbeing?

Of course, one of the ways we acquire these things is through gifts. We can reduce our use through gifting experiences, rather than things and asking others to do the same for us. Research supports the fact that experiences are better for our wellbeing than more 'stuff'. Just think back on your own life and the things you'll probably be drawn to are not what you've owned but what you did.

Utilities is another area. Using less water can be as simple as taking a shower in preference to a bath, only filling the kettle with enough water for your drink, using a water butt in your garden, or recycling grey water for use outside. From a business perspective we can ensure our workplaces are using water effectively by auditing use and making improvements.

Switching to a green energy supplier, installing solar power, improving building insulation, curtains and draft excluders, LED lighting and using less power by switching off appliances when not in use are all ways of reducing electricity. Ensuring we have efficient HVAC systems and turning down thermostats by 1 degree to reduce heating bills are others.

Transport can easily be reduced. If more companies were to trust employees and move to remote working, than has been the case to date, we could drastically cut the miles from commuting very quickly. I hope the pandemic has 'forced' this situation a little, but fear there will still be many companies that are slow to catch on. The advances in remote technology, particularly video conferencing, have also made it possible for companies to drastically reduce air, train and road miles for meetings and conferences. As individuals, we can also choose to walk and cycle more when the opportunity presents itself.

What other areas can you think of where you can reduce use as an individual or in your workplace?

If we can't reduce our use we can think more creatively about getting more out of what we do have.

REUSING, REPAIRING, REPURPOSING AND RECYCLING

By reusing, repurposing, recycling and repairing we can save money, help people in our local community through donations, save the energy required to produce a new item, conserve finite resources used to produce new goods and reduce waste to landfill.

One idea that overlaps both reducing use and encouraging reuse is to think about 'hiring' or 'sharing', rather than 'owning'. How many items do you own that you have used only once, or less than a handful of times? Could you have possibly hired these things? The internet has made it easier for people to connect and in so doing share idle or under-utilised assets. Parkopedia (people renting out their driveways for parking) and AirBnB (people renting out their houses or spare bedrooms) are just two examples of the growing 'Sharing Economy'. Along the same lines a growing number of people are now questioning use of private vehicle ownership. Think about how often your vehicle sits idle.

Where could the sharing economy present new opportunities for you and your business? How can we encourage greater reuse of 'stuff'?

If things can't be reused then perhaps they can be repaired. Clothes, furniture, electrical and mechanical products can all be repaired. Many of the things we throw away haven't actually reached the end of their life. Repair workshops are springing up all over the world. Examples in the UK include therestartproject.org and repaircafe.org whilst in the European Union repair.eu is a coalition of organisations active on the cause of repair. This includes iFixit Europe which offers a free, publicly editable online repair manual for almost anything.

From an organisational perspective new repairability requirements recently adopted in the EU represent a turning point in the way we produce and use our products. The repair.eu website explains that "As of 2021 all TVs, monitors, fridges, freezers, washing machines, washer-dryers, dishwashers and lighting products placed on the EU market will have to meet minimum repairability requirements aimed at extending their lifetime."

It is said that 'one person's trash is another person's treasure'. Repurposing is the act of using something for a purpose other than its original intended use. It is an example of where environmental wellbeing meets with mental wellbeing (creative thinking). 'Upcycling' is one way this is commonly referred to. When we think about it there are many things that can be re-purposed and upcycled. Shipping containers being used as housing or old cruise liners being converted to moored restaurants/hotels are just two bigger examples. Ideas can be big and small for both business and personal activities. When we repurpose things we can save the energy required to transport and dismantle the old item and also the potential cost of producing a new one.

If we can't reuse, repurpose or repair then we can focus on recycling. Recycling helps reduce our reliance on raw materials, avoid landfill and subsequent CO_2 emissions. There is so much that can be recycled including food, plastics, electronic goods, metal, glass and paper. One of the biggest problems for the recycling process is when items are put in the incorrect container as this can slow down the process and reduce the quality of recycled materials. So when we get involved we must make sure that things are put in the right places!

We've now looked at some of the key things we can do as individuals and organisations to adapt to our changing environment but governments must also play their part. Adaptation requires a coordinated response from individuals, communities, businesses and government. However at the national and international levels, what appears to be clear, is that we need to adapt more quickly. In respect to climate change and reducing biodiversity, the scientists have set targets relating to various different scenarios and countries appear to be 'going through the motions' by tailoring their approach to the responses of other countries rather than setting an example and taking a lead.

Business and particularly governments need to play a stronger role. As outlined in the chapter on Cultural Wellbeing, when we are in a crisis situation we need leadership to be more directive. Discussion and debate have their place but now is a time when we need stronger direction and action.

As an example, air travel is believed to be one of the biggest contributors to carbon emissions. Some groups argue that we should therefore stop flying altogether. At the present time this call seems to be falling on deaf ears as air miles increase around the world. However, taken to the extreme, if we *did* all stop flying then the airline industries would crumble, many tourist destinations would die, and the world would become a less connected place. The problem is exacerbated because air travel has a largely positive affect on our wellbeing but a largely negative effect on the wellbeing of the planet.

This is where governments and businesses need to take the lead. It seems to me we have three options as follows:

1. **No flying.** If not, so be it but, how do we overcome the disruption to trade, tourism and the loss of employment in the airline industry? An international response from governments will be required to manage this.
2. **Limited flying.** If I can still fly then how many air miles can I fly before my travel becomes too burdensome on the environment? What if I don't fly? Could governments put in place a system where individuals who want to fly more can purchase air miles from people who don't fly? This would have the added advantage of re-distributing some wealth between individuals whilst also limiting air miles flown to acceptable levels. Would governments then need to support the airline industry and invest in finding alternative solutions to carbon based fuel? Current targets for innovative carbon free flights appear to be set for 2045-50 but this is too late. Scientists tell us we need to reduce emissions much quicker than this.
3. **Fly as much as you want.** This appears to be the de facto response from governments across the world to my knowledge. I am aware of work across some governments to limit air miles schemes in 2020 onwards but the overall response has no real intention or commitment as evidenced by the increasing number of air miles flown each year.

My personal view is that Option 2 above provides the most responsible approach, where we balance our wellbeing with that of the planet. However, governments and businesses across the world are taking a very 'laissez faire' option 3 approach, which will lead us to places where we don't want to go.

I'm not eradicating responsibility as an individual, far from it. Personally, I have reduced meat in my diet, use single use plastic less (although I'm not always sure whether plastic is single use or not, are you?), recycle (although I'm not always sure what packaging can or can't be recycled due to poor labelling), compost, drive less than 5,000 miles per year and conduct as many meetings as possible using online video to avoid unnecessary travel, invest ethically, buy less (but know I have more than I need and am still not sure whether an electric toothbrush is better for wellbeing than a sustainable bamboo one?)

However there are things that are very difficult to influence as an individual. It could be argued that individuals should stop using products with palm oil in. This is very noble and I respect anyone who does this. However, for me, and I'm sure many others, it is highly impractical when we are told that virtually every product that crosses our path contains or uses palm oil to some extent. I might be wrong here but the sheer time, energy and additional cost taken to find out which products contain palm oil, then research and source products which don't, is overwhelming.

We can all do our bit as individuals but, the points in parentheses in the paragraph above demonstrate the requirement of businesses, organisations and governments to take more of a lead. The UN has already done an excellent job of outlining what we need to do at the international and national levels, and below I've extrapolated from the SDGs the key aspects that relate specifically to environmental wellbeing.

FOOD

- Reduce waste and deliver sustainable, efficient and resilient agriculture, fishing and food production

- Provide year round access to safe, nutritious and sufficient food for all

WATER

- Sustainable management of fresh, waste, marine, ocean and water-related ecosystems, including mountains, forests, wetlands, rivers, aquifers and lakes. This will be achieved by reducing pollution, protection measures, better harvesting, treatment and sanitation, desalination, improving water quality, recycling and increased water-use efficiency
- Universal and equitable access to safe and affordable water supplies

NATURAL ENVIRONMENT AND BIODIVERSITY

- Reduce the impact of cities paying special attention to air quality and municipal and other waste management
- Implement sustainable management and restoration of all types of terrestrial and inland freshwater ecosystems and their services, in particular forests, wetlands, mountains and dryland. Combat desertification and achieve a land degradation-neutral world
- Prevent loss and maintain the genetic biodiversity of seeds, cultivated plants, flora and fauna, farmed and domesticated animals and wild species

PRODUCTION AND CONSUMPTION

- Implement inclusive and sustainable production through

effective management of natural resources, improved procurement, adoption of environmentally sound business and industrial practices, reducing waste and improving its management
- Safe and secure working environments for all workers
- Promote responsible consumption

INFRASTRUCTURE AND TRANSPORT

- Safe, affordable, accessible, resilient and sustainable transport systems and infrastructure that supports economic, social and environmental links across borders and between urban, peri-urban and rural areas
- Universal and affordable access to the Internet

HOUSING AND THE BUILT ENVIRONMENT

- Universal and inclusive access to integrated and participatory human settlement planning that provides safe, affordable, sustainable, energy efficient housing, buildings, basic services, resources, green and public spaces
- Protect and safeguard the world's cultural and natural heritage
- Improve resource efficiency using local materials where possible
- Improve mitigation, adaptation and resilience to climate-related extreme events and other economic, social, environmental shocks and disasters

ENERGY

- Improve energy efficiency, advance cleaner fossil-fuels and accelerate the transition to renewables
- Develop an energy infrastructure that provides universal access to affordable, reliable and modern energy services

I hope, from reviewing this list, you see the areas where your business or organisation can contribute.

It's interesting that during the corona-virus pandemic we are seeing a renewal and recovery of the natural world. The rivers of Venice have flowed clear and with wildlife for the first time in hundreds of years. Carbon emissions are at an all-time low. Traffic is virtually nonexistent (which makes the few essential travel trips we make pleasurable). The perpetual smog of Beijing has actually lifted.

This relatively short period has provided a glimpse of what might be achieved if we can continue our efforts going forward. Imagine what a more sustained program of reduced flights, travel, and consumption could do? If we were to adapt, how could that benefit us all in the long term?

As outlined earlier in the book, these adaptations and mitigations are largely designed to help us survive and manage risks. They are designed, as the UN states, 'to decouple economic growth from environmental degradation'.

They aren't designed to help us move closer to thriving. What if we turn this on its head? Could we *couple economic growth with environmental flourishing*? This brings us to the topic of renewal.

RENEWAL

		Wellbeing Domains - 'Territories' - Interconnected areas of our lives							
		Mental Our thoughts	**Emotional** Our emotions	**Physical** Our actions	**Spiritual** Our spirit	**Social** Our communities	**Cultural** Our way	**Environmental** Our spaces	**Economic** Our trade
Wellbeing Dimensions 'Highways' Intertwined routes we use to navigate our lives	Creating meaning	Thinking	Feelings	Behaviour	Identity	Friendship	Way of life	Affinity	Needs
	Achieving potential	Focus	Control	Mastery	Motivation	Teamwork	Governance	Cultivation	Impact
	Nurturing relationships	Regard	Empathy	Interaction	Stories	Trust	Belonging	Cohesion	Fairness
	Building resilience	Flexibility	Agility	Health	Growth	Support	Diversity	Adaptation	Integrity
	Enriching lives	Imagination	Wisdom	Energy	Purpose	Empowerment	Integration	Renewal	Freedom
		Wellbeing Factors - 'Signposts' - Interconnected things that can help us improve wellbeing							

"The earth will not continue to offer its harvest, except with faithful stewardship. We cannot say we love the land and then take steps to destroy it for use by future generations."

POPE JOHN PAUL II

> "Like music and art, love of nature is a common language that can transcend political or social boundaries."
>
> JIMMY CARTER

Where the previous section on 'adaptation' focused on the things we need to do to survive, and ideas for change at both individual and group level, this section focuses on what we can do to thrive and activities likely to be driven more at the group, national and international levels.

These opportunities we have to improve our environment are promoted less well and yet here lies fantastic growth opportunities. Every industry needs to be challenged to re-imagine its business model with wellbeing at the heart. This will ensure that businesses not only tackle the problems but seize the opportunities. What we need is transformation, not incremental change.

'Leave it in a better state than you found it'. That was advice I often used to hear in my childhood. Unfortunately, I think we are going to leave the world in a worse state than we found it, unless we act quickly with real commitment. But how about we do more than that?

How about we renew our environment and make it even better than it is now? That will require lots of investment, growth and innovation, music to the ears of those who might be worried about de-growth scenarios, which we'll discuss in the next chapter. However, each of the elements I discuss in this section will require investment that can provide fantastic growth opportunities aligned to environmental protection.

From an environmental perspective, renewal goes two ways. Our environment plays a huge part in helping us renew, heal and revitalise. But to continue to benefit we must play our part in renewing, healing and revitalising our environment.

In the media, much of the early rhetoric during COVID 19 has been about how we move 'back to normal'. But what if we don't move back to normal? What if we use this tragedy to find a new better way?

It is pleasing to see that the rhetoric appears to be changing to **#buildbackbetter**. This is really what this section, and the whole book, is about. Many of the actions we discussed in the previous section on adaptation will help us to restore our planet, but what more can be done to ensure we flourish with our environment?

FALLING BACK IN LOVE

If you had the choice of two rooms in which to stay would you prefer one with a lovely view of the landscape or one with no view? Which patients do you think generally recover better when bed bound in hospital - ones with a view of nature or ones with no view?

The answers to these questions are, hopefully, obvious and linked to our deep rooted, evolutionary and genetic affinity with nature. Our biological programming to connect with nature is known as Biophilia, a term popularised by American biologist Edward O. Wilson in his work of the same name in 1984. The popular nature-nurture concept and environmental psychology both recognise the important role that nature and our environment play on the way we think, feel and behave with others.

Numerous other studies reveal that connecting with nature helps us:

- Better regulate our emotions and uplift our mood
- Improve motivation, energy levels and memory
- Build attention, focus and problem solving skills
- Reduce stress and alleviate hyper-tension

For example, in Japan, research[1] has shown that people who spend more time in nature through the practice of 'Forest bathing', or Shinrin-yoku, benefit from better nervous system function, heart condition and reduced bowel disorders than those who don't. Other research in this field suggests improvements to stress recovery effects in the autonomic nervous system and increased immune function.

The principles of biophilia are also recognised by The International Wellbuilding Institute™ (IWBI™) in their ninth concept - "How Building and Community Design Impact on Our Minds" - when they describe how our built environments can "support direct access with nature using plants, water, light and views, and indirect access to nature using natural materials, patterns, colours or images."

Following the theme of this book, we should also remember that our environments can mentally inspire and renew us. Images, motivational quotes, inspirational art, areas to relax, take breaks or even sleep can all help us re-energise.

So building on a point made earlier, the first step to revitalising our planet is to fall back in love with it. We need to think differently, re-engage with nature, and see ourselves as part of it and not separate. Education can play a big part here and I cover that in greater detail in the final Chapter 'Vision for the Future'.

For now though let's look at some of the ways we can move towards thriving. To be fair to the UN, I think that, of all the eight wellbeing domains, the environment is where they come closest to recommending actions that will help us thrive. However, I still believe there is more of a focus on problems and survival rather than opportunities and thriving. Subsequently the following sections mirror much of what they recommend with a few additions.

FOOD

In this area the UN SDGs include plans for progressively improving land and soil quality and this will be key to continuing to benefit from the rich harvest our land provides. They also recommend moving towards a more plant based diet. However where we really need leadership to help us thrive is in answering the following question, using the eight domains of wellbeing as guidance:

1. In respect to meat, fish, dairy and plant based food what is the optimal diet for the human population going forward when we take into consideration all of the potential contributory factors such as population growth, resource availability, climate change, nutritional content, health and so on?

Very fortuitously, in researching this topic I came across a group who have answered this very question, well almost. The EAT-Lancet Commission[2] brought together 37 world-leading scientists from across the globe to answer the following:

Can we feed a future population of 10 billion people a healthy diet within planetary boundaries?

In answering the question the commission considered physical health and environmental factors from a comprehensive range of studies across the world. I would argue that the answer would also benefit from a mental, emotional, spiritual, social, cultural, and economic wellbeing overlay, however it is the best attempt I've seen and provides a 'reference' diet for the whole world to work from going forward.

The findings, unsurprisingly, propose a transformation of eating habits, food production and waste reduction. Fundamental to this is a move to a greater proportion of plant-based food, although the diet recommended can flex from omnivore to vegan, and incorporate geographical and cultural preferences. Whilst it was clear that diets across different regions of the world vary considerably, all regions were consuming less fish, vegetables, fruit, legumes, whole grains and nuts than recommended in the 'reference' diet.

The commission has produced useful briefs for all people: in cities, farmers, food professionals, healthcare professionals and policy makers so wherever you fit, in respect to your leadership role, there is something for you.

To help us thrive this will need to deliver the maximum effectiveness of food consumption between locally grown and imported. Food choices also have an impact on our water use, so having a plan for consumption of food types that have a lower water footprint makes excellent sense.

WATER

For those of us fortunate enough to live in developed nations some of our key concerns during COVID-19 may well have focused on 'social distancing' and whether or not we should wear face masks.

However, for 1 in 3 people in the world, access to safe clean drinking water may well have been at the forefront of their minds. 2 in 5 people do not have access to basic hand washing facilities with soap and water. Amazingly more than 673 million people practice open defecation. There is much we need to do to transform access, use, and management of our water resources!

Most of our water is used by agriculture for irrigation of crops and by the energy industry for cooling power plants generating electricity. Smarter irrigation techniques using advanced technology and other changes to agricultural practices are beginning to make a difference here. Moving to renewables will also help us use less water than electricity development.

Ways we can reduce our water footprint are largely linked to the things we have already discussed. Reviewing and reducing travel, food, energy and product consumption are all key ways to reduce water use. The water used to produce fossil fuel based energy, certain food types and in particular meat, gasoline based fuel, and for flying is substantial.

But we can't do it alone and this is where technology can help in transforming our use and management of water in the world. These include the use of:

- A range of developing technologies to improve the filtration and purification of water
- Biomimicry, such as copying the processes by which mangrove plants and euryhaline fish extract seawater using minimal energy
- Smart monitoring to reduce the loss from water leaks
- Waste water treatment processing to remove nutrients for use as fertilisers, leaving water that can be re-used in business or for drinking

NATURAL ENVIRONMENT AND BIODIVERSITY

When there is a strong connection between a rich diversity of animals and plants, ecosystems are healthier, more productive and resilient. Loss of any species in this chain weakens the connections and the subsequent health, productivity and resilience of the ecosystems such as mountains, deserts, wetlands, forests, oceans, rivers and coral reefs.

TRANSFORMING AGRICULTURE

Agriculture "takes up one third of the world's landmass and endangers 62% of all threatened species globally." In their report[3] "Integrating Agroecological Production in a Robust Post-2020 Global Biodiversity Framework", over 360 scientists from 42 countries are calling for a transition from current agricultural practices to agroecological principles.

These principles include:

- Better regional and local planning of diversified farmlands of varying sizes
- The reduced use of synthetic pesticides
- More effective use of fertilisers
- Diversified cropping

- Use of technological innovations
- Eco-certification and agricultural policies
- Zero deforestation
- Eco labelling
- Innovative investment models
- The involvement of indigenous people and local communities
- Measuring agricultural output against a broader set of measures (I suggest the eight domains of wellbeing!)

Whilst these recommendations have, at the time of writing, yet to be accepted by the UN, it seems that José Graziano da Silva, Director-General of the Food & Agriculture Organisation of the UN, is thinking along similar lines[4], "We have to innovate and transform agriculture. It is fundamental to produce food in a way that preserves the environment and biodiversity. Business as usual is no longer an option."

GOVERNING THE 'GLOBAL COMMONS'

In addition to transforming agriculture we must become more collaborative globally in how we manage our shared resources, or 'Global Commons'. These Global Commons have traditionally included resources beyond the control of a nation state, in particular the oceans, atmosphere, Antarctica and Space. However, it has become clear that this definition is no longer sufficient. Damage to the Amazonian rainforest, seen by many as the 'planet's lungs' has demonstrated that resources 'owned' by a few countries can have a big impact on all of us. The internet is another, albeit unnatural resource, that demonstrates the requirement for a joined up approach. So the first step forward is to define what we mean by 'Global Commons' and the UN is the best vehicle for achieving this.

As we have advanced technologically, and human activity has

increasingly encroached into each of these common areas, there is also a need to revisit and update the international laws and policies required to manage and protect each.

DE-EXTINCTION AND REWILDING

Beavers, Bison, Pine Marten, White Storks, White Tailed Eagles are some of the species which have been, or are on the verge of being, re-established in Britain. In densely populated areas of Europe, Wolves are now thriving. Re-introducing these species can help restore the natural balance.

Intriguing technological advances in cloning and gene editing means the prospect of bringing back extinct animals is now closer than ever. This type of technology can also be used to protect animals close to extinction. 'Back Breeding' is one technique, where animals that are closely related and look similar to those that have gone extinct are bred over successive generations to 're-create' the lost species. Quaggas, a Zebra-like creature in South Africa, is one such example.

Other techniques include assisted reproduction, cloning, and stem cell science. For example, Harvard Medical School is planning on creating a Mammoth by editing its genes into elephant cells. If successful, they will create, not a mammoth, but an elephant whose DNA has been altered so it can live better in colder environments. You might like to call it a 'mammophant'.

As outlined above, the benefits of bringing extinct animals back is that they can help to restore balance to ecosystems through the unique roles each play. There are of course ethical concerns, but just as IVF has become accepted, the hope of medical researchers is that so too will their techniques.

PRODUCTION AND CONSUMPTION

If consumption and population growth trends continue on their expected trajectories, by 2050 we will need 3 planets with the resources of Earth to provide for our needs. It just doesn't work, does it? To counter this, the UN is calling for us to shift our production and consumption patterns to a more sustainable course. As you know, I largely support the UN SDGs, but I want us to go further.

I call for us to shift our consumption patterns to a course for thriving. There's a subtle difference.

For example, cigarettes can be produced sustainably but they won't help us thrive. Here's what Philip Morris International's (PMI), Chief Sustainability Officer, Huub Savelkouls had to say about cigarette smoking in April 2019, "Thanks to today's advances in technology, cutting-edge science and substantial investment, PMI has developed a range of smoke-free products with the potential to **significantly reduce the harm** associated with cigarette smoking."[5]

Note here that he's not talking about no harm. He's talking about providing products to the public with reduced harm. These 'smoke-free products' include a range of 'vapes', the likes of which are commented on by Michael Blaha, M.D., M.P.H., Director of Clinical Research at the Johns Hopkins Ciccarone Center for the Prevention of Heart Disease, in an article[6] which describes "an outbreak of lung injuries and deaths associated with vaping", particularly in respect to black market or modified devices. The article goes on, in respect to all vaping, that "You're exposing yourself to all kinds of chemicals that we don't yet understand and that are probably not safe."

If we don't understand them, and they're probably not safe, why are we using them?

In a similar vein, processed food can be produced sustainably, but eating too much of it won't help our health. Motor vehicles can be produced sustainably but manufacturing more and more of them may not help us thrive.

What we need to do is produce and consume enough of what is positive for our net wellbeing and the planet, whilst reducing or stopping the production and consumption of things that are negative. Granted this may require appropriate periods of change for both producers and consumers, but we began to understand that smoking is bad for us back in the 1950s. That's seventy years! In these times, where we have much greater knowledge and imperatives to change, we must move more quickly.

One possible solution I've seen put forward by many, including many reports to the UN, is to 'internalise externalities'. This could include taxing consumers and/or producers for goods or services with high carbon production, therefore making them more expensive and/or less profitable. Whilst this may be preferable to the current situation and I'm sure would have an impact, it could restrict high carbon producing goods to those who can afford it. It also wouldn't significantly reduce the carbon producing goods! On the other hand, it may also force providers to leave less profitable markets which otherwise added to the wellbeing of people. Neither of these scenarios is really what we desire. Whilst this approach may have value as a stepping stone, perhaps there is a better way forward?

I refer back to the example I provided on the airline industry in the section on 'adaptation'. What we need to do is assess the overall contribution to wellbeing. The answer is not to restrict flying to only those who can afford it, or to significantly burden airlines with costs that force them out of business. If we believe that flying has a net positive effect on our wellbeing, then we must invest in airlines to produce carbon free fuel more quickly. In the meantime, we must find innovative ways to restrict flying to levels in line with scientists recommendations for climate change.

I've also heard calls to blindly cut production and consumption by up to 50%. But just cutting production and consumption like this would be harmful to the lives of billions across the planet. We need to be smarter and more nuanced. We need to tie economic production to environmental protection and development.

- In food, we need to increase our consumption and production of plant based whilst reducing our intake of meat
- In energy, we need to increase production and consumption of renewables whilst reducing fossil fuel based energy
- In housing, the built environment and infrastructure we need to invest in developments that deliver improved wellbeing through sustainable designs that embrace nature
- We need to produce and consume more experiences that help us engage with our environment whilst reducing the impact on it

The way to achieve these changing production and consumption patterns is through a combination of education, greater legislation, improved governance, new business and economic models which use the eight domains of wellbeing to influence, individual, organisational, community, national and international transformation. I'll cover this more in the final chapter 'Vision for the Future'.

INFRASTRUCTURE AND TRANSPORT

Infrastructure includes the physical systems of a business, region, or nation such as the building facilities, communication networks, utilities and transport. I've already discussed water and will come onto the built environment and energy, so in this section we'll focus on transport and communication.

Transport is recognised by the UN as a key enabler of economic growth and improving people's lives through better access to markets and services like health, education and finance. At present the provision of transport routes and services across the world is unequal. According to a World Bank report in 2006[7], more than 1 billion people, or one-third of the global rural population, still lacked access to all-weather roads and transport services. In respect to air travel, although it is difficult to calculate exact figures, it is clear that many people across the globe have yet to step foot on an aeroplane. In addition to the social inequality, there are also many other negatives associated with transport including contribution to greenhouse gas emissions, pollutants, environmental degradation, deaths and casualties from accidents and illicit flows of contraband.

In recognition of these challenges and in response to the UN SDGs a global initiative, Sustainable Mobility for All ™ (SuM4All™)[8], has emerged. As outlined on their website, SuM4All is a multi-stakeholder partnership that acts collectively to help transform the transport sector. Its ambition is to make mobility:

1. **Equitable**—ensuring that everyone has access to jobs and markets through good quality transport regardless of their economic or social status
2. **Efficient**— to allow people and goods to move from place to place quickly and seamlessly
3. **Safe**—by halving the number of global deaths and injuries from road traffic accidents and other modes of transportation
4. **Green**—by lowering the environmental footprint of the sector to combat climate change and pollution

These are great ambitions and to build on this I urge those involved to also remember the sheer pleasure, emotional freedom, imagination and cultural inspiration that transport can embody. We need our transport to inspire us too!

As mentioned earlier, one of the ways that we can improve transport is by reducing any unnecessary journeys. We can do this through digital connectivity. I'm sure many of us have seen the benefits of remote working, facilitated by video conferencing and other online services, during COVID-19 lockdown. But digital can also help us in a number of other ways such as the enablement of the sharing economy, mentioned previously, on-demand services, and efficiency of transport services through passenger information systems and real-time traffic management systems.

Aside from transport, digital also helps us communicate more effectively, particularly through the internet. Many of us wouldn't know about the SDGs without access to the internet![9] However access to the internet is not distributed fairly, as outlined by Forest Whitaker, UNESCO Special Envoy for Peace and Reconciliation, "In the developed world, for example, over 80% of individuals use the Internet; in the developing world, less than 35% do. The remaining 65% are often poor and remote communities or disenfranchised groups." So a key priority is to provide universal access to the internet. However, this must be achieved in a responsible way.

Perhaps knowledge is one of the most valuable, and dangerous, things we own. Spreading knowledge openly, freely, and transparently across the world will help us learn, innovate, and understand each other better. Of course, knowledge can also be used to misinform and spread hate, so we must ensure people are educated effectively and that our digital services are governed and legislated appropriately.

This is a key challenge currently as recognised in the report of the UN Secretary-General's High-level Panel on Digital Cooperation[10]. Effectively there is no obvious authority for emerging developments such as the Internet of Things (IoT), Artificial Intelligence (AI) and differences in political ideologies about how the internet should be run. The report recommends, amongst other things, "updated mechanisms for global digital cooperation" with enshrined "shared values, principles, understandings and objectives for an improved global digital cooperation architecture."

HOUSING AND THE BUILT ENVIRONMENT

Did you know that we've basically been using the same brick design in our buildings for the last 5,000 years?

Let's face it, the brick is the fundamental building block (literally) of the construction industry. Bricks use clay, which strips land topsoil and inhibits plant growth. This clay is shaped and baked in kilns, often heated through fossil fuels which contribute to carbon emissions. The bricks are then transported to construction sites, contributing even further to emissions.

A Scottish start-up, Kenoteq[11], is bringing to market its sustainable equivalent, the K-Briq, which is made by moulding crushed construction waste, mixed with water and a binder. The K-Briq, which is comparable if not superior in quality to its standard equivalents, can be produced in a multitude of colours producing less than a tenth of the emissions and can be manufactured close to site reducing transport costs.

If there is room for improvement in the most fundamental building block of construction then the scope for change must be huge. The basic requirement, which the UN covers, is good accommodation for all people. This will be a great step forward but to thrive we need much more.

We need built environments that are inspiring and beautiful, where people always have access to natural spaces and wildlife close to where they live. In the UK, the Wildlife Trusts have set out a fantastic vision and practical guidance on the types of built environments we should aspire to in their "Homes for People and Wildlife"[12] – how to build housing in a nature-friendly way. Ideas centre around core themes of improving the integration of wildlife and nature with the built environment, greater access, improved health and wellbeing, effective water management, pollution and climate control and measurable gains for wildlife. Practical ideas for businesses might be growing 'green walls', roof gardens, planting trees and plants for 'pollinators', raised beds for growing vegetables or anything that brings nature closer.

But we can also be more creative in finding different ways for living. Co-housing is a 'newish' way of living where people come together intentionally to buy, build or renovate buildings. These often cater for a range of individuals, families and other living arrangements providing shared facilities such as laundries, gyms, social and guest rooms. Due to the shared nature, and often the attitudes and beliefs of residents, this can prove an extremely environmentally and economically friendly way of living, but also provides a real sense of community. Notable 'communities' have already been established in Denmark, USA, Canada, France and Germany, where, in the university town of Tübingen more than 80% of new builds are co-housing developments. Traction is also gaining ground in other countries such as the UK.

'Seasteading'[13] is another idea pioneering a course for different ways of living. Regardless of the political views of those leading the way in this area, with a rising population, it surely makes sense to investigate opportunities for building 'floating cities' on the sea.

ENERGY

Fossil fuels are gradually being phased out and the costs for renewable energy are falling quickly. If we can harness the energy of the sun effectively there is enough to provide for everyone in the world for free. The introduction of electric/autonomous vehicles, whilst in infancy, is increasing and will largely replace private cars and mass transit. Investment in new, carbon free, fuels for aircraft are estimated to be available from 2040-50.

From commercial innovations like solar glass[14] to large scale international developments such as the European Union's Hydrogen Strategy[15], energy is transforming quickly. Europe is leading the way and "in the first half of 2020, and for the first time, Europe generated more electricity from renewable sources than from fossil fuels."[16]

In the near future, we will see the combination of hydro, solar, wind and bioenergy, electricity, and hydrogen, with the latter bridging the important gap to "decarbonise industrial processes and economic sectors where reducing carbon emissions is both urgent and hard to achieve."[17]

Of course we must balance the need for speed of change with understanding the 'systemic' implications of adopting these new technologies. For example, hydrogen can be used to power vehicles, generate electricity, and produce heat without carbon emissions. It is almost certainly a better option than fossil fuels. However, some of the environmental consequences of using hydrogen remain unexplored, such as how it impacts on land surfaces or chemical balances in the atmosphere.

An adaptive and flexible approach, utilising a number of fuel sources and technologies, will be fundamental to success.

CHAPTER SUMMARY

Climate change provides us with very strong reasons to become more environmentally active. But, regardless of whether you believe in climate change or not, throughout this chapter I've demonstrated that by becoming more environmentally active we can improve our mental, emotional, physical, spiritual, social, cultural and economic wellbeing.

In many ways we already know what to do, we just aren't doing it, or at least not quickly enough. We know that we need to change and yet many of us still seem to resist or act very passively.

Part of the reason for this is our biased, rigid and incorrect thinking and beliefs at individual, organisational or national levels. Below I've attempted to debunk some of the most common.

Group	Belief	Reality
Individuals	Increasing wealth brings increasing happiness	Wealth on its own does not bring sustainable happiness. Wellbeing, incorporating wealth, is a better term to describe overall success. For good wellbeing we need a healthy environment.
	Whatever I do to help improve the environment it won't make that much of a difference	If we all make an effort we can make a difference but it will require action at individual, organisational and national levels.
	If I get more stuff (better car, better house, nicer clothes) I'll be happier	You may be happier for a short period if you get nice things but our overall wellbeing relies on deeper meaningful experiences and relationships. We can be just as happy with 'enough' as we are with 'more'.
	If I have less because I'm earning less and the economy isn't growing as fast I'll be less happy	For some people who aren't earning very much at present this may well be true. However if we focus on using our time more effectively on things that build our wellbeing and get rid of things in our lives that aren't really adding to our wellbeing we'll be even happier. We can help the people who need it by more fairly distributing wealth and wellbeing.
Organisations	We must maximise profit at the expense of all else for our business to be successful	Being financially sound is important but if our business is damaging the environment and treating people unfairly is it really successful?
	Our environmental impact is secondary to our economic impact	What good is a business if you haven't got a planet to put it on?
National governments and politicians	We must keep growing our economies at the expense of all else	Governments have a responsibility to help citizens maximise wellbeing, which productivity is a part of, not just productivity alone.
	If we reduce our carbon emissions and reliance on fossil fuels more quickly than other nations we'll become less competitive. If we are less competitive we'll all be less happy	If we take the lead and focus on wellbeing we may go through a period of difficulty. Change can be difficult. But if we are honest with citizens and help them through the change we can all come out the other side with higher levels of wellbeing. Change can also be a driver of new, better growth.
	My fate as a politician is tied purely to the economy. If the economy suffers because we prioritise the environment I and my party will get voted out	Your fate as a politician is tied to the wellbeing of people. Your role is to represent and lead people to a better future. As a leader you must present a vision for this better future and that is one where we can all thrive. Growth focused on wellbeing can replace the void left by growth focused on wealth.
	We must always do what is best for our national citizens	When the balance of wealth and wellbeing between nations becomes too unfair it leads to greater tension and conflict. We must therefore balance the needs of our own citizens with those in other countries and the future of our planet.

The great news is that we know what to do. I'm personally optimistic. From doing the research it is clear that we have many clever people in different domains across the world doing fantastic work to deliver innovative solutions that solve some of our most pressing problems. This isn't so much a question of knowledge, it's a question of attitude and action. If we can change and take collective responsibility we can thrive in, and along with our environment.

However, in order to do this we will need to take a different approach to our economy. This is the subject of our next chapter. Before we move onto this here are a few thoughts for your reflection.

KEY CONCEPTS TO IMPROVE OUR ENVIRONMENTAL WELLBEING:

Improving 'Affinity'

- Get back into nature
- Make sure we 'feel at home'. If we don't, move.
- If we can't move then change what we can in our environment

Improving 'Cultivation'

- Use the eight domains of wellbeing to improve our environment:

mental, emotional, physical, spiritual, social, cultural, environmental, and economic factors

- Consider the International Wellbuilding Institute™ (IWBI™) 11 concepts:

air, water, nourishment, light, movement, temperature, sound, materials, mind, community, innovation

- Use the 5 S methodology - Sort, Set in place, Shine, Standardise, Sustain, Safety

Improving 'Cohesion'

- Think about how to integrate people rather than segment them
- Involve the people who will use the environments in the design
- Develop, unique expressive environments with strong identities

'Adapting'

- Review and refine our activities
- Reduce our use where possible
- Reuse, repair, repurpose, recycle

'Renewal'

- Fall back in love with nature
- Change our diet using the 'reference diet' as a basis
- Use water more efficiently
- Buy local where possible
- Consume less stuff
- Produce responsibly
- Reduce travel
- Integrate wildlife and nature into our homes, workplaces and communities
- Use renewable energy

KEY BEHAVIOURS:

Where do you score on the following attributes that can help develop greater Environmental Wellbeing?

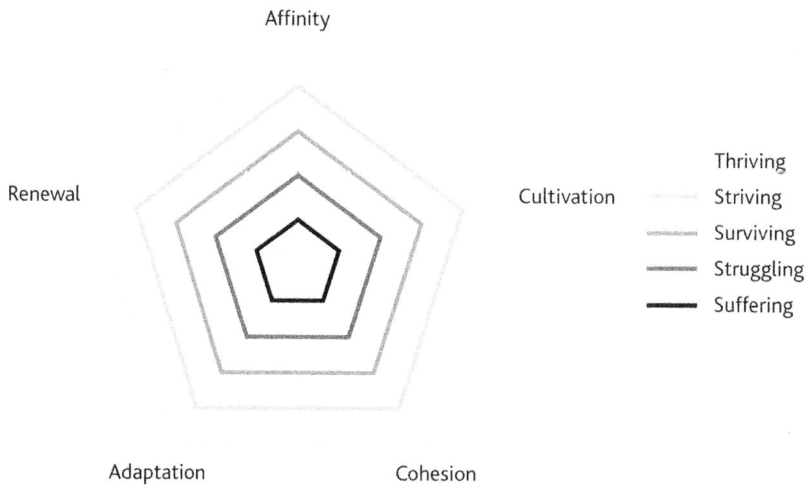

What would you like to do differently?

CHAPTER TWELVE

IMPROVING ECONOMIC WELLBEING

Wellbeing Domains - 'Territories' - Interconnected areas of our lives

Wellbeing Dimensions 'Highways' Intertwined routes we use to navigate our lives		Mental Our thoughts	Emotional Our emotions	Physical Our actions	Spiritual Our spirit	Social Our communities	Cultural Our way	Environmental Our spaces	Economic Our trade
	Creating meaning	Thinking	Feelings	Behaviour	Identity	Friendship	Way of life	Affinity	Needs
	Achieving potential	Focus	Control	Mastery	Motivation	Teamwork	Governance	Cultivation	Impact
	Nurturing relationships	Regard	Empathy	Interaction	Stories	Trust	Belonging	Cohesion	Fairness
	Building resilience	Flexibility	Agility	Health	Growth	Support	Diversity	Adaptation	Integrity
	Enriching lives	Imagination	Wisdom	Energy	Purpose	Empowerment	Integration	Renewal	Freedom

Wellbeing Factors - 'Signposts' - Interconnected things that can help us improve wellbeing

---

"The greatest wealth is well-being."

LAILAH GIFTY AKITA

> "The market came with the dawn of civilization and it is not an invention of capitalism. If it leads to improving the well-being of the people there is no contradiction with socialism."
>
> MIKHAIL GORBACHEV

I use the term economic to apply to individual, organisational, community and national wellbeing. After all, we all benefit from, or are part of, the economy. Consequently the principles we'll discuss in this chapter can be equally applied to all of these groups.

Economics continues to be one of the greatest influences on the world as evidenced by the unprecedented interventions by international governments to support our economies during the corona-virus pandemic. But what are our economies actually for?

The history of the word economy can be traced to the ancient Greek 'Oikonomia', which means 'management of household'. In line with this the Greeks thought the purpose of the economy was to produce and distribute food, water and other goods primarily for preserving human life. In other words an economy is there to satisfy our **needs**.

In more recent modern history Adam Smith, a pioneer of political economy, and Jeremy Bentham a social reformer and founder of utilitarianism, both expressed views about the role of an economy in meeting, not only people's basic needs but also higher level needs. Coming from a different economic perspective, Marx, when arguing for socialism and communism proposed that goods and services be distributed "to each according to his *need*, from each according to his ability." So the concept of needs is widely recognised across different political spectrums.

As individuals we satisfy our needs (italicised in the following list) and benefit from financial and economic wellbeing in numerous ways and at many levels, including things such as:

- Having enough money for *food, shelter and clothing*
- Being able to live in *secure* neighbourhoods
- *Feeling more in control of our safety and destiny* from reduced money worries
- *Opportunities to experience growth* from new experiences
- *Increased self-esteem and status* from the respect of others
- *Feeling good* about giving to and helping others

But meeting individual needs is also good for communities, organisations and nations. Improved relationships, physical and mental health, better productivity and more 'thrifty' financial management. Let's face it nations have evolved over the years through the coming together of people from all walks of life to create better, more secure lives for themselves, loved ones, and the communities around them.

If economies are understood in terms of how they meet our needs then we must measure their **impact** using a much broader range of measures. For individuals we may express economic wellbeing more as 'financial wellbeing'. Within this we may measure income and expenditure, assets such as houses and investments, and liabilities such as credit card debt and mortgages. Organisations measure financial wellbeing using indicators such as cash flow, profit & loss, capital, assets, dividends and return on investment. Communities, particularly large cities, are now more likely to measure financial wellbeing in line with corporations. Finally nations measure economic wellbeing using measures such as GDP, inflation and trade deficit/surplus.

But all of these measures really miss the point. It is the same as taking a person's pulse to try to establish the quality of their life. Of course a person needs a pulse to live but this tells you nothing about how well their life is going. Perhaps Jim Collins described it best at an organisational level. In his book *Good To Great*[1] he describes profit in the most healthy and aligned way to wellbeing I've come across:

'Enduring great companies don't exist merely to deliver returns to shareholders. Indeed, in a truly great company, profits and cash flow become like blood and water to a healthy body: They are absolutely essential for life, but they are not the very point of life.'

We must remember that the very point we do all this stuff is because we have needs. But our needs are often perceived in relation to others and if scarce resources are shared **unfairly** it can lead to poor relationships. Of course this is also affected by the **integrity** of an economy. A lack of transparency and poor ethics can lead to mistrust with the system and at its worst systemic failure. But an economy also goes through good and bad times and needs to have integrity in terms of resilience. Everybody needs a rainy day fund as we have experienced through the Coronavirus pandemic!

Finally an economy needs to enrich people through improving the quality of our lives. If it doesn't we should consider whether that is real **freedom** or not.

So, there is a growing realisation that to be truly successful an economy must:

- Provide us with opportunities to meet our **basic and higher levels needs.** This will be as both a participant (giving to) and beneficiary of (receiving from) the economy
- Help us achieve our potential through **positive impact** on the welfare of all people, society, nature and our planet
- Help nurture relationships built on trust and **fairness** balancing both individual and collective needs
- Build resilience for people and planet with **integrity** that is moral, protects us from increasing risks and works within planetary boundaries
- Enrich people's lives by delivering real **freedom.** Outcomes that help us thrive

When our economy meets the criteria above we will be truly

prosperous. If our economy fails to meet these criteria for some, or many people across the world, it may result in greater **destitution**.

So far I've talked about an economy here as if it were a separate entity from us, but of course we are both participants and beneficiaries of an economy. We must contribute in order to benefit from the goods and services it provides. We should expect to both give to and receive from the economy. Rights and responsibilities!

Let's now take a deeper look at each of these components of a wellbeing economy.

NEEDS

		Wellbeing Domains - 'Territories' - Interconnected areas of our lives							
		Mental Our thoughts	Emotional Our emotions	Physical Our actions	Spiritual Our spirit	Social Our communities	Cultural Our way	Environmental Our spaces	Economic Our trade
Wellbeing Dimensions 'Highways' Intertwined routes we use to navigate our lives	Creating meaning	Thinking	Feelings	Behaviour	Identity	Friendship	Way of life	Affinity	Needs
	Achieving potential	Focus	Control	Mastery	Motivation	Teamwork	Governance	Cultivation	Impact
	Nurturing relationships	Regard	Empathy	Interaction	Stories	Trust	Belonging	Cohesion	Fairness
	Building resilience	Flexibility	Agility	Health	Growth	Support	Diversity	Adaptation	Integrity
	Enriching lives	Imagination	Wisdom	Energy	Purpose	Empowerment	Integration	Renewal	Freedom
		Wellbeing Factors - 'Signposts' - Interconnected things that can help us improve wellbeing							

"Everybody needs beauty as well as bread, places to play in and pray in, where nature may heal and give strength to body and soul."

JOHN MUIR

What is the best way of describing our needs and how well our economies currently meet them? I'd like to look at this by revisiting Maslow's work and combining it with the domains of wellbeing.

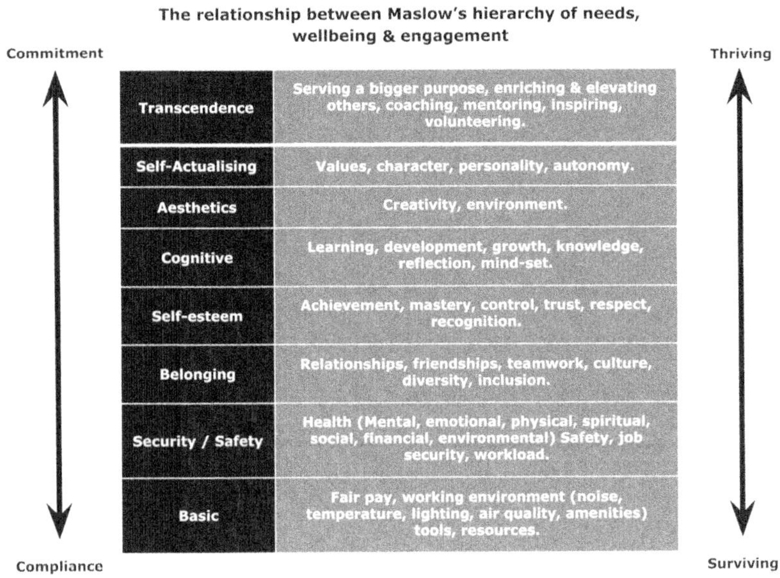

BASIC NEEDS

We all have basic needs such as food, water and shelter. Access to these things is often determined by our income so within this section I also include fair pay. Breaking it down even further it is hopefully obvious that in order to live well we also need clean air, low noise levels, good lighting and amenities that make life at least comfortable.

So how well are our economies doing? In many parts of the world economic activity has led to rising standards of living. There is less poverty now than ever before. However when we look at some of the key issues outlined in the chapter 'Course Correction', it is clear that we can do better. In respect to food, every year one third of the world's food is being wasted, according to a 2013 report from the Food and Agriculture Organisation of The United Nations. There are still too many people who go hungry and too many who are obese. As outlined earlier, over 70% of the world's population suffer from water scarcity for several months each year. Even in developed economies we continue to suffer from homelessness. Air quality in many major cities around the world is below safe levels and temperature rises are causing catastrophic natural disasters.

If an economy is deemed successful when it meets the needs of all it's people then we surely should not be celebrating just yet.

Many would argue that the world is a safer place now than it has ever been. It seems strange writing this as I sit in isolation at home amidst one of the biggest pandemics the world has ever known. It is clear that we still face many threats to our security across the world from incommunable diseases, invisible viruses, cyber attacks, intrusive state surveillance, economic sanctions and the potential loss of jobs due to automation. Whilst many of us do feel safer now we should not 'rest on our laurels'. Of course, the biggest threat to our security is climate change and there will be ever greater and more expansive impacts if we don't put in place sufficient plans to slow emissions quickly enough.

Physically and mentally our economies should provide us with opportunities to contribute. However many of the jobs and activities are actually damaging our physical and mental health, as evidenced by the rise of mental health issues across the world and levels of obesity previously mentioned. Sacrificing our mental and physical health at the expense of earning enough money to live is no longer acceptable or necessary.

So our economies are not even meeting many of our basic needs for people across the world.

HIGHER LEVEL NEEDS

But economies should not just be meeting our basic needs. They should also be meeting our higher level needs. Economies should be building strong relationships between countries, communities and individuals. As we've already covered, strong relationships are built on trust, empowerment and fairness. In essence strong relationships are built when everyone wins.

And yet our economies are not built in ways that enable everyone to win. Sanctions, unfair pay, tariffs, protectionism, unfair taxation and an unfair distribution of wealth are increasingly tearing at the fabric of societies across the world and leading to poorer relationships and lower levels of trust. Cultures and environments are being lost or diminished due to unsophisticated economic practices.

Self-esteem is being eroded through people being trapped in jobs where there is little achievement, growth or spiritual development. Rather than encouraging virtuous actions our economies still produce vice and addictions.

In short our economies have the ability to help the human race transcend our current existence to a new level. At the moment I fear that our direction of travel is towards dystopia. Let's turn that around and start moving towards utopia. We may not get there but as Norman Vincent Peale, the minister and author of *The Power of Positive Thinking* said, "Shoot for the moon. Even if you miss you'll land among the stars."

In order to get there, our economies need to grow outwards and upwards. By that I mean that they must provide for all people across the world but also meet our basic and higher level needs. That will be real economic 'growth'. Not the Gross Domestic Product, quantity over quality focused growth that dominates our thinking at present.

IMPACT

		Wellbeing Domains - 'Territories' - Interconnected areas of our lives							
		Mental Our thoughts	**Emotional** Our emotions	**Physical** Our actions	**Spiritual** Our spirit	**Social** Our communities	**Cultural** Our way	**Environmental** Our spaces	**Economic** Our trade
Wellbeing Dimensions 'Highways' Intertwined routes we use to navigate our lives	Creating meaning	Thinking	Feelings	Behaviour	Identity	Friendship	Way of life	Affinity	Needs
	Achieving potential	Focus	Control	Mastery	Motivation	Teamwork	Governance	Cultivation	Impact
	Nurturing relationships	Regard	Empathy	Interaction	Stories	Trust	Belonging	Cohesion	Fairness
	Building resilience	Flexibility	Agility	Health	Growth	Support	Diversity	Adaptation	Integrity
	Enriching lives	Imagination	Wisdom	Energy	Purpose	Empowerment	Integration	Renewal	Freedom
		Wellbeing Factors - 'Signposts' - Interconnected things that can help us improve wellbeing							

"Before you begin scrambling up the ladder of success make sure it's leant against the right building."

STEPHEN COVEY

It was largely as an outcome of World War II, with the invention of Simon Kuznet's Gross Domestic Product (GDP), that economic focus was diverted to productivity, supporting war efforts and then post-war growth. This more modern expression of economics is built around two core ideas. One, that resources are scarce and, two, that society must use them efficiently.

However the limitations of this approach are increasingly being recognised and in the past few decades interest in measuring the success of an economy in respect to its impact on the wellbeing and happiness of people has risen back to the surface. It seems that there is growing consensus that we have our 'ladder of success' leant against the wrong building!

The ineffectiveness of an imbalanced financial focus was most famously recognised on the world stage by Robert Kennedy back in 1968 during his presidential campaign trail when he said, "The GNP does not allow for the health of our children, the quality of their education, or the joy of their play." Since this time there have been evolving solutions to provide more rounded measures.

In 1990, the Human Development Index[1] was introduced to expand 'the richness of human life, rather than simply the richness of the economy in which human beings live.' First published in 2007, the Legatum Prosperity Index[2] benchmarks 149 countries around the world across 12 distinct categories. Other examples where wellbeing is being measured at an international level include the OECD How's Life Index, The World Happiness Report, and the Gallup World Poll, but there are many others.

At a national level, Gross National Happiness (GNH)[3] was a term coined by His Majesty the Fourth King of Bhutan, Jigme Singye Wangchuck back in the 1970s. This concept implies that: "sustainable development should take a holistic approach towards notions of progress and give equal importance to non-economic aspects of wellbeing." The Kingdom now regularly measures GNH and uses it to form policy. This has been followed to lesser or greater degrees by England, Scotland, Wales, France, Iceland, Canada and New Zealand.

This economic refocus has been highlighted even further by the interventions seen during the COVID-19 crisis. The actions taken by governments across the world reflect a human race that desires to protect and enhance the basic and higher level needs of **all** citizens.

As we saw in the diagram at the beginning of this chapter, if our basic and higher level needs are met then we will be more engaged and likely to achieve our potential economically. To do this we need to have a positive impact both individually and collectively. Positively improving our life and the lives of others by increasing wellbeing across all of the eight domains. This brings us onto how we measure wellbeing.

In their excellent 2016 review of wellbeing measures[4], Myles-Jay Linton, Paul Dieppe and Antonieta Medina-Lara revealed 99 self-report measures for assessing wellbeing in adults. Within the measures reviewed they identified 196 dimensions (what I refer to as 'signposts' in this book) and six thematic domains (what I also refer to as domains). Having reviewed[5] these domains and dimensions (signposts) I am confident that the CANBE Wellbeing Model accommodates each one.

Within the study the authors make many valuable points, including:

1. Improvement and measurement of wellbeing has become a key policy and government objective in the UK
2. There is no group that oversees the development of wellbeing although the Organisation for Economic Development (OECD) has made some effort to formalise the approach
3. There is disagreement as to the definition of wellbeing although the authors reference "the quality and state of a person's life."[6] The boundaries between health and wellbeing remain blurred
4. "Wellbeing should be understood as a multidimensional construct, reflecting themes that often overlap."

5. There is inconsistent agreement on how wellbeing should be measured, with varying priorities amongst disciplines and each taking different approaches
6. There is some agreement in scientific literature about domains including biological, psychological, social, economic and spiritual
7. There is a need for both highly focused and widely scoped measures

These points are based on the analysis of self-report measures for assessing well-being in adults but what about national and international measures? Below is a sample of measures, one national (UK Measuring What Matters) and three international (OECD How's Life, Gallup World Poll and The Legatum Institute Prosperity Index) that seek to measure wellbeing.

	Mental	Emotional	Physical	Spiritual	Social	Culture	Environment	Economy
UK ONS Measuring What Matters	• Personal wellbeing • Health • Education and skills	• Personal wellbeing	• Personal wellbeing • Health • What we do	• Personal wellbeing	• Personal wellbeing • Relationship	• Personal wellbeing • What we do • Where we live • Governance	• Personal wellbeing • Where we live • Natural environment	• Personal wellbeing • What we do • Personal finance • The economy • Education and skills
OECD - How's life	• Subjective wellbeing • Health • Knowledge and skills • Human capital	• Subjective wellbeing	• Subjective wellbeing • Health • Human capital	• Subjective wellbeing	• Subjective wellbeing • Social connections • Social capital	• Subjective wellbeing • Civically engaged • Social capital	• Subjective wellbeing • Housing • Environment quality • Safety • Natural capital	• Subjective wellbeing • Income and wealth • Work and job quality • Work life balance • Economic capital
Gallup World Poll	• Education and families • Wellbeing	• Wellbeing	• Health • Wellbeing	• Religion and ethics • Wellbeing	• Engaged citizens • Education and families • Wellbeing	• Engaged citizens • Comms and technology • Education and families • Governance and politics • Law and order • Religion and ethics • Social issues • Wellbeing	• Engaged citizens • Comms and technology • Education and families • Environment and energy • Food and shelter • Health • Law and order • Wellbeing	• Business and economics • Engaged citizens • Food and shelter • Wellbeing • Work
Legatum Prosperity Index	• Living conditions • Health • Education	• Living conditions	• Living conditions • Health	• Living conditions	• Safety and security • Personal freedom • Social capital • Living conditions	• Safety and security • Personal freedom • Governance • Social capital • Enterprise conditions • Living conditions	• Safety and security • Market access and infrastructure • Economic quality • Living conditions • Health • Nature and environment	• Investment environment • Enterprise conditions • Market access and infrastructure • Economic quality • Living conditions

As you can see the eight domains correlate well with the topics and measures being used by these separate national and international bodies. This demonstrates the growing widespread agreement about the things that contribute to a good life and wellbeing at both personal and collective levels. Now is the time to consolidate that learning.

Here's how I believe the CANBE Model contributes to and answers many of these challenges.

- Firstly, it can help us improve the measurement of

wellbeing through a shared language and understanding of what wellbeing is. As such it provides a basis for agreeing a definition and getting a better 'line of sight' between individuals, teams, organisations, communities and nations. This shared understanding will, I believe, increase engagement and advance a more joined up and consistent approach to the measuring and management of wellbeing which will ultimately lead to better outcomes.

- The framework provides a multidimensional construct that encourages users to think systematically about overlapping themes and factors that contribute to wellbeing.

- It builds on existing agreement amongst scientific literature about the domains but simplifies the psychological domain, for reasons explained earlier in the book. The inclusion of social, cultural, environmental and economic dimensions recognise the collective nature of wellbeing and the influence of external factors on individuals. Spiritual and emotional wellbeing, which are often glossed over, very lightly covered, or even missed by many surveys at the national and international levels, are important additions. Who we are as individuals and collective groups is an important part of our wellbeing including our identity, character, personality, values, beliefs, stories, motivation and purpose. As we've seen earlier in the book our rational thought is often hijacked by our emotions so it is the spiritual and emotional dimensions that can often drive our behaviours. We should do more to understand these factors.

- It provides a framework for measuring wellbeing both

objectively and subjectively, allowing for both highly focused and widely scoped measures. By consistently measuring objective and subjective aspects of well-being across personal, organisational, community and national levels, we can obtain a richer picture and understand the systemic factors that are contributing to better lives for all. This is important so that we understand not only an individual's assessment of their own experience but also the factors in each setting which may be contributing to greater wellbeing.

- In terms of subjective measures it could provide a richer understanding of wellbeing through the use of the 'suffering to thriving' scale as opposed to 'satisfaction with life' which is most often used now in surveys.

Let's now look at this in practice. At a very basic level we can use the dashboard to get a high level view of our wellbeing. Where would you put yourself in each of the domains? Are you thriving, striving, surviving, struggling or suffering?

		Wellbeing Domains - 'Territories' - Interconnected areas of our lives							
		Mental Our thoughts	Emotional Our emotions	Physical Our actions	Spiritual Our spirit	Social Our communities	Cultural Our way	Environmental Our spaces	Economic Our trade
Wellbeing States	Thriving								
'Indicators'	Striving								
	Surviving								
States of wellbeing we move through	Struggling								
	Suffering								

To begin to uncover a more detailed analysis we can use the 'dimensions' and 'signposts' as guides for the types of measures we should include.

Wellbeing Dimensions 'Highways' Intertwined routes we use to navigate our lives	Creating meaning	Thinking	Feelings	Behaviour	Identity	Friendship	Way of life	Affinity	Needs
	Achieving potential	Focus	Control	Mastery	Motivation	Teamwork	Governance	Cultivation	Impact
	Nurturing relationships	Regard	Empathy	Interaction	Stories	Trust	Belonging	Cohesion	Fairness
	Building resilience	Flexibility	Agility	Health	Growth	Support	Diversity	Adaptation	Integrity
	Enriching lives	Imagination	Wisdom	Energy	Purpose	Empowerment	Integration	Renewal	Freedom
		Wellbeing Factors - 'Signposts' - Interconnected things that can help us improve wellbeing							

One of the most extensively used measuring methods in organisations is the 'Balanced Scorecard' originated by Drs Robert Kaplan and David Norton.

In describing the scorecard Kaplan and Norton, in line with the more balanced approach of the CANBE Model, recognised the limitations of measuring financial performance alone, "These financial measures are inadequate, however, for guiding and evaluating the journey that information age companies must make to create future value through investment in customers, suppliers, employees, processes, technology, and innovation."[7]

The typical measures in a scorecard include financial, internal efficiency measures, customer and innovation and learning and it is the responsibility of the leadership team to choose the appropriate ones, ensuring they are aligned with achieving the strategy.

I believe this framework is perfectly capable of including measures that are representative of the eight domains at an organisational level. Here is an example of how the model can actually be used to develop a scorecard including qualitative and subjective measures across groups. Please note that some of these measures cross different domains and many can be used at individual, organisational, community and national levels.

	Mental	Emotional	Physical	Spiritual	Social	Culture	Environment	Economy
Individual	• Intelligence Quotient (IQ) • Creativity Quotient (CQ) • Mental distress	• Emotional Quotient (EQ) • Positive & negative affect	• Health markers • Functional assessment • Self evaluation	• Level of motivation / engagement • Feeling purposeful • Sense of growth	• Positive relationships • Levels of trust • Treated with respect	• Ability to be self • Political voice • Sense of belonging	• Access to & quality of facilities • Sense of safety/ security • Carbon footprint	• Income, savings & investments • Feeling financially secure
Organisation	• Levels of mental health • Growth mindset	• Instances of conflict	• Health orientation • Sickness & absence • Effective	• Level of engagement • 'Lived' purpose	• Policies & procedures • Access to support	• Policies & procedures • Levels of diversity • Effective governance	• Air, water, temperature, material, noise quality • Supplier audit • Health & safety • CO2 emissions	• Profit, cashflow, Dividend, ROI, brand value • Provision of financial education • Pay ratios / Fair Pay
Community	• Provision, access to & quality of services	• Provision, access to & quality of services	• Provision, access to & quality of services	• Religious participation • Sense of identity	• Levels of volunteering • No. of clubs/ activities	• Functioning of services • No. of cultural events • Pride • Participation & inclusion	• No. of parks & recreation facilities • Levels of crime	• Diversity & composition of local business • Demographic composition
Nation	• Levels of mental distress • Levels of entrepreneur-ship	• Levels of happiness / sadness	• Levels of health	• International reputation • Pride in country	• Levels of isolation	• Levels of corruption • Freedom of expression • Electoral participation	• CO2 emissions • No. of National parks / protected areas	• GNP • Trade deficit/ surplus • Employment/ Unemployment • Confidence in future

This table of measures is not conclusive but hopefully demonstrates the ability of the eight domains to accommodate a full range of both qualitative and quantitative measures at different levels of analysis. Measuring wellbeing is not an exact science and approaches are still developing but I urge all leaders to move to this model of measurement now.

If we can agree that wellbeing is a better focus for human development than narrow economic growth, or even sustainable development, then we must measure both the negative and positive aspects of our impact to ensure our contribution is net positive.

My suggestion, in addition to measuring 'impact on us' is that we increasingly measure our 'impact on others'. This can be achieved at the individual, team, organisational, community and national levels. Many measures now focus predominantly on our personal wellbeing, or the wellbeing of our organisation, community or nation. But what about the impact we are having on others? If we take more and leave less for others our wellbeing might well be higher. However the other people may be left suffering. Successful wellbeing impact is when we all benefit together.

Imagine a workplace where employees are encouraged to spontaneously feedback on how the behaviours of others have impacted on their wellbeing. Each employee could use the simple dashboard below, where others score them based on how their behaviours had either hindered or helped and, over time, a picture of their contribution to the wellbeing of others and the workplace would build.

		Wellbeing Domains - 'Territories' - Interconnected areas of our lives							
		Mental Our thoughts	Emotional Our emotions	Physical Our actions	Spiritual Our spirit	Social Our communities	Cultural Our way	Environmental Our spaces	Economic Our trade
Wellbeing States 'Indicators' States of wellbeing we move through	Thriving								
	Striving								
	Surviving								
	Struggling								
	Suffering								

What was the outcome of your interaction with X in any of the following areas?

MENTAL WELLBEING - FOR EXAMPLE:

- Thriving- helped you reflect, think better, focus more, build your self esteem, overcome obstacles, open up to new ideas
- Suffering- left you worried, stressed, anxious or ruminating, distracted, with lower self esteem, feeling like you want to give up in the face of adversity, closed down to new ideas

EMOTIONAL WELLBEING - FOR EXAMPLE:

- Thriving- helped you understand your feelings better, feel good, take a step back and control your emotions, build empathy with others, manage your emotions flexibly
- Suffering- ended with you feeling bad, losing control of your emotions, lacking empathy for this person or others, not wanting to budge over your feelings

PHYSICAL WELLBEING - FOR EXAMPLE:

- Thriving- helped me develop good habits and take action, master new skills, communicate more effectively, be more healthy, feel energised
- Suffering - influenced me to develop bad habits and procrastinate, perform worse, communicate less effectively, be unhealthy, lose energy

SPIRITUAL WELLBEING - FOR EXAMPLE:

- Thriving- helped me to understand myself better, be myself, be more motivated, understand the bigger picture, grow as a person, be more purposeful
- Suffering - do things not aligned with who I am, become less motivated, become more confused, become smaller or neglect an opportunity to grow, feel less purposeful

SOCIAL WELLBEING - FOR EXAMPLE:

- Thriving - was a good friend, worked well in the team, built high levels of trust, provided excellent support, empowered me and others
- Suffering - created enemies, disrupted teamwork, eroded trust, was unsupportive and disempowering

CULTURAL WELLBEING - FOR EXAMPLE:

- Thriving - encouraged good governance, belonging, diversity, inclusion, and integration
- Suffering - caused conflict, poor governance, feelings of exclusion, separation and a lack of appreciation for differences

ENVIRONMENTAL WELLBEING - FOR EXAMPLE:

- Thriving - made it feel like home here, helped cultivate a better environment, used our spaces, technology and resources to collaborate effectively, adapted well to our surroundings and circumstances, sourced, reviewed, recycled, reused, repaired resources effectively to ensure we operate sustainably
- Suffering - made it feel unwelcoming here, used our spaces, technology and resources ineffectively, resisted and refused to adapt to changes to surroundings and circumstances, used resources ineffectively or wasted them.

ECONOMIC WELLBEING - FOR EXAMPLE:

- Thriving - helped ensure my needs for resources, information, financial and non-financial rewards are met, helped me have a positive impact on business and deliver what I need to, was fair, acted with integrity both morally and to protect long term interests of the organisation, is progressive
- Suffering - didn't help me get what I need or acted counter to my needs, had a negative impact on business and my delivery, acted unfairly or without integrity, stalled progress or is regressive

Feedback could be delivered anonymously or transparently depending on preferences. This outcome-based approach focuses on the actions of the person and not who they are, so would deliver valuable feedback to help behaviour change. As a real time dashboard, it would also help managers have better performance reviews on a more regular basis, providing information about things that they often won't see or be aware of, especially with more and more workers operating remotely.

Used as a supplement to what employees are actually delivering this would reveal the unsung heroes whose activities currently go unnoticed but whose actions help bind companies together on a daily basis. It would also help unearth those employees who, whilst delivering results, may be stepping on others to achieve. Typically there will be a large portion of people who sit in the middle and of course those who are delivering whilst also helping others thrive, your star performers! When aligned to an organisational dashboard measuring workplace wellbeing and performance, this could be an extremely powerful tool to understand the impact of individuals and teams.

But we should also use this model to challenge businesses operations. Earlier in the book I used this approach to demonstrate how we might make decisions on the airline industry, but this should equally be applied to all other industries. Some might argue that this could stifle innovation, but I would counter that innovation isn't really innovation worth pursuing unless it delivers greater wellbeing. In fact by setting the bar slightly higher and asking companies to prove how they are delivering, or will deliver, greater net wellbeing we may even increase innovation. Here's a simplified model for doing just that. Why not score your own business or organisation right now?

Consider your overall business impact across the eight domains of wellbeing on employees, suppliers, investors, customers, the community and the planet:

1. What are the positive impacts your business is delivering?
2. What are the negative impacts?
3. Overall are you causing suffering, struggling, surviving, striving or thriving? Score your business or organisation accordingly.
4. Total all your scores across the eight domains to arrive at your net wellbeing score.

		Wellbeing Domains - 'Territories' - Interconnected areas of our lives								
		Mental Our thoughts	Emotional Our emotions	Physical Our actions	Spiritual Our spirit	Social Our communities	Cultural Our way	Environmental Our spaces	Economic Our trade	
Wellbeing States	Thriving	+2	+2	+2	+2	+2	+2	+2	+2	
	Striving	+1	+1	+1	+1	+1	+1	+1	+1	
'Indicators'	Surviving	0	0	0	0	0	0	0	0	
States of wellbeing	Struggling	-1	-1	-1	-1	-1	-1	-1	-1	
we move through	Suffering	-2	-2	-2	-2	-2	-2	-2	-2	
Wellbeing Impact	Net impact									Total net Wellbeing

SCORE

+10 to +16	Your business is contributing to **thriving**. How can you keep improving and share your practices with others?
+6 to +9	Your business is contributing to **striving**. What more can you do to improve?
-5 to +5	Your business is only contributing to **survival**. Consider radical change.
-6 to -9	Your business is causing **struggling**. Implement radical change or cease trading.
-10 to -16	Your business is causing **suffering**. Transform or cease trading.

This is a very simplified version and there are cleverer people than I who could develop this model based on some of the measures I've suggested earlier in this chapter. For example, we may wish to 'weight' scores to allow for greater importance. The environmental impact of our businesses would fit this category in our present predicament!

I've shared this idea largely to spark debate, but with a genuine desire for us to see the success of businesses measured and audited on their contribution to net wellbeing and not purely on profit. I hope this demonstrates how this type of framework could be used to refocus our businesses and organisations on what is truly important.

Throughout this section I've demonstrated how the model can be used by individuals, teams, organisations, communities and even nations. The strength of this lies in the consistency and clarity it would bring to all levels and groups in society, in defining what is most important.

One of the key motivators to help deliver the greatest impact is 'fairness'. If we feel that we are being rewarded unfairly for a particular task, we are much less likely to 'give our all'. If deals between organisations are unfair, they will be much more likely to fail or deliver sub-optimum outcomes. If one country treats another unfairly, it will lead to resentment between nations and between the people of those nations.

FAIRNESS

		Wellbeing Domains - 'Territories' - Interconnected areas of our lives							
		Mental Our thoughts	**Emotional** Our emotions	**Physical** Our actions	**Spiritual** Our spirit	**Social** Our communities	**Cultural** Our way	**Environmental** Our spaces	**Economic** Our trade
Wellbeing Dimensions 'Highways' Intertwined routes we use to navigate our lives	Creating meaning	Thinking	Feelings	Behaviour	Identity	Friendship	Way of life	Affinity	Needs
	Achieving potential	Focus	Control	Mastery	Motivation	Teamwork	Governance	Cultivation	Impact
	Nurturing relationships	Regard	Empathy	Interaction	Stories	Trust	Belonging	Cohesion	Fairness
	Building resilience	Flexibility	Agility	Health	Growth	Support	Diversity	Adaptation	Integrity
	Enriching lives	Imagination	Wisdom	Energy	Purpose	Empowerment	Integration	Renewal	Freedom
		Wellbeing Factors - 'Signposts' - Interconnected things that can help us improve wellbeing							

"Being good is easy, what is difficult is being just."

VICTOR HUGO

"Fairness does not mean everyone gets the same. Fairness means everyone gets what they need."

RICK RIORDAN

As Isaac Prilleltensky, Professor of Educational and Psychological Studies and Dean of Education and Human Development at the University of Miami points out, in his paper "Wellness as Fairness"[1], justice and fairness should be considered as important factors in developing greater wellbeing.

This is because different levels of justice help to influence well-being outcomes. Interestingly, he describes how these various levels of justice and fairness can lead to thriving, coping, confronting, and suffering respectively, closely reflecting proposals put forward in this book.

But I also believe that higher levels of wellbeing can help to achieve outcomes of greater fairness. Whilst I haven't been able to find any research on this, it makes intuitive sense to me that if people are thriving there will be less need to be 'unfair'. If our needs are being met across all the domains of wellbeing then the motivation to gain an advantage or 'get one over on others' would likely diminish.

I've included fairness in the section on economic wellbeing as it is often associated with the fair distribution of resources. However, as with all other 'signposts' in the book, fairness is linked to all other domains of wellbeing.

There is considerable evidence that fairness and justice support wellbeing at individual, organisational, community and national levels. It is perhaps no surprise that the 'egalitarian' nordic countries we see topping the World Happiness Index[2] are also some of the fairest and most just in the world, as recorded by the World Justice Project[3] and the Social Justice Index[4]. Indeed the World Happiness Index suggests "that people are happier to live in societies with less disparity in the quality of life."

I use the word fairness over and above equality because no person is equal with another, or ever will be. We are all different. The strive for equality has been distorted and misguided and, I believe, will eventually lead to negative consequences. Rather than celebrating differences between us and playing to these strengths we seem to be in the process of breaking them down. This is not diversity, it is homogeneity. You know the feeling when you try to force two magnets together of the same polarity! They repel each other. Only last night I watched an 'Economist' video about problems in South Korea. Population growth has dropped below 1 child per couple, when as recently as 2011 it was 6. A contributory factor is young women and men becoming disillusioned with each other due to more modern conceptions of their prospective roles in society.

Following this line of thought it is clear that, whilst we share many human characteristics, we all have subtle differences in needs, abilities, preferences and motivations. I propose that what matters is not that we are treated equally but that we are treated fairly.

Another argument against the strive for equality is that it just isn't human nature. We compete for status, power, recognition and even admiration for being different amongst our peers. As we explored earlier, emphasis differs between individualistic and collective nations, but the fact remains that each of us attach different levels of importance to status and power than others.

We live in unequal societies. It is important to recognise this. We have monarchy, lords and ladies, oligarchs, 'followers' and 'leaders', the rich and powerful (Top 1%), the sexes, black and white, LGBT and straight people, indigenous and immigrant.

The check and balance for this is not equality. Trying to treat all these different groups equally will just cause tension. The check and balance is fairness. Fairness empowers people to be different, to have more (or less), money, power and status, to be what they want to be, as long as this isn't causing undue suffering to others.

But 'the world just isn't fair' I hear you say. Of course it isn't. It never will be totally fair, just as it won't be equal. However it is fairer today than it was 200, 100 or even 30 years ago. During this time we have seen the abolition of slavery, the emancipation of women, the reduction of poverty, less conflict and the development of the United Nations based on 'human rights' for all. Our role now is to continue on our journey towards ever greater fairness.

But what is fairness? Here we can draw from the concepts of

distributive and procedural justice. In short, distributive justice is what we get. This can be seen from the perspective of how fairly benefits and costs, rights and responsibilities, burdens and privileges, are allocated to each of us. There are two main arguments as to how these distributions should be determined. The first is that everyone should get what they need. The second, that everyone should get what they merit. Although often put forward as opposing arguments, these aren't necessarily contradictory and can operate effectively together.

If everyone were to get what they need and then those people who work hardest, take greater risks, or put in additional effort were rewarded on top for their merits, I'm sure most people would agree that this would be a fair society. This was reflected by Minouche Shafik, Director, London School of Economics and Political Science and former Deputy Governor of the Bank of England in an interview with the World Economic Forum in 2019 where he said, "In today's economy, too much of what happens to you depends on which family you're born into and the opportunities that brings. What most people would like to see would be a society and an economy in which everyone was guaranteed a minimum, so nobody would be absolutely destitute. But also that, if you worked hard and tried hard, you could advance yourself regardless of which family you were born into."[5]

I mentioned previously that fairness is both what we get and how it is given. How it is given is the procedural element of justice which Isaac Prilleltensky says, "refers to fair, transparent, informative, respectful, and,... participatory decision making processes. Decisions affecting individuals ought to follow due process and they should be impartial." He goes on to explain that "people's dignity and self-respect are highly dependent on both" distributive and procedural justice. "Wounds to the soul may be as harmful as wounds to the body."[6]

In essence, a fair society is one where all people can thrive by both giving and receiving according to their capabilities, merits, and needs.

However, currently as far as I can see, there are four problems to achieving this goal.

1. Not all people are getting what they need or deserve, as evidenced already in this Chapter.
2. People are being rewarded disproportionately for their 'merits', for 'merits' that aren't delivering greater 'net' wellbeing, or even a lack of 'merits'. Oxfam states that "the world's 2,153 billionaires have more wealth than the 4.6 billion people who make up 60 percent of the planet's population"[7]. But even on a more local level we can all identify areas where some people are paid far more than others for the same work, or for work that in comparison delivers less essential benefits. In fact some people may even be getting rewarded for eroding wellbeing. Just think of shareholders invested in companies which have damaged the environment. On the other end of the scale we see criticism of the 'benefits society' with reports of people being rewarded for contributing very little.
3. The role of luck is being brushed under the carpet and/or confused with merit. As Barry Swartz, the Dorwin Cartwright Professor of Social Theory and Social Action at Swarthmore College, says in his TED presentation "What Role Does Luck Play In Your Life?": "There are an awful lot of good people who just aren't going to make it." In a just and fair system, "people get what they deserve." He goes on to say that, "we hate the thought that really important things in our lives are not under our control...Lots of people also deserve successes like ours who haven't had it. Working hard and playing by the rules is no guarantee of anything. What do we owe people who struggle, work hard, and are less lucky than we are?"[8]
4. Finally, an unfair balance of power rests with those who

may be resistant to change due to fear of losing their advantages.

The question, then, is what extra can we do to keep moving forward on our journey to a fairer society?

You won't be surprised to learn that the complex answers lie within the CANBE Model. However, I believe there are four key areas where we can improve. I have written more about these in the chapter 'Vision for the Future' but for now here are thoughts relating specifically to fairness.

FAIRER EDUCATION

By improving education and aligning it to the CANBE Wellbeing Model we can expand people's capabilities to achieve better outcomes for themselves, but also develop citizens that are more compassionate, altruistic, and fair towards others.

For example, by helping people think better we can improve decision making to increase fairness. Reducing bias is an obvious example here, but encouraging people to use a combination of head, heart, and gut will also lead to more calculated risk and better choices. We can actually educate people to be 'luckier', through developing more optimistic outlooks and helping build resilience, two of the key traits associated with 'lucky' people. Greater confidence, empathy, compassion, support and empowerment are all keys to seizing opportunities when they present themselves.

Manouche Shafik explains further, "A lot of research now shows that it's the first thousand days of life that matter enormously for life outcomes. So very early years education, nutrition at a very young age, interventions at that point can have huge benefits in terms of people's major health and educational outcomes and career prospects. So we aren't doing enough at the very beginning." He goes on, "And our educational systems are still very unequal. People who are better off can hoard opportunities and keep them for their own children, through things like private schooling and private tuition. We also could do much, much more when people finish school to support them so that, if they lose their job, they're able to acquire new skills quite easily to find a new one."

FAIRER GOVERNANCE AND LEGISLATION

Why should governments focus on a fairer distribution of wealth and wellbeing? There are three basic reasons:

1. Poverty reduction increases the happiness of poorer people at greater rates than increasing the wellbeing of already wealthy people
2. As previously stated, there is a positive relationship between fairer societies and wellbeing, and yet there is increasing vocalisation of the damage caused to social cohesion, health, education, and access to other services due to the growing concentration of wealth and power
3. Removing obstacles and providing people with increased capability and opportunity to 'improve their lot' is good for everyone

It was the Great Depression of the 1930s and 1940s that demonstrated a requirement for greater Government involvement in providing for the welfare of all citizens. Prior to this Governments had a largely "laissez faire" attitude towards providing a safety net.

Post World War II, international consensus on this topic saw the introduction of the Declaration of Human Rights and specifically Article 22 which recorded social security as a universal right.

In the modern age governments play a role in providing for the welfare of all individuals through public services such as healthcare, education, transport and infrastructure but they also set the rules which determines how the private sector plays its part in delivering a better quality of life for all.

Focused and courageous governance and legislation can help to tackle some of the key current failures such as:

- Growing disparity in income and wellbeing between countries and within populations
- Market distortions
- Corruption

It is likely that a combination of the following solutions can help play a part in delivering greater fairness. Of course, different solutions may work for different countries in relation to each of their specific circumstances. I'd also like to point out that none of these solutions will work on their own. This, I believe, is a failure of arguments so far. They tend to be for or against, based only on scrutiny of an idea in isolation.

For example, people against Universal Basic Income (UBI), the idea that every person in a nation should get a basic income regardless of status, often argue that it is a disincentive for people to work, or that people will spend the money unwisely. However, as outlined throughout this book we need to approach things systematically. We need a revolution and transformation in how we approach these issues. If UBI were introduced alongside better education, which helped people find work they enjoyed, included better financial education, extolled the virtues of contribution to society, combined with automation which took over more mundane jobs, then we get a much different picture.

UNIVERSAL BASIC INCOME

Whether UBI works or not has never really been fully proven nor disproven, but what we do know is that most, if not all, governments across the world are failing to provide an adequate safety net for citizens that need it most. The role of the government is to find a way to provide that safety net, as poor finance can lead to suffering, and an important part of wellbeing is to be financially resilient.

Since the 1960s there have been many ideas put forward in this area, including negative income tax, public ownership of productive assets (what if we all owned a robot that could work for us!), minimum income (which differs from UBI in that it only guarantees income to those who need it), and other ideas along the same theme.

What I would say is that if we apply fairness principles, accommodating both people's needs and their merits, then a Universal Basic Income seems unfair whereas a Guaranteed Minimum Income seems more aligned. Giving everyone money regardless of whether they NEED it seems unfair whereas providing a minimum income for those that do seems much more sensible.

Perhaps the biggest test along these lines is Spain's recent introduction of a guaranteed annual income for 850,000 of its poorest citizens. On 15 June 2020, spurred by the economic fallout of coronavirus, it launched a website offering monthly payments of up to €1,015 (US $1,145) to the nation's poorest. The scheme, which is intended to outlast the pandemic, is being watched closely by economists and governments across the world.

It is now time to act and it looks like Spain may be leading the way. governments across the world must stop delaying and start delivering.

FAIRER DISTRIBUTION OF WEALTH AND WELLBEING

I think it is well recognised that a 'safety net' of the sort mentioned above will help improve the quality of people's lives, but income's effect on wellbeing cannot be seen in isolation. After all there are plenty of both happy peasants and unhappy millionaires.

Our overall quality of life then, is heavily influenced by all eight domains of wellbeing. Amartya Sen, Thomas W. Lamont University Professor, and Professor of Economics and Philosophy at Harvard University, in his book, *Development As Freedom*, proposed a theory of global justice based on expanding people's 'freedoms' and 'capabilities'. He argues that by expanding people's ability to help themselves, combined with removing any constrictive social, political, and economic barriers, we can achieve a better world for all.

Of course education is a big part of this but I believe it is the government's role to help individuals remove any barriers and build capabilities in each of the eight domains. So what are these freedoms and capabilities and how can governments do better? Well, to provide a few examples:

- A fairer system of quality education for all, based on wellbeing, will expand people's capabilities across all eight domains and give them more freedom to choose vocations aligned to their specific skills and characteristics
- Government legislation to make it easier for us to recycle expands our capability to look after the environment
- Government legislation and influence on diversity education to expand our knowledge, understanding and capability to get along with others
- Government regulation to ensure people on low incomes aren't penalised by having to pay more for accessing energy, utilities and credit as is often the case currently

One other obvious example, where the government can make a difference in the growing rift between the rich and poor, is in taxation.

TAXATION

In addition to providing security governments, can also seek to redistribute wealth. Thomas Piketty[9], in his 2013 book *Capital in the Twenty-First Century*, which relies on data going back 250 years, argues that the rate of capital return in developed countries is persistently greater than the rate of economic growth, resulting in an ever-rising concentration of wealth which is not self-correcting. He further argues that to address this problem, governments must intervene, and he proposes redistribution through a progressive global tax on wealth.

Other ideas in this area include, shifting greater taxation to things we want to discourage, such as excessive use of natural resources, or resources adding to climate change, and away from things we want to encourage, such as greater employment. It is clear to many that the gap between the rich and poor is growing and that governments must now take action to alleviate the problem. In addition, people are increasingly uneasy about the loopholes and inadequate global tax rules which allow rich corporations and individuals to avoid their tax responsibilities.

It is important to state this concentration of wealth not only affords the rich access to experiences and quality of goods and services not available to others, but it also gives them a more powerful voice. The use of wealth to pervert or obtain advantageous justice, or in lobbying government representatives for favourable policy outcomes is tearing at the heart of democracy across the world.

MANAGING IMPERFECTIONS

Markets are recognised as the greatest anti-poverty engine there is and can help to deliver greater wellbeing. However, they are imperfect and, left to themselves, they can fail to deliver on that promise. As economist John Maynard Keynes argued, the invisible hand of the market needs assistance from the visible hand of the state.

One key problem is that the true costs of products and services aren't being effectively built into their price. One prime example would be the value of a pack of cigarettes. The cost of a pack to the individual is far less than it is to society, which picks up the bill for poorer health as a result of smoking across the nation.

We should also remember that this works the other way round. The benefits people get from 'socialising' at a local market are often not reflected in the price due to cost pressures imposed by internet-based models of shopping.

Moving to a wellbeing based model of accounting where both the 'true' costs and benefits of products and services are reflected in prices will help us alleviate this problem. Fair Trade is an organisation set up to reflect the fact that the way we view costs and benefits currently doesn't always lead us to the best outcomes.

FAIR TRADE

The fact that there is a growing Fair Trade Organisation[10] suggests that, this organisation at least, believes that trade isn't fair. It is also a demonstration of market failure, being set up to counter the collapse in world coffee prices over 25 years ago, and protect the small-hold farmers who were earning less than the cost of growing their coffee.

Today the organisation certifies schemes for some of our favourite products including bananas, chocolate, gold, coffee, flowers, tea, wine, juice, sugar, spreads and oil, herbs and spices, clothes and beauty, further demonstrating the exploitation and failure of these markets on a wide scale. Their principles include fair pay, decent working conditions, sustainability and fair terms of trade.

The 'simplified' problem they are working to address is that, in the competitive markets outlined above, many of the 'players' are focused on driving down costs and as such driving down prices to maintain market share.

The obvious result from this is that producers, many of them in nations being impacted disproportionately by climate change, are left with smaller profits and incomes. When this is combined with the impact of climate change on many of their crops the outcome could well be one where everyone loses. Producers left with unviable businesses and consumers left with less produce, or paying higher prices anyway due to lower supply. Of course, some may argue that as prices start to rise again this will encourage the re-entry of producers to increase supply and bring back down prices. But these people probably won't have suffered the same impacts on their lives as the producers. Is this really the way we want to live our lives? Do we really want to exploit others to get the lowest prices?

So what is the solution? We need to intervene in the markets. Individuals need to understand the results of constantly driving down prices and be willing to accept a higher and fairer price so that everyone can win. In doing so many consumers may require further support to their income so that they can afford higher prices as outlined in the section on fairer distribution of wealth and wellbeing. Businesses need to collaborate to set prices that are fair but enable them to compete, and governments must ensure that laws and regulations enable them to do that.

Unfortunately this is not the case at present. Many consumers are largely ignorant to the issue, or unable to afford higher prices; businesses are constrained by competition laws which disable them from collaborating on prices and governments are slow to act.

It should be noted that there are criticisms of fair trade which largely centre on the discrepancies between policy and practice. For example, the scheme can be open to corruption, with co-operatives failing to pass on the full benefits to small-hold farmers. Another issue is the use of the Fair Trade mark as a marketing ploy to inflate prices, as opposed to a genuine approach to business.

However whilst there may be learning we need to do along the way the principles of fairer trade can only be of benefit to us all in the longer term. On this basis it is encouraging to see the European Union support for Fair Trade, and in particular the Scottish Government commitment to Scotland as a 'Fair Trade Nation'[11]. In both areas policies are being aligned to the UN SDGs recognising the economic, social and environmental impacts that fairer trade can have.

As with the UN SGDs this increasing focus on 'fairness', at the international and national levels, will increasingly permeate down to our organisations.

FAIRER ORGANISATIONS

So how can organisations play their role in improving fairness? As mentioned previously, by consistently applying principles of transparency, open communication, respect, inclusivity, participatory decision making, impartiality and dignity organisations will be well on their way to becoming fairer. Organisations also have a huge role to play through provision of decent work, terms of employment, fair rewards and benefits. Organisations can either inspire us or sap our energy, largely dependent on how we are treated. By giving people a chance, when otherwise they might be disadvantaged, organisations can help people advance in society.

Other than the factors just mentioned some specific opportunities to increase economic or financial fairness include the following:

FAIR PAY, REWARDS AND BENEFITS

A Chartered Institute of Personnel and Development (CIPD) press-release headlined *"Top Bosses' Pay Overtakes Average Worker's Entire 2020 Pay In Just 3 Days"* alerted us all to the fact that, in the UK, top bosses earn in 3 days what the average full-time employee does in a year[12].

It is no surprise that, from 1 January 2019, recently passed legislation requires these large 'listed' UK incorporated companies with more than 250 employees to report on pay ratios. First results have begun to be seen in 2020, leading to the sorts of headlines seen above.

This legislation sprung from public and political concern about 'excessive' pay. Ironically, growing evidence supports the point that staff are less productive where decisions on pay are felt to be unfair and gaps are larger between top and bottom.

Auditing and changing pay ratios, paying at least the minimum, but preferably a living wage[13], closing the gender pay gap, or any gaps that exist where one group of employees may be being paid unfairly in relation to another, are all actions organisations can take to improve financial fairness. Of course this should also be extended to rewards and benefits.

EMPLOYEE OWNERSHIP

Extending the spirit of fairness further, organisations are increasingly embracing a model of employee ownership. The Employee Ownership Association in the UK states growth at just under 10% per annum[14]. This is not a new model but it is growing in popularity. In the UK, perhaps one of the most well known exponents of the model is the John Lewis Partnership, the largest employee-owned business in the UK, with gross sales of over £11.7bn and a workforce of over 80,000 Partners.

This spirit of fairness is based on employees having 'skin in the game'. If the business does well, I do well. If the business doesn't do so well then neither will I. It is important to recognise this element of fairness. It is about both give and take, rights and responsibilities, gains and pains.

FINANCIAL EDUCATION

One way we can be fairer is through sharing knowledge. It is worth mentioning financial wellbeing a little more here as it fits into the domain of economic wellbeing. Financial wellbeing has become a more popular topic in the workplace and the focus is mainly on helping people to make the best use of their money. This is a fantastic initiative that I fully support.

However, we should remember that financial education becomes a very blunt tool if people are paid unfairly in the first place, or if the money they do earn is created by being in a job that is causing poor mental and physical health. Likewise if the money people earn is acquired or invested in ways that damage the environment then the reason for financial wellbeing is diminished. My point is, whilst it is a good idea to manage our finances prudently, perhaps we should be thinking a little wider about what we are managing them prudently for!

FAIRER MEASUREMENT

Following fairer education, fairer governance and fairer organisations the fourth key area where I think we can improve is moving to a well-being focused model as a measure of success for individuals, organisations, communities and nations. This, I believe, will help improve fairness across each of the eight domains. By measuring net contribution to wellbeing we would be rewarding people and organisations more proportionately, and disincentivising or stopping those who are damaging wellbeing.

I mentioned previously that fairness should be based on both needs and merits. If we substitute the word 'merits' for impact then we can begin to see fairness as rewarding people who have a positive impact on the world around them. This, in essence, was the subject of the previous section in this chapter.

Positive relationships are built when people have fair access to resources, information, wealth and wellbeing. It is a shame having to write about fairness. The fact that we require legislation and accreditations, badges and logos to help promote that we are 'fair' is testament to the fact that there is still much to do to make the world fairer. Perhaps one sign that the world is becoming even fairer will be the disappearance of all these names, accreditations, and badges.

This will be a sign that our leaders have great integrity. After all, saying that you are fair because people are watching and actually being fair because you think it's the right thing to do are two separate things!

INTEGRITY

		Wellbeing Domains - 'Territories' - Interconnected areas of our lives							
		Mental Our thoughts	**Emotional** Our emotions	**Physical** Our actions	**Spiritual** Our spirit	**Social** Our communities	**Cultural** Our way	**Environmental** Our spaces	**Economic** Our trade
Wellbeing Dimensions 'Highways' Intertwined routes we use to navigate our lives	Creating meaning	Thinking	Feelings	Behaviour	Identity	Friendship	Way of life	Affinity	Needs
	Achieving potential	Focus	Control	Mastery	Motivation	Teamwork	Governance	Cultivation	Impact
	Nurturing relationships	Regard	Empathy	Interaction	Stories	Trust	Belonging	Cohesion	Fairness
	Building resilience	Flexibility	Agility	Health	Growth	Support	Diversity	Adaptation	**Integrity**
	Enriching lives	Imagination	Wisdom	Energy	Purpose	Empowerment	Integration	Renewal	Freedom
		Wellbeing Factors - 'Signposts' - Interconnected things that can help us improve wellbeing							

"The ultimate measure of a man is not where he stands in moments of comfort, but where he stands at times of challenge and controversy."

MARTIN LUTHER KING, JR.

"Little progress can be made by merely attempting to repress what is evil. Our great hope lies in developing what is good."

CALVIN COOLIDGE

Integrity is the quality of moral principles, and also the state of being whole and undivided. Before we delve deeper, there are some important questions we must consider.

The first is, should we consider economics and ethics, or morality, together? Economists have wrestled with this challenge since the dawn of economics. Whilst some economists may still try to remain value neutral I believe that the majority would now consider ethics, values and human behaviour as valuable factors in contributing to the development of economic policy. After all, if the purpose of an economy is to satisfy our needs, and these are based on both rational and emotional decisions, shouldn't we then consider our economy in this context.

The second question then becomes, 'whose ethics?' Again in this area there are many historical, religious, cultural, intellectual, normative/social and political theories and approaches. Is any one of them right or wrong? No. They each have pros and cons in the eyes of their champions and critics.

This is where I believe economics based on wellbeing can provide us with an evolutionary framework for ethical considerations. Is it right or wrong? No. But **it is** a framework that builds on the wisdom of many cultures, religions, intellects, and political approaches and is also flexible enough to adapt to the circumstances of our time.

Is it better than purely relying on economic indicators and leaving our destiny in the hands of the 'free market'? Yes, I believe it most definitely is. The 'free market', as a concept, does not have ethics. So to argue that we should 'let the market decide' is, by its very nature, unethical. It is our attempt to deflect difficult decisions away from ourselves to a concept. We must take responsibility for our own actions. If we are making redundancies, raising prices, or making other difficult decisions it is not 'driven by the market'. It is driven by us.

As outlined throughout the book we have come a long way in many areas but we can do even better and there are still many challenges. We have missed targets for reduction of carbon emissions and protection of biodiversity. Our current ethics and integrity seem somewhat misplaced. I believe a wellbeing focused economy would provide us with the critical lens to facilitate a course correction.

RESILIENCE

The second way we can view integrity is based on the resilience of our economic and financial state to overcome obstacles, unforeseen events, and plan for a better future together.

According to research[1] "no country currently meets basic needs for its citizens at a globally sustainable level of resource use." So, we're not even managing to maintain the integrity of our economic system now, let alone threats from pandemics, climate change, or other unforeseen events.

One area where we can improve is in managing what we have much better.

MANAGING FINITE RESOURCES PRUDENTLY

If we are to manage our resources prudently the first thing we need to know is 'what's in the cupboard'. Unfortunately we currently only have one supplier. It's a monopoly, and that one supplier is planet Earth. Earth is our 'goose' and we need to protect the 'golden eggs'.

I've searched and, whilst there are many different organisations with what appear to be partial data on available resources in the world, there doesn't appear to be one definitive database on what is available to us.

Now I appreciate that this may be constantly changing as new resources are found, resources are used, and new innovation changes our requirements, but surely this is the first step. I also appreciate that this is a complex task, with materials currently in use (such as the metal in the cars we drive) being available for recycling and therefore accountable as part of our overall metal stock. However, we need a definitive, open, and transparent database of what we have available to us, and I would expect that to be managed by each country and ultimately the United Nations.

If there is one I apologise, but I would expect to find it very easily by searching the internet on 'world database of available resources' or such similar terms. Currently this is not the case. My hunch that there isn't one is also supported by the OECD Global Material Resource Outlook to 2060 report which states "unfortunately, material stock accounting data are not readily available."[2]

Unless we have this database, it will be difficult for any business, community, nation or economic region to plan effectively. In essence we might want something but other individuals, businesses or nations might want it too, and eventually there may not be enough to go round!

In the OECD report it projects that, "in the absence of new policies' global material use will almost double from 2017 to 2060 with increases reflected across metallic, non-metallic, biomass and fossil fuel categories. This will lead to the 'doubling of greenhouse gas emissions, pollution to the soil, water and air and toxic effects on humans, and aquatic and terrestrial ecosystems."

It goes on to make useful policy recommendations for governments to counteract some of the challenges posed above. I paraphrase these below:

1. Encouraging and incentivising resource efficiency along product value chains
2. Improve data and analysis of resources
3. Supporting businesses in their supply chain management efforts
4. Strengthening international co-operation

5. Alleviating barriers to trade and investment in environmental technologies
6. Harmonising environmental labels to reduce costs and improve understanding

Following this, it is then interesting to note the EU Commission *"Critical Raw Materials Resilience: Charting a Path Towards Greater Security and Sustainability"* report[3], which states "Access to resources is a strategic security question for Europe's ambition to deliver the Green Deal. The new industrial strategy for Europe proposes to reinforce Europe's open strategic autonomy, warning that Europe's transition to climate neutrality could replace today's reliance on fossil fuels with one on raw materials, many of which we source from abroad and for which **global competition is becoming more fierce**."

The report goes on to acknowledge the requirement to reduce and reuse materials before finally recycling them and the necessity to scale up the circular, regenerative and renewable economies. Other useful elements from this strategy that can be applied by individuals, organisations or countries include the following:

- Understand resource use. Where do our resources come from, or could they come from, and what are they used for?
- Prioritise resources. Which are most important?
- Understand where we might be able to substitute one resource for another.
- Diversify our supply chain. Make sure we've got more than one supplier so we're less at risk if things become difficult
- Ensure we source responsibly
- Become more self-sufficient in extracting, processing and refining materials, and therefore creating more jobs. Can

we produce resources ourselves that are currently being outsourced?
- Be innovative and create new resources and materials

What is slightly disconcerting is the strength of certain suppliers. For example, China currently provides 98 % of the EU's supply of rare earth elements (REE) and the EU is also "75% to 100% reliant on imports for most metals."

For me, this situation combined with the increased pressure on resource use in future, highlights the importance of increasing cooperation, as opposed to competition on the international stage. This is reflected by the EU when it states 'Conflicts arising from, or aggravated by, access to resources are also a recurrent source of international tension.'

Another way to manage the integrity of our resources and help the planet into the bargain is responsible production and consumption.

RESPONSIBLE PRODUCTION AND CONSUMPTION

Whilst we don't have a full audit of the planet's resources organisations such as Global Footprint Earth[4] measures how fast we consume certain resources and generate waste compared to how fast nature can absorb waste and produce the equivalent new resources.

They demonstrate that 'since the 1970s, humanity has been in ecological overshoot, with annual demand on resources exceeding what Earth can regenerate each year. Today humanity uses the equivalent of 1.6 Earths to provide the resources we use and absorb our waste.' In 2020, "Earth Overshoot day" was on August 22nd[5]. Due to coronavirus this is a slight contraction from the previous year!

So there is a definite requirement to consume less in certain areas. If we consume and it doesn't improve our wellbeing then surely that is unnecessary consumption? Why would we consume something if it doesn't improve our lives? And yet we do, week in and week out.

What could we stop consuming that wouldn't detract from our wellbeing and may even improve it?

The most obvious answer to this is 'too much', or to put it another way, greed. Gandhi said, "There is enough in the world for all our needs, but never enough for one man's greed." We need to know when enough is enough. As we explored earlier: food, clothes, cosmetics, alcohol, drugs, fuel, heating, and water are all obvious examples.

Of course, businesses have a role to play here too. Irresponsible marketing that encourages consumption against the interests of public wellbeing should be challenged and stopped. There is a balance to be found between quantity and quality. Producing goods which last, and/or can be repaired, rather than planned obsolescence is another.

GLOBALISATION AND LOCALISATION

Following this we must strike a better balance between globalisation and localisation. There is room for both. Globalisation offers economies of scale, efficiencies, knowledge sharing and distribution of products and services that may not otherwise have been available to us. Localisation provides uniquely crafted local products and can help to reduce the strain on our ecological systems.

In a similar vein, building on the principle of 'subsidiarity', which I covered in the section on 'Governance', we must become more agile in using centralised and decentralised governing mechanisms. It has become apparent through the pandemic that the relationships between the World Health Organisation (WHO), national and regional governance has worked to varying degrees of success, but that perhaps more power could have been distributed to local authorities in meeting the demands of their unique and specific circumstances. Being able to flex more to local and regional requirements will make us more resilient.

SAVING AND INVESTMENT

There are many ways we are actually poor judges of what is good for our wellbeing. Affective forecasting is a concept that describes how we can often be poor judges in the present about what will bring us happiness and improved wellbeing in the future. Having worked in the Life & Pensions industry, I know only too well how many people struggle to plan for their retirement, because it is so difficult to imagine how much money they'll need to secure a good level of wellbeing in the future. Many can also be inhibited and/or biased towards prioritisation of present expenses.

For example, we are often prone to instant gratification. We may eat the whole chocolate bar now rather than saving some for later in the week. In a similar vein, we often relate consumption to happiness. We may feel a little low or bored and find ourselves online, purchasing that new item we've wanted for a while, but don't really need. Whilst we may get an instant 'hit' of happiness, actually in the longer term this isn't what is necessarily best for our wellbeing, or the planet.

Often these behaviours are results of poor habits and not thinking things through. In the chapter on Mental Wellbeing we explored some of the advantages of being 'present minded', but of course we should also divert some of our attention to the future from time to time. We can't know what will happen, but we can plan for different scenarios to give ourselves the best chance to adapt and overcome any obstacles.

From an economic perspective this brings us to saving and investing. It is important to get people to a point where they can save and invest. Raising people out of poverty is a great start but if those same people are hit by catastrophes like failing crops, wildfires, floods or other unforeseen events, they can soon be dragged back down again. This is why we all need a 'rainy day fund' and a 'nest egg' for the future. Of course a minimum guaranteed income, or a scheme of the sort, would provide people with exactly this type of safety net, should things go wrong.

Building on this, knowing and sticking to a budget is a good starting point and there are many apps and tools available now to help us with just that. The next step is to cut out any wasteful spending. The more we cut, the more we can save, preparing us for any troubles that come our way. Once we've saved enough for a rainy day fund we can begin to invest. These financial skills should be taught in schools. Raising students' financial capabilities will help them become much more responsible citizens in the future so that they have a better chance of becoming economically self reliant.

When we do invest, one of the things we can do is to choose ethical or impact investing. This is when we choose to invest in companies that do no harm, or are focused on making positive social and environmental impacts in balance with a financial return.

At a macro level governments should begin investing across the eight domains of wellbeing to counter any disinvestments in areas that are not sustainable. For example, a recent study, commissioned by Campaign for Nature, found that the "economic benefits of protecting 30% of the planet's land and ocean outweigh the costs by at least 5-to-1."[6]

From a mental and emotional wellbeing perspective, investing in supporting people out of distress but also generating greater creativity and helping people feel good are key examples.

Physically there is room for massive improvement in all areas: diet, exercise, sleep and relaxation. In the UK, we are currently having a big debate about whether children in need should be receiving free school meals out of term time. This situation has obviously been exacerbated by COVID-19. Providing meals for children that need it would be an investment in their future.

Continuing with food, there is a massive project required to change the diet of the nation. Using the 'reference diet', mentioned previously, this could be an investment in higher energy levels of people, fewer dietary related health conditions, sustainable agriculture, greater social cohesion and diversity, protection of the environment, all whilst contributing positively to the economy.

MANAGING RISKS

The World Economic Forum's Global Risks Report 2020[7] makes for sombre reading. Climate change, environmental degradation, species decline, a slowdown of the global economy, cyber attacks, disease, domestic political unrest, growing nationalistic policies and widening inequality are all noted amongst key risks that threaten global stability.

Now, more than ever, we need greater international co-operation, flexible and adaptive thinking, combined with courageous action. And yet what we seem to be getting is exactly the opposite. Fractures in the global community with China and America's continued trade dispute, outdated systems, thinking that is failing to keep up with technological advances, missed targets for CO_2 emissions, and biodiversity loss.

The window of opportunity for change is getting smaller and smaller. We must act now. Wellbeing, as a universal vision, can help bring us together, provide a platform and capabilities to think differently, and a basis for our leaders to make more ethical decisions.

BECOMING MORE THRIFTY

Perhaps a concept that best brings together the thinking outlined so far in this section is that of thrift. Thrift is a word that is probably derived from Old Norse, meaning 'to **thrive**'. Dictionaries define it as '**careful** management, especially of money', 'healthy and vigorous **growth**', '**avoiding waste** and **saving** money for the future'. Words associated with thrift include providence, meaning 'to **provide**', 'having **foresight**', and prudence, meaning '**discretion**', '**caution**'.

Unfortunately, in the modern world, thrift is probably most associated with austerity and frugality, but this should not be the case. "The paradox of thrift" is a mainstream economic concept that suggests if people save more, there will be lower demand for goods and services, and therefore lower output. As income and output must be equal this will lead to a downward spiral of lower savings and output.

As you can see from the definitions above this is an unbalanced view. People who believe in this theory have taken the word savings and focused only on that, and yet the word also denotes growth, thriving, careful management and avoiding waste. Of course, if we were all to just save then things would come to a grinding halt. However that is not what thrift means. If we are thrifty we will still take risks but with discretion and caution. We will save and invest for the future but we will also spend now to achieve healthy and vigorous growth.

I see being thrifty or thrifty economics as:

'Careful management of money and resources, to avoid waste and achieve healthy growth, so that we can thrive now and in the future'.

The current economic interpretation of thrift suggests we should spend, spend, spend and that 'vice' is better for our economy. The definition above proposes that we build our economy on 'virtue'. When investment, entrepreneurship, consumption and production are combined with virtue the increase to wellbeing can be transformative.

I hope you can see the strong correlation between thrift and the actions we need to take from an environmental, social, and economic basis to improve individual and collective wellbeing.

Thrift is also a concept that will help us achieve more freedom as individuals, organisations and nations.

CHANGING MINDSET

This is perhaps the biggest challenge we face to increase economic integrity but I'm confident we can do it. As we know from earlier sections in the book, resilience is about adopting a flexible mindset. It's about being agile with our feelings, being healthy and growing through experience.

COVID-19 is testing us all economically. But perhaps now is the best time to challenge our thinking. If we can meet our needs, ensure we contribute positively to wellbeing, keep working on being fairer, and develop our economies based on virtue, in a way that balances people, purpose, profit and planet we can shake off the shackles to become the best version of ourselves.

Wellbeing is success. Not wealth, celebrity, fame or any other measure. Wellbeing will set us free.

FREEDOM

		Wellbeing Domains - 'Territories' - Interconnected areas of our lives							
		Mental Our thoughts	**Emotional** Our emotions	**Physical** Our actions	**Spiritual** Our spirit	**Social** Our communities	**Cultural** Our way	**Environmental** Our spaces	**Economic** Our trade
Wellbeing Dimensions 'Highways' Intertwined routes we use to navigate our lives	**Creating meaning**	Thinking	Feelings	Behaviour	Identity	Friendship	Way of life	Affinity	Needs
	Achieving potential	Focus	Control	Mastery	Motivation	Teamwork	Governance	Cultivation	Impact
	Nurturing relationships	Regard	Empathy	Interaction	Stories	Trust	Belonging	Cohesion	Fairness
	Building resilience	Flexibility	Agility	Health	Growth	Support	Diversity	Adaptation	Integrity
	Enriching lives	Imagination	Wisdom	Energy	Purpose	Empowerment	Integration	Renewal	Freedom
		Wellbeing Factors - 'Signposts' - Interconnected things that can help us improve wellbeing							

"Between stimulus and response, there is a space. In that space is our power to choose our response. In our response lies our growth and our freedom."

VICKTOR FRANKL, AUSTRIAN NEUROLOGIST AND PSYCHIATRIST

"The great revolution in the history of man, past, present and future, is the revolution of those determined to be free."

JOHN F. KENNEDY, 35TH PRESIDENT OF THE UNITED STATES OF AMERICA

"Freedom is nothing but a chance to be better."

ALBERT CAMUS, FRENCH AUTHOR, JOURNALIST AND PHILOSOPHER

Freedom from want, one of the "Four Freedoms"[1] proposed by President Roosevelt in his Annual Message to Congress of January 6, 1941, is as relevant today as it was back then, albeit under much different circumstances.

Imagine a world where we were all free from want. This surely is a much better goal than a misplaced focus on growth for growth's sake.

If we are to be free from want we must understand what currently traps or cages us. The obvious example here, as recognised by the UN SDGs, is poverty. So we must work to reduce poverty and many of the activities planned by the United Nations and outlined in this book will help to move us in this direction.

But it is not only the poor or destitute that are caged or trapped. Many so-called 'wealthy' people also feel caged and trapped.

- Trapped by debt
- Trapped by a lack of quality opportunities to work
- Trapped in mundane jobs
- Trapped in expensive lifestyles
- Trapped by the fear of losing what we have
- Trapped by "keeping up with the Joneses"
- Trapped by fixed beliefs
- Trapped by addictions
- Trapped in relationships

- Trapped by "having to" rather than "choosing to"
- Trapped in lives that are comfortable and safe but are far from actually "living"

Please note: I am not comparing the plight of someone with nothing to someone who seemingly has everything here. I'm merely pointing out that we should not just assume that economic freedom is all about reducing poverty.

We are trapped by many things both within our individual control but also under the control of society, our cultures and the economy. This is why, to achieve economic freedom, we need activity at individual, organisational, and national levels.

What can we do as individuals to help achieve economic freedom? Well we can use the CANBE Model to change the way we think, feel, and act. Do we really need another pair of the latest shoes? Should we really drink another glass of wine? Could I work for myself and turn my passions into my own business rather than relying on others for work? Unfortunately, many of us have been educated and brought up in ways and circumstances that might make these changes more difficult, which is why it is so important we revolutionise the way we both teach and parent as quickly as possible. More on this in the next chapter.

One big problem holding us back is fear and confusion amongst the general population, in developed nations at least, about what the future holds. This, in some regards, is why we are not changing quickly enough. It is interesting that the World Happiness Report 2020[2] found that the "UN SDG 12 (Responsible Consumption and Production) and SDG 13 (Climate Action) have, in fact, strong negative correlations with self-reported measures of human wellbeing." I believe this represents the fear people feel that changing consumption patterns and taking action to reduce climate change will negatively impact the quality of their lives.

We need to dispel this fear and paint a picture of a brighter future. When we look at this in the context of the key problems discussed at the beginning of the book, what might that look like? Freedom from want, freedom from boredom, freedom from the 'rat race'. In essence a progressive economy is one where it works for us, rather than us working for it.

What we should progress towards is greater economic freedom. The opportunities for growth lie in this area. Some people argue that we should focus on de-growth, consuming less. If everything remained the same, then I think this argument would hold true.

However, everything isn't staying the same. We are ingenious. It's less about whether we are doing anything to change (we are), and more about whether we are changing quickly enough (we're not).

Of course, many of the traps we fall into as individuals are also reflected in our organisations. Too much debt, jobs that are mundane, expenses that have run away with themselves, fixed beliefs that our organisations should focus on profit and growth above all else, fear of losing market share or keeping up with competitors, focus on products and services that we're not really good at, serving customers that we should really let go, dealing with unreliable suppliers, feeling like we 'have to' rather than 'choosing to' and forgetting why we're really in business in the first place.

All of these traps turn our organisations into institutions more like prisons rather than places where we really want to be. As leaders we can choose to free ourselves and our teams from these shackles. When we do this our organisations will begin to contribute to economic freedom and we will be freer.

Let's take a look at some of the other solutions we can take at organisational and national levels.

CLEVER, TARGETED, WELLBEING-FOCUSED GROWTH

Arguments abound about whether we can achieve abundance in a post-scarcity world or whether we should focus on de-growth. These arguments, whether from climate activists or capitalist champions, tend to be very 'blinkered' and narrow in focus. Climate activists may argue we should stop flying, for example, without considering the mental, emotional, social, cultural and economic benefits that flying provides. If we all stopped flying whole areas would be decimated due to lack of tourism.

Hard line capitalists, on the other hand, espouse economic benefits with little concern for the environment. Currently only about 1 billion of our 7 billion world population fly regularly. Expanding the market, whilst continuing to use the current fossil based fuels, would be foolish at best and catastrophic at worst, due to the effect of carbon emissions on the climate. Unfortunately this is what we are doing at the moment.

However, if we can quickly solve the problem by designing improved fuels, the opportunities for growth and improved wellbeing are tremendous. In the meantime, we should be much more demanding about reducing emissions in this industry, whilst ensuring companies are supported and sustained until such time as the new fuels are found.

The reality is that economic growth does provide the wealth and technologies needed to lift people from poverty. However it is also a reality that unfettered, unsophisticated growth will continue to add to the many problems already covered.

At the moment our view of growth is a little like the scattergun approach. All growth is good. But not all growth is good! Cancer is definitely not good growth; the excessive sprouting limbs on plants are trimmed by the prudent horticulturist in order for the plant to thrive and direct its energies most efficiently. We need to be smarter and more sophisticated in where and how we choose to grow.

One way we can do this is to review business practice and opportunities against the CANBE Wellbeing Model as I previously demonstrated in the section on 'Impact'.

Any new or existing organisation should be challenged to provide an assessment of their overall net contribution to wellbeing using this format. Assessments should be independently reviewed and actions for improvement implemented. In certain circumstances, activities should be ceased or declined. Growth opportunities should be focused on those areas deemed to provide the greatest positive impact on wellbeing. So where are some of these growth areas:

- Automation and Artificial Intelligence
- Technology development to support wellbeing
- Repairing, upcycling, and recycling
- Climate change mitigation
- Environmental management, protection and renewal
- Sustainable agriculture
- Transport, infrastructure, architecture, planning and building for wellbeing
- Creative industries
- Education for lifelong learning and retraining
- Renewable energy
- Experience based leisure and entertainment
- Sustainable tourism
- Flying (if we can develop environmentally friendly fuels)
- Holistic health, focused on prevention (sleep, diet, exercise, relaxation)
- Caring for others
- Coaching and talking therapies
- Protecting culture and promoting diversity
- Local governance
- Local produce and services
- Organisational auditing and compliance to ensure delivery of net wellbeing

Even this incomplete list demonstrates that there are plentiful opportunities for growth and creating opportunities for people to contribute in ways that will be beneficial for our collective wellbeing.

If you think about your own industry and experience where can you see opportunities for growth?

A NEW MODEL OF BUSINESS

What is good business? As I've already mentioned there are numerous different models and organisations with a view on what this should look like, and in my mind, what binds them all together is an aspiration for greater wellbeing. An economy that serves the needs of people in balance with our planet requires a new archetype of enterprise.

Therefore I propose a new all-encompassing model of business: The 'Wellbeing Business'. Organisations will demonstrate a commitment to delivering a net positive benefit across all eight domains of wellbeing for the individuals they employ, suppliers, customers, investors, communities, nations and the planet on which we all rely for our resources. And no, I'm not going to set up yet another certification scheme to monetise this! All businesses should be wellbeing businesses. This book and the CANBE Model provide the framework to work towards this, but each organisation will have their own specific challenges.

They may be circular, social, conscious, Benefit Corps, state owned, privately owned, for profit, not for profit, limited, partnerships, sole trader, employee owned or any other model. What will join them together is an unwavering focus on improving wellbeing. I'll provide a blueprint for what these organisations might look like in the next chapter, 'Vision of the Future.

VALUING CONTRIBUTION RATHER THAN WORK

We should value people for who they are and what they contribute rather than what they own, their job role or where they work. Millions of people do selfless practical things each day to help and benefit others with limited or no financial reward. Being a good friend or neighbour, volunteering, parenting and caring are just a few examples. However if we free people up we might be surprised with the creativity and entrepreneurship this leads to. Many people have created small businesses from their hobbies and passions. If we value contribution rather than work perhaps many more will follow?

I've tried to provide solutions throughout this book, but in this case I'm not sure what the answer is here. However, I do believe that from a wellbeing perspective it builds on core principles of giving people more autonomy, flexibility, using their core skills and strengths, intrinsic motivation, and more, so I'm sure this would be a positive step forwards.

Perhaps this could work through a combination of the following factors:

- A Guaranteed Minimum Income to enable people to do more of what they love
- A crypto-currency that enables each of us to reward people that we believe are contributing to the wellbeing of others
- Flexible, modular working where jobs are shared, people work fewer days, remote working is encouraged
- Automation and AI that increase productivity, removes mundane tasks and frees people up to contribute in ways that are more representative of who they are

This brings us neatly to the next point.

AUTOMATION AND ARTIFICIAL INTELLIGENCE (AI)

The jury is out about whether AI will take away or create more jobs. But this is ridiculous. Surveys and articles are treating this as if there is some undeniable force controlling whether or not we create new jobs or allow many of them to become redundant. What they all seem to be forgetting is, it is OUR decision. AI won't create jobs, we will. Automation won't take jobs away, we will.

AI and automation are enablers, we are the masters. It is up to us to decide how we want AI and automation to work for us. If we decide to let the free market forces make our choices for us then who knows. Perhaps we will lose jobs, perhaps we won't. However if we take the reins and decide for ourselves we can make this work however we want to.

Artificial intelligence and robots will perform tasks that are either too mundane, repetitive or complex for us and we will focus on what we love to do. We will work less and create more. At present many organisations are using AI and automation to reduce costs, particularly in manufacturing. We need to accelerate our pace of change and move from cost reduction to value creation. We must embrace change and not feel threatened by it. Educating people to be more resilient and flexible in their thinking will help.

We would all like to work less wouldn't we? We'd all like to be freer. That doesn't mean we don't want to contribute. It means we have more choice about what and when we do things. It means we do more things we actually enjoy and excel at.

Perhaps, if we approach this with a constructive mindset that's exactly what we can achieve. What if we accelerate AI and automation and get them to do even more of the things we don't want to do? What if we split more jobs and share them between people? What if we create new jobs that people would like to do?

Who would like to become an Environmental Protectionist? Who would like to be paid for looking after elderly relatives at home rather than paying others to look after your nearest and dearest? Who'd like to become a robotic engineer?

Who would like this technology to help us achieve an age of well-being where everyone in the world can thrive?

CHAPTER SUMMARY

As we've seen, our economies have helped to improve the lives of many across the globe. However, I'd argue that for many our economies are, at best, enabling us to survive. Many, many more are suffering.

The question then, is how can we organise our economies so that they help us thrive mentally, emotionally, physically, spiritually, socially, culturally, environmentally and financially.

In its Global Economic Outlook Report of June 2020, Laurence Boone, the OECD's chief economist says, "Governments must seize this opportunity to engineer a fairer and more sustainable economy, making competition and regulation smarter, modernising government taxes, spending, and social protection. Prosperity comes from dialogue and cooperation. This holds true at the national and global level."[3]

This will be an economy where all our **needs** are met, both basic and higher level. It will be characterised by a clear understanding of **impact** on net contribution to wellbeing at individual, team, organisational, community, national and planetary levels. We can achieve this by using the CANBE Model as a framework to measure wellbeing and thinking more systematically about the impact of our actions across the eight domains.

Our contributions will become more **meaningful** as they will be based on our unique strengths and capabilities. We will do more of what we love, and with greater engagement, creativity, and imagination, will be inspired as individuals and as a human race to **achieve our full potential**.

Through wellbeing education focused on building people's capabilities, improved welfare and modern, progressive taxation and regulation, a wellbeing economy will be **fairer** to all and managed with **integrity** both in terms of ethics and **resilience**.

This will help build our economies around **stronger relation-**

ships within people and between nations where trade is based on mutual gain.

Finally I put forward a vision for a wellbeing economy as one which enriches our lives. By that I mean we will be freer.

- Free from distress
- Free from fear
- Free from weariness
- Free to be ourselves
- Free from isolation
- Free from conflict
- Free from environmental destruction
- Free from wants and destitution

Coronavirus has given us all a chance to re-evaluate our lives and consider the challenges we face as a human race. Now is the time to #buildbackbetter. This is the subject of the final Chapter. Before we move onto this here's a chance to reflect on this chapter.

KEY CONCEPTS TO IMPROVE OUR ECONOMIC WELLBEING:

Meeting our 'Needs'

- How well are our needs being met across the 8 domains of wellbeing?
- How well are we meeting the needs of others in a similar fashion?

Improving our 'Impact'

- When we measure our individual, collective and national impact using the 8 domains of wellbeing is it net positive? Where can we improve?

Improving 'Fairness'

- How well are we applying the principles of needs and merits?
- How well are we ensuring responsibilities, rewards, benefits and costs are distributed fairly and that processes used to do this are impartial, transparent, open and inclusive
- Are we challenging unfair practice and corruption wherever we see it?

Improving 'Integrity'

- Use the CANBE Wellbeing Model to inform your decision making and then communicate about it
- Manage resources prudently
- Produce and consume more responsibly
- Review and re-balance our purchase of global and local products and services
- Embrace automation and AI
- Save and invest in each of the eight domains of wellbeing
- Plan for an increasing number of risks
- Be more thrifty

Greater 'Freedom'

- Help those less fortunate than ourselves
- Reduce poverty and debt
- Reduce unnecessary expenses
- Lose our attachment to stuff
- Stop comparing ourselves to others
- Examine our beliefs about the relationship between money, wealth, the economy and wellbeing
- Stop consuming the things that aren't good for us

- Let go of poor relationships
- Choose to do; don't have to do
- Step outside our comfort zones
- Value contributions of others to wellbeing

KEY BEHAVIOURS:

Where do you score individually, as a team, organisation or nation on the following attributes that help develop greater Economic Wellbeing?

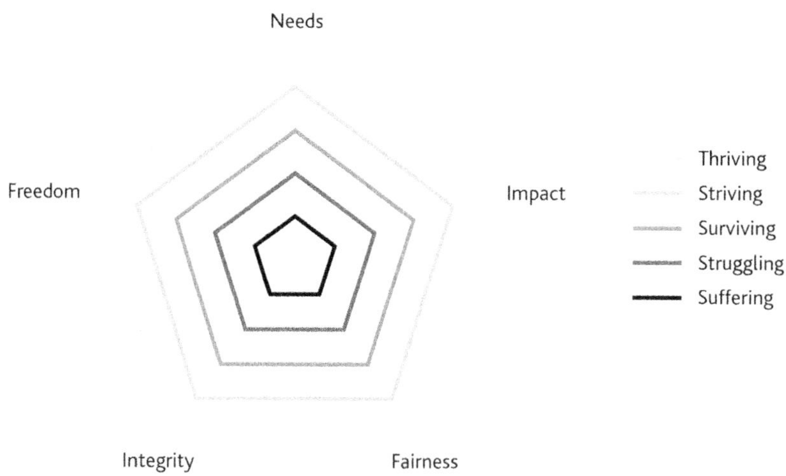

What would you like to do differently?

CHAPTER THIRTEEN

A VISION OF THE FUTURE - #BUILDBACKBETTER

	Wellbeing Domains - 'Territories' - Interconnected areas of our lives							
	Mental Our thoughts	Emotional Our emotions	Physical Our actions	Spiritual Our spirit	Social Our communities	Cultural Our way	Environmental Our spaces	Economic Our trade
Thriving	Creative	Composed	Vital	Fulfilled	Engaged	Harmonious	Flourishing	Prosperous

'A **world where we can all thrive.'**

We are now at a critical point. We have the opportunity to form a unified and inclusive global society. A society that works symbiotically with technology and the planet as a whole. The journey to this future will be uncertain. It will take a leap of faith and courage to get there. To help people navigate this uncertainty, take a leap and move forward with courage, we need a positive vision of the future.

I believe **'a world where we can all thrive'** is that vision.

In order to help us get there and build on the 17 UN Sustainable Development Goals I put forward eight wellbeing goals (one for each of the eight domains):

1. **We are creative and imaginative**
2. **We feel at ease with ourselves and each other**
3. **We are physically vital**
4. **We are spiritually fulfilled**
5. **We are socially engaged**
6. **We are living in cultural harmony**
7. **We are living in flourishing environments**
8. **We are economically prosperous**

I hope you can see that the goals and measures I've already outlined in this book aren't contradictory to the UN SDGs. In fact, they are complementary. But these goals take us past surviving towards thriving. These goals can work at an individual (I feel at home here), workplace (increased trust, increased diversity) community (reduced isolation) or even national level (Gross National Wellbeing).

What this book provides is intuitive, experience based and scientifically backed ideas for how we can progress towards these goals. To achieve this vision we will require action at many different levels. Leaders must learn to think systematically about all eight domains of wellbeing.

What follows is an exploration of how leaders can make changes at all of these different levels using the CANBE Model as a guide. I've used diagrams to explain the journey from our old/current story to a new one. There is much great work already underway, in many areas, to take us closer towards this new story. As leaders, we will be at different stages on this journey, and we may even be travelling closer to the new story than the old. If that is the case I congratulate you. If not I urge you to consider how you might change.

WELLBEING-FOCUSED PEOPLE

Individuals story

Old/current story		New story
Success measured by wealth, celebrity, fame	➡	Success measured by wellbeing
Too many stressed, anxious & burnt out people	➡	More relaxed, composed and engaged
Too many obese or starving people	➡	Healthy nutritious diets for all
Too many unhealthy people	➡	More healthy
Too many spiritually unfulfilled	➡	More spiritually fulfilled
Too many isolated people	➡	More connected
Cultural bias either to rights or responsibilities	➡	Rights & responsibilities
Individual or Collective Me,me,me or We,we,we	➡	Interdependent Me,we,world
Environmentally passive	➡	Environmentally proactive
Work/Job | Career | Income	➡	Contribution | Projects/Portfolio/Journey | Value
Train for career	➡	Lifelong learners

"Be the change you expect to see in the world"

GANDHI

COVID-19 has taken many lives and is one of the largest international tragedies in many of our lifetimes. Many people have died, leaving devastated families behind them.

However, times of tragedy can also help us grow and come back stronger. This pandemic has forced us to recognise our 'key workers' and celebrate 'local heroes'. I say forced because I don't believe the majority of us praised or celebrated this group the way we are now before the virus struck. If you did I apologise. Amongst this group are:

- Health and care workers including frontline staff, volunteers and those who from part of the supply chain
- Education and childcare including teachers, support staff, and social workers
- Key public services including justice, religion, charities delivering frontline services undertakers, journalists and broadcasters
- Local and national government staff responsible for the COVID-19 response or for essential public services
- Food and essential goods like medicines including production, distribution and sales
- Public safety and national security including the armed forces, police, fire, prison and border security
- Transport staff who keep the road, rail, air and water services going
- Utilities such as oil, gas, electric, water and waste disposal
- Communication services such as broadband, telecommunications and the postal service including field workers, call centres and data infrastructure
- Essential financial services such as banks, building societies and financial infrastructure

In the UK, at least, it is the frontline health workers who have taken the 'lion's share' of praise from the public. Whilst I have supported, donated to, and applauded them myself, it is, I believe, another demonstration of how we seem to get 'fixated' on one group. If you like, the frontline health staff have become our 'celebrities' of the moment. And yet, what you realise, when you review the full list, is that we all need each other. We are all interdependent. Let me take this moment to praise all of the other people on this list, not only in the UK but across the world. Thank you.

There are also many omissions from this group. No musicians, footballers, artists, writers, CEOs, entrepreneurs, influencers, famous people, people on the rich list. Quite often, these are the people we become 'fixated' with. We see these people as successful and reserve our praise and adoration for them.

Of course we need these people too. That's the point. We all need each other. We need people to help us think, feel, act, connect, grow, love, build, tell us stories and enrich our lives. But perhaps now is the time to re-evaluate our perception of the worth of one group over and above another. Perhaps it is time things got fairer.

As we move through the stages of COVID-19 the common rhetoric I hear is "things should never go back to normal" or "what will be the new normal?" I put it to you that the new normal should be a focus on wellbeing as success, and not a return to the fixation with wealth, celebrity, fame, and influence.

COVID-19 is also challenging many of our habits and beliefs. I've talked to many neighbours and friends who are enjoying home-working, the extra time they have with close family, the slower pace of life and getting back to nature. I've seen more people on 'my heath-land' walking than ever. Don't they know that this is my nature reserve?

Joking aside, I believe what we are finding during COVID-19 is the importance of wellbeing. Whether it be mental, emotional, physical, spiritual, social, cultural, environmental or economic, all conversations I've heard can be categorised into one of these domains.

So going forward my answer to the question "What is the new normal?" is quite simple. The new normal is a focus on wellbeing.

- Reducing the number of burnt out stressed people in the workplace. Being more creative
- Ensuring people have nutritious healthy diets
- Improving fitness levels
- Helping people to understand and be themselves
- Ensuring people can be connected
- Recognising that we all have rights as well as responsibilities
- Recognising our reliance on each other and the planet
- Recognising that work is a means to an end not the end itself. Being more flexible to ensure works fits in with life
- Continuous learning throughout life

As individuals we are all doing our best in the context of our own personal beliefs, values, culture and systems that surround us. The problem is we need to change. If collectively we keep doing what we are doing, then in essence, we are sleep-walking over the edge of a cliff with our children, grandchildren, and near ancestors tied to us.

So my call is for us all to up our game. What more can we do? This book has provided the framework and practical tools to help us change. By identifying where we are doing well and where we could do better, we should now know how to improve both personal and collective wellbeing. The question is where will we now lead ourselves and others?

Of course individuals cannot change everything themselves. One of the key areas to start this change is through our education. We need our educational establishments to develop citizens who think, feel and act in improved ways so that we can all thrive going forward.

WELLBEING-FOCUSED EDUCATION

> "Education is the most powerful weapon which you can use to change the world."
>
> NELSON MANDELA

> "Every person of learning is finally his own teacher."
>
> THOMAS PAINE

When I refer to education, this includes all forms from infant through to adult, and as such, all institutions from universities to schools to adult learning facilities. In fact, universities are recognised by English School historian, Ivor S. Goodson, as particularly important to the change process as they are responsible for determining the content that influences activities lower down the educational chain.

This section is indebted to the fantastic book 'Sustainability, Human Well-Being and the Future of Education' edited by Justin W. Cook from Sitra, The Finnish Innovation Fund, Helsinki, Finland. Finnish education has been recognised around the world for its innovative and pioneering approach, putting wellbeing and sustainability at the centre of its thinking. Contributors to the book are educational experts from across the world, in particular, Finland and the USA.

What is encouraging, to me at least, is that the recommendations put forward are very consistent with the drive and focus of *The Age of Wellbeing*.

The main points I believe the book makes are as follows:

1. Current education is based on the historic needs of the industrial age and must change to keep up with the new challenges and opportunities of our modern age
2. Education can play an extremely important role in helping us change the future of society
3. To do this it will need a renewed purpose, best represented by expanding the capabilities of learners to lead lives that both contribute to and benefit from sustainable wellbeing
4. Transformative change, as opposed to just doing things better, or doing better things, will be difficult and require systemic support from individuals, communities, organisations and governments

In describing the transformative change required, the book tells a story of what education is now and what it should become. I've summarised this in the diagram below:

Education story

Old/current story	New story
Conveyor belt providing workers for industry based on knowledge	A 'think tank' producing change makers for a better society based on knowledge, character and skills
Places of learning	Learning organisations networking learners, communities, businesses and others
Learner goes to a physical space	Learning is available in virtual and physical spaces
Teacher as authority figure imparting knowledge	Teacher as facilitator learning with student
Silo, subject based learning 'Taught'	Real world problem and opportunity based projects 'Experienced/embodied'
One size fits all learning	Personalised learning tailored to each individual
Learners polarised and segmented based on age, level and achievements	Diverse, integrated learners
Knowledge based on 'rational' and 'external' Authority and reason. 'Head'	'Rational', 'emotional', 'external' and 'internal' knowledge. Authority, reason, experience and intuition. 'Head, heart, gut'
Learners with fixed mindsets and skills	Resilient learners. Transferable skills and growth mindsets
Standardised tests and assessments	Personal growth and ongoing performance dialogue. Short courses

As I see it, this new story supports wellbeing in the following ways: firstly it will be better for the wellbeing of the learner. More personalised, diverse, tailored learning delivered through a multitude of media will be more engaging and motivating. A focus on the growth mindset of the learner will help to build resilience and adaptability, exactly the traits required in our modern ambiguous world. Less testing and more ongoing performance dialogue will also give learners more space to make mistakes, reflect, and grow. I believe this will also have a positive impact on the levels of stress, depression, and anxiety experienced by many.

It follows that this new approach will also be better for the wellbeing of teachers. Less focus on targets, greater variety of project based learning, diverse groups of students and more personal development will free teachers up and raise their profile once again to become "pillars of the community."

Of course this will also be beneficial for the wellbeing of society. "Learning organisations" can provide resources to more than just our youth. Greater ties with business, communities, and other organisations will bring people closer together with learning focused on benefiting all parties.

Where do I see the CANBE Model fitting with this?

		Wellbeing Domains - 'Territories' - Interconnected areas of our lives							
		Mental Our thoughts	Emotional Our emotions	Physical Our actions	Spiritual Our spirit	Social Our communities	Cultural Our way	Environmental Our spaces	Economic Our trade
Wellbeing States 'Indicators' States of wellbeing we move through	Thriving	Creative	Composed	Vital	Fulfilled	Engaged	Harmonious	Flourishing	Prosperous
	Striving	⬆	⬆	⬆	⬆	⬆	⬆	⬆	⬆
	Surviving	Alert	Impulsive	Weary	Satisfied	Connected	Tolerant	Desolate	Poor
	Struggling	⬆	⬆	⬆	⬆	⬆	⬆	⬆	⬆
	Suffering	Distressed	Disturbed	Drained	Unfulfilled	Isolated	Conflicted	Degrading	Destitute
		⬆	⬆	⬆	⬆	⬆	⬆	⬆	⬆
Wellbeing Dimensions 'Highways' Intertwined routes we use to navigate our lives	Creating meaning	Thinking	Feelings	Behaviour	Identity	Friendship	Way of life	Affinity	Needs
	Achieving potential	Focus	Control	Mastery	Motivation	Teamwork	Governance	Cultivation	Impact
	Nurturing relationships	Regard	Empathy	Interaction	Stories	Trust	Belonging	Cohesion	Fairness
	Building resilience	Flexibility	Agility	Health	Growth	Support	Diversity	Adaptation	Integrity
	Enriching lives	Imagination	Wisdom	Energy	Purpose	Empowerment	Integration	Renewal	Freedom
		Wellbeing Factors - 'Signposts' - Interconnected things that can help us improve wellbeing							

Well, I believe the CANBE Model is a great framework to add to these expert opinions in the following ways:

1) It can act as a framework for considering the 'real world problem and opportunity based projects'. These problems and opportunities will come from the domains of wellbeing. Here are just a few broad examples but learners will obviously determine these based on their own needs and they will be much more tailored, age appropriate and specific to their circumstances.

- Mental - how do we reduce levels of stress and anxiety in our community? How can we increase levels of creativity?

- Emotional - how can we increase empathy between particular groups?
- Physical - how can we develop better eating habits? How can we make exercise available for all?
- Spiritual - what is the story of me/my organisation/my community? What is it to have purpose?
- Social - what is a friend? What makes a good team? How can we increase trust?
- Cultural - how can we manage diversity better?
- Environmental - what can we do to reduce climate change?
- Economic - how can we share resources fairly?

2) The model provides a framework for the growth and development of learners. Discovering, practicing and embodying skills and habits that contribute to wellbeing should be the new focus of education. A survey released in February 2020 by the Youth Sport Trust Charity[1] revealed a strong appetite amongst parents, with children aged 18 or under, for schools to focus on the wellbeing of pupils as a priority over academic attainment. For example, whatever the project or subject being studied learners will benefit from better thinking, focus, regard, flexibility, and imagination. We would also want our learners to be emotionally composed, physically vital, spiritually fulfilled, socially connected, culturally harmonious, living in flourishing environments and economically prosperous, wouldn't we?

I urge leaders in education, business, government or in any area responsible for educating others to consider the following.

To counter growing stress and anxiety we need to build better and more flexible thinking, self-regard and resilience into the curriculum. We need to get our learners imagining a better future and creating ideas for getting there. However, evidence suggests that rather than schools developing students with good mental health the emphasis on exams and academic attainment is having a detrimental effect.

In line with technological developments, we need to focus more on human competencies in communication, creativity, empathy, and social skills including things like negotiation, persuasion, kindness, caring and compassion for each other.

To prevent growing obesity, and mental health issues already mentioned, we need to raise the importance of exercise, diet, sleep and relaxation. However, it appears the opposite is true. Statistics from the government's annual school workforce census show that, in English state-funded secondary schools, 51,600 hours of physical education provision were lost from timetables between 2010 and 2017.

Spiritually we need to support people in identifying their strengths, personality, character and what makes them, them. We need to get more square pegs into square holes and round pegs into round holes. Cultural diversity, experience in nature and the environment, as well as greater financial and economic awareness, should also play a bigger part in what we are teaching.

It seems there are clear reasons for changing and that we will also need to implement these changes with pace.

Whilst this picture remains a little hazy what does appear to be clearer is the view that jobs will change dramatically. There is little doubt that repetitive, routine, rules-based jobs will come under increasing threat. Even some jobs involving human interaction are at risk with AI advances in the processing of natural language. Tom Hulme, General Partner at Google's venture capital arm, has been quoted as saying "Sixty-five per cent of children entering primary school today will ultimately end up working in completely new job types that don't yet exist."

So we have both a need and urgency for change, but we cannot put too high expectations on education without simultaneous change in ourselves, our communities, our businesses, and our governments. Change must happen at all levels. Outside of what I have discussed elsewhere in this book, parenting is one solid example of where education will need to be supported. Perhaps there should be a more formal process for supporting parents?

Supporting this point, one of the key lessons from the book *Sustainability, Human Well-Being and the Future of Education* is that education cannot be expected to deliver the change required all on its own. It will require the systemic support of parents, businesses, communities, and governments.

WELLBEING-FOCUSED BUSINESS AND ORGANISATIONS

Business story

Old/current story		New story
Profit maximising	➡	New models balancing people, purpose, profit and planet
Focused on building wealth	➡	Focused on building wellbeing
Change management- Doing things better, or better things	➡	Networked continuous learning organisations Transformation - imagining new solutions
Draining and controlling	➡	Energising and trusting
Human labour and intellect Automation based cost reduction	➡	Human, machine and AI collaboration Knowledge, data and technology driven to deliver value
Employees	➡	Employees working with gig economy, freelancers project/task based work
Uniform, hierarchical, siloed and rigid to maintain power at centre	➡	Diverse, flatter, integrated and agile to distribute greater autonomy
Employee fits to work - 40 hr working week in workplace	➡	Work fits to employee - flexible hours and locations
Investment in people seen as a liability	➡	Investment in people seen as an asset
Unfair distribution of wealth	➡	Fairer distribution of wealth

The future of good business is to build greater wellbeing. As we've already explored, there is no doubt that good businesses play an important role in building the wellbeing of individuals, communities, and nations. This means rather than focusing on profit-maximising and creating wealth, businesses will increasingly focus on profit-making or cash flow – and creating wellbeing. The CANBE Model facilitates this and is consistent with all other models being put forward. It is for the benefit of all, purpose led, sustainably focused, socially and community-oriented, conscious, circular, supportive of profit and not-for-profit, aligned with the UN SDGs and different political approaches to achieving the goal of wellbeing.

To do this, organisations will need to transform. We will move from incremental improvement to a totally new way of working. This will involve businesses reaching out more to engage with educational institutions and the community to research and co-create better solutions that deliver benefits across the eight domains of wellbeing.

In fact, if businesses do not deliver a net positive benefit to wellbeing, we will question whether they should operate at all or ensure they put in place measures to quickly turn things around.

Linked to changes in education, we will shift mindsets of future workers from solving problems to become both problem and opportunity focused, using greater imagination and creativity. A great example of the change required is our current focus on mental health. Most interventions and support are targeted at stress, anxiety, depression; what I'll describe as the "problem end" of the spectrum. There is much less emphasis being put on creativity and imagination, the "opportunity" end of the spectrum. It is ironic that the current approach we are taking to mental health is clouded by negativity bias! Future mental health initiatives will cater much better for the full spectrum, both problems and opportunities.

Organisations of the future will be more trusting of employees and other categories of workers. Current habitual processes such as inflexible working, the 40 hour working week, and office-based work will be challenged and replaced. In fact, all obstacles to autonomy, competence, and relatedness, which we discussed earlier in the book, will be removed.

Rather than feeling drained and controlled, workers will feel energised and trusted. Even as I write this, I am aware of people being asked to return to the workplace as lockdown restrictions are relaxed, when they have proved the success of working from home. As we move 'back to normal' it is a great time for businesses to challenge existing processes and give employees greater respect and trust.

This will be enhanced by the accelerated introduction and embracement of AI and automation to reduce the requirement for people to perform mundane and repetitive tasks. AI and automation will move from a focus on cost reduction to value creation in line with the mindset change from problem to opportunity focus. Managed wisely, this technological transformation will lead to a new age of good work and improved quality of life. However, if managed poorly, there will be a greater risk of widening divisions in skills, wealth, and wellbeing.

There will be fewer employees and a greater mix of freelance, temporary, and contract staff bringing unique skill sets as and when required. This will, in turn, enhance the flexible sharing of work across a broader spectrum of people. In essence, work will begin to fit with the worker. Organisations will become flatter, more agile, and will empower workers.

Work will become more 'spiritual' in several ways. Firstly, there will be clearer links between the purpose of an organisation and its contribution to wellbeing. This increased visibility and understanding will provide workers with greater belief, pride, motivation, and engagement. Secondly, workers, through improved wellbeing-focused education, will be more self-aware of their personality, character, strengths, and weaknesses. As a result we will have more workers doing jobs that they are actually suited to and passionate about. Third, employers will be more focused on the growth of workers as people, not just for technical skills.

The workplace of the future will also be more egalitarian. People will better understand that large discrepancies in relative pay lead to resentment and under performance. Work will become more 'we' rather than 'me' with a much greater emphasis on teamwork and collaboration rather than star performers and competition. If

COVID-19 has taught us nothing else, every role is important and should be valued. Star sports people, entertainers, and celebrities earning hundreds of thousands each week seems very misplaced and unfair in relation to the low wages of the many 'key workers' who kept our countries going in one of our most difficult times. This greater understanding of our interdependence will lead to 'fairer' levels of pay for all with more worker ownership. Wealth will begin to be re-distributed with the workplace playing a key role.

The contribution of people to wellbeing, outside of the usual workplace, will receive increasing recognition both from an understanding and financial perspective. Parenting will be elevated in importance with greater time off, plus financial and educational support to ensure that efforts leverage the changes to education.

WELLBEING-FOCUSED COMMUNITIES

Communities can be described in many different ways including geographically/territorially, virtually, by interest, or by values. Here I refer to the geographic/territorial description and include small rural communities (villages) as well as towns and cities.

Communities are more than the sum of their parts. Aggregating individual wellbeing scores will tell you about the overall wellbeing of members of the community but it won't capture the community 'spirit'. Wellbeing grows from the relations between individuals and the places where they live, work and play.

Increasing urbanisation is pulling people away from rural areas towards the major conurbations. This has both pros and cons. On the plus side, major conurbations can be more effective and efficient at providing work, utilities, and resources for their populations than the spread out networks required for rural dwellings.

However, as we've seen from COVID-19 and continuing conflict across the world, large densities of population can be much more susceptible to epidemics and other catastrophes. Resilient planning will hopefully see a diverse range of both rural and urban dwelling places going forward.

If interest in individual and national wellbeing are gaining traction, then community wellbeing can be described as the 'poor cousin'. In the UK, the Centre For Thriving Places[1] is beginning to fill the gap but even so research into the topic is still very much in its infancy.

As such, I've based the table below on personal experience of having helped lead my own community response to improving wellbeing (albeit we didn't call it that at the time), and generalisations from news about what is happening to some communities in the UK. Of course, your own community may be totally different to this and there will be large discrepancies between communities that may have been ravaged economically and those that are prospering. However, I believe many of these generalisations hold true.

Community story

Old/current story		New story
Increasing mental health issues	➡	Increasing creativity and imagination
Lacking real focus or built on economy	➡	Focused on building wellbeing
Reduced focus on physical fitness	➡	Increased focus on physical fitness
Lacking real identity and spirit	➡	Strong identity and spirit
Increasing isolation	➡	Increasing connectedness
Segmented groups and areas	➡	Integrated groups and areas encouraging greater cultural diversity
Threats to environment and community assets	➡	Protection and cultivation of community environment and assets
Fragile local economies impacted by urbanisation, AI, population changes, environmental degradation	➡	Resilient local economies
Unfair access to resources	➡	Fairer access to resources

The main way I believe communities of the future will change is by focusing on wellbeing. The CANBE Model provides a framework to enable communities to thrive. Below I've taken measures used by The Centre for Thriving Places and mapped these against the CANBE Model. I've also added in a few additional measures as an example of the types of things communities of the future will focus on.

		Wellbeing Domains - 'Territories' - Interconnected areas of our lives							
		Mental Our thoughts	Emotional Our emotions	Physical Our actions	Spiritual Our spirit	Social Our communities	Cultural Our way	Environmental Our spaces	Economic Our trade
Wellbeing States	Thriving	Creative	Composed	Vital	Fulfilled	Engaged	Harmonious	Flourishing	Prosperous
	Striving	↑	↑	↑	↑	↑	↑	↑	↑
'Indicators'	Surviving	Alert	Impulsive	Weary	Satisfied	Connected	Tolerant	Desolate	Poor
States of wellbeing we move through	Struggling	↑	↑	↑	↑	↑	↑	↑	↑
	Suffering	Distressed	Disturbed	Drained	Unfulfilled	Isolated	Conflicted	Degrading	Destitute

Example Community Wellbeing Measures							
Education IQ	Education IQ	Fitness	Identity	Trust	Governance	Safety	Quantity of work
Mental Health	Empathy	Mortality	Religon	Connection	Diversity	Housing	Income
		Life expectancy		Isolation	Way of life	Transport	Unemploy-ment
		Illness and disability		Participation		Green space	Local business
		Comms				Sustainability	Resources

Reflecting the overall population, mental health is an area which will receive increasing attention going forward. Communities will support the full spectrum, from helping those with stress and anxiety to developing more creativity and imagination. As greater pressure is exerted on rural communities from urbanisation and loss of industry, this creativity and imagination will become increasingly important for finding new ways forward.

Linking back to the required changes in education; the increased focus on emotional intelligence in schools and the workplace will help to facilitate a calmer community where people listen to each other's views with greater empathy and respect. People will communicate more effectively and communities will benefit from greater collective wisdom to address local issues and solve problems together.

Spaces will be designed with behavioural science to encourage greater lifestyle fitness and physical activity including relaxation, improved diet and exercise. People will feel more at ease.

Unfortunately many communities have lost their sense of identity due to factors such as loss of industry, people being forced to move frequently, and second home owners with no sense of commitment to the area. Future communities will build new stories based on heritage, shared values, beliefs and a renewed sense of purpose. Faith will become more encompassing, binding people together rather than driving them apart.

Investment in spaces and activities where people can connect will be enhanced by technology, helping them understand the sorts of people they might like to connect with. Communities will have a greater variety of both virtual and physical spaces in which to connect and provide more opportunities to give and receive support.

There will be closer connections between schools, communities, businesses and other organisations. For example, a key requirement for communities to operate successfully is spaces where people can meet, debate issues, learn from each other and take action. By becoming centres of learning for the whole community schools can provide these spaces as well as more opportunities for adult education and upskilling the population.

By making use of a full range of technologies, combined with face to face interaction, communities will become more inclusive and participative. Diversity will be welcomed and celebrated. Schools and businesses will play an even greater role in facilitating this through improved education and policies. AI and technology will be used to anticipate and plan for population changes so that each community is adequately resourced and prepared. This technology will also bring greater transparency, accountability, and participation in governance at local, regional, and national levels, helping to increase trust.

Communities will become more environmentally aware and active. From protecting community assets such as parks, open spaces, waterways and facilities to ensuring that waste and pollution are minimised, communities will be more aesthetically pleasing and healthier places to live. Transport will be cleaner and more accessible to all. Walking, cycling and electric vehicles will help to reduce noise and CO_2 emissions with the added benefit of encouraging greater physical activity.

Housing and shelter will be diverse, imaginative, and well designed, catering for the full range of needs of community members. From tree houses, to glamping, to converted container units, affordable single apartment complexes for young people through to rented and privately owned housing. As populations increase we will consider floating dwellings to make use of the vast untapped water area on earth. This flexible range of solutions will stimulate a fantastic mix of permanent and temporary residents ensuring a balance between stability, belonging and the influx of new ideas. People will have choices about where they live and feel safe, secure and invigorated all at the same time. Dwindling high streets, libraries, public houses and other establishments will be repurposed as housing, places where people can meet and/or enterprises.

Communities will benefit, in the future, from an enhanced social security system. There will be no poverty. This will give people hope. Poverty drains the power away from communities and the individuals that live in them. By providing a financial platform, we will release the energy and imagination of people in their communities to find new ways to grow economically. This will be based on local strengths, assets and the identity of a community. Local economies will be more diverse and resilient. They will benefit from the unique skills of community members who will be freed up from mundane and repetitive tasks to contribute in ways that are more authentic and true to themselves. Supporting this economic resilience, and in line with sustainable development, communities will strike a balance between localisation and globalisation. Where products can be sourced locally to support local businesses they will. Where products are required from outside the local area they will be sourced using advanced technology and delivered using clean distribution.

Greater devolution of powers and budgets with the support of skills, expertise, and knowledge from regional and national levels will enable local management of community assets, neighbourhood plans, and action to change for the better. A new range of community-based roles are exactly the sort of thing that might provide for some jobs lost through the acceleration of AI and other technology. These jobs would aim to give people a voice, provide specific expertise in bringing them together, and focus on the betterment of local services and projects to improve community wellbeing.

With more power and autonomy, communities of the future can thrive but they will require the support, skills, and investment from regional and national governance.

WELLBEING-FOCUSED GOVERNANCE AND NATIONS

Governance story

Old/current story	New story
Prioritising economy	Prioritising wellbeing
Ideological | Traditional | Stuck in the past Linear thinking	Pragmatic | Modern | Progressive Systems thinking
Emotionally charged Opposition and competition	Wisdom Consensus and collaboration
Opaque and self serving	Transparent and virtuous
Not representative or connected Distrusted and disempowering	Representative and connected Trusted and Empowering
Centralised power Playing to the popular vote - hesitant Nationalism	Distributed power Courageous and selectively interventionist Internationalism
Environmental responsibility	Environmental renewal
Unfair	Fair

As we explored earlier, governance comprises all of the processes of government, a state, market or network over society including systems, leadership, law, technology and economy. So from an organisational perspective it would also include systems, policies and procedures, technology, leadership, and management.

We've also discussed general principles and actions that can be taken to improve wellbeing. Better thinking, improved emotional intelligence, improved physical health, spiritual fulfilment, social connection, cultural harmony, environmental sustainability and economic prosperity. Good governance in the future will focus on delivering these things to meet the needs of all people. It will focus on wellbeing as a priority above profit or economic development.

To do this will require a change in thinking. In future, we will focus on improving the lives of people and then flexibly choosing the best path to get there rather than dogmatically sticking to 'entrenched' ideologies. Sometimes this will require a more collective response, sometimes more individual. Sometimes things might be better delivered by the private sector, other times the public sector. Sometimes we should be told, other times we should be involved.

This change will also require us to think increasingly systemically. This is where the CANBE Model can be very helpful. Whilst I don't claim it has all the answers, what it does do is encourage leaders to think more across all of the domains and to join up the dots. Climate change is not just a CO_2 issue. It is linked with how we think and feel about the environment, consumerism and materialism, population growth, our cultures, economies and many factors that need consideration.

On too many occasions across the world we see leaders in conflict and political systems that create opposition and competition leading to bad outcomes for the people. Governance and leadership of the future will be more collaborative. Our leaders will win back the respect of people for their considered wisdom. Their decisions will be based on the shared virtues and values of humanity across the world.

Digital technology will enable more knowledgeable, participative, and creative politics where people can get involved in co-creating solutions and feel more empowered. This will be enhanced by a more flexible division of responsibility based on the principle of subsidiarity that we discussed earlier in the Cultural Wellbeing chapter.

As part of this, we will move towards the UN taking a more

powerful role in the governance of global issues. It will increasingly play a role in aligning the interests of people, organisations, and nations with the interests of the global society. We can begin to see this with the traction gained in respect to the Sustainable Development Goals, but this power will be extended further into responses to climate change, disaster relief, regulation of international trade, human rights and responsibilities, migration, prevention of pandemics, global peacekeeping and counter-terrorism. Global issues require a global response. This will be aided by nation states achieving a better balance between the governance within their borders and the requirements of an interdependent world.

The highest profile example of this at present is obviously climate change. As we move to a focus on wellbeing, national governments will come to their senses and work to achieve universal compliance with the targets set.

Nation states, regions and communities will increasingly realise that they have an important role to play in supporting the wellbeing of people. Social, cultural, environmental and economic factors, which are out of the control of any one individual, can have a massive impact on our wellbeing. Where required nation states will become more adept at selectively and courageously intervening. One such example will be in the area of universal social security. This will likely be accelerated by the COVID-19 pandemic resulting in large scale redundancies, lower growth, or even a depression, and the increased use of automation and AI. Nation states will intervene to provide more welfare where required which will include a form of basic income.

Another key area where national governments will do better is in the management of externalities and public goods. This will be linked to developments in the sharing economy, more efficient use of limited resources, and the growth of thrift. International efforts will resist any splitting of the internet for ideological purposes. Knowledge will be seen as a common good and shared accordingly across the world for the benefit of all.

Governments will be stronger with regulation and guidance to quickly remove single use plastics, reduce packaging, and move more quickly from fossil fuel based energy to renewables. The food and beverage industry will be challenged to improve diets across the world. A focus away from materialism and consumerism will see us review every product and service offering against a set of wellbeing criteria to establish whether it is net positive for human wellbeing. If these products or services are found wanting there will be stronger checks, balances and penalties.

As we realise that the opportunities for growth lie in sustainable business, investment will shift increasingly quickly towards solving these challenges and environmental renewal. Ultimately governance will become more fair with the aim of delivering a thriving world for all.

CONCLUSION

We're approaching a "critical point" in regard to the wellbeing of both our species and the planet as a whole, and we need to change quickly. But there is hope. We *can* change. It is not yet too late to turn things around.

The biggest challenge we face is not re-landing on the Moon or travelling to Mars, attractive and glamorous as these concepts are. The biggest challenge we face is changing ourselves.

But how to do it? The UN Sustainable Development Goals can help us survive perhaps, but they are insufficient to deliver *thriving* in our future world. And we all want to thrive, not merely survive.

To thrive we need to improve the way we THINK, FEEL and ACT as well as our social, cultural, environmental and economic systems. To deliver this will require consistent, long term, synchronised change by individuals, communities, organisations and governments. No one element can be expected to change successfully on it's own. And the best way to do that is to focus on wellbeing.

Wellbeing is malleable in the hands of those that work towards it and provides people of differing nations, religions, cultures, political beliefs and personalities with a unifying vision of a 'thriving world for all'.

The CANBE Wellbeing Model provides us with a common will, language, and understanding of the steps that can take us towards this vision with strategies to shift from surviving to thriving across all eight domains of wellbeing: *mental, emotional, physical, spiritual, social, cultural, environmental* and *economic.*

It is, however, *only one solution* and I invite you to help me build on it. This is my call to wellbeing.

A CALL TO WELLBEING

Here's what I'd like to see. I'd like to see the world change to one where we can all thrive. But in doing so I must reflect on the advice of Gandhi and Rumi:

> "Be the change you wish to see in the world."
>
> GANDHI

> "Yesterday I was clever, so I wanted to change the world. Today I am wise, so I am changing myself."
>
> RUMI

These pieces of advice are sage and I am doing my best to change in many areas of my life. This, I find, is an ongoing process and harder in some areas than others. But I also believe that in order to change we need help. After all we're all connected and if you change, you change the people around you, even if only a little.

As we've seen through the book there are also external social, cultural, environmental and economic factors that must change in order to free up individuals like you and I.

The good news is that this change is already happening. The door is open and many people have already stepped across the threshold into the Age of Wellbeing. Passionate individuals across the world are speaking up and taking action. As we've read throughout the book there are also many organisations, communities, towns, cities and even nations embracing the vision of a world with greater wellbeing.

The time to get involved is now.

INDIVIDUALS

Please use this book to be the change wherever you can. Get involved with one or more of the activities outlined below. Help those around you. Get coaching to help you get to where you want to be.

PHILANTHROPISTS

Help by providing leadership, money and expertise to support the ideas and initiatives outlined in this section.

COACHING ORGANISATIONS

I'd like to speak with large international coaching organisations about adopting the wellbeing approach so that we can train thousands of coaches to help other individuals, leaders, organisations communities and groups to improve wellbeing.

WELLBEING ORGANISATIONS

I am aware of many fantastic wellbeing organisations across the world who are already operating successfully. We should explore coming together to help leverage strengths and energise our influence.

BUSINESS LEADERS

Become a wellbeing focused business. Use the coaches outlined above to help you. B Corp, and Blueprint for Better Business are two organisations operating in this area and, of course, please feel free to get in touch with me!

COMMUNITY LEADERS

Focus your communities on wellbeing. Use the coaches outlined above to help you. Engage with organisations like Network of Wellbeing, Thriving Places Index or the equivalents in your own countries.

EDUCATIONAL LEADERS

Challenge your governments to focus on wellbeing education. Develop wellbeing trials in your schools. Introduce wellbeing philosophy into the school curriculum. Be wellbeing teachers. Use the coaches and experts in your communities. Engage with businesses.

COMMUNICATION LEADERS

Embrace and promote the wellbeing agenda. Communicate responsibly.

POLITICAL LEADERS

Regardless of your political persuasion, remember your responsibilities to represent and support the wellbeing of all people. Engage with the Wellbeing Economy Governments partnership (WEGo) to share expertise and policy practices.

UNITED NATIONS LEADERS

Build on the SDGs to embrace an approach that takes us towards thriving by focusing on wellbeing. Remember people would rather thrive than focus on sustainable development. A world where we can all thrive is a much stronger message.

This is my call to build a world with greater wellbeing. I hope you will join me, and the many others, on our journey to a world where we can all thrive.

ABOUT THE AUTHOR

David created the CANBE Wellbeing Model based on over eight years of research, a life-long passion for personal improvement and a vision for a world where we can all thrive. He is the founder of Improveon, a wellbeing coaching, consulting and speaking organisation working with individuals, teams and leaders.

He has broad experience of leadership and strategy having experienced positions in FTSE 100 companies, sport and the community. Over the last 30 years has read widely around leadership, neuroscience and wellbeing including many of the best sellers.

Online courses including The Science of Happiness (Berkeley University), Social Wellbeing (The University of Edinburgh), The Science of Happiness (Yale) and Mindfulness for Wellbeing (Monash University) have helped to build on his knowledge.

His love of challenges and keeping fit have seen him conquer three mountains (small'ish'), two marathons (long'ish'), a ride around Dorset (hard'ish'), a 1 mile swim (wet'ish') and a sky-dive from 13,000 ft (scary'ish').

On a personal level he has been married for twenty three years, has two adult sons and continues to reside in Dorset.

For further information visit:

www.improveon.co.uk

AFTERWORD

Thanks for reading. If you enjoyed this book, please consider leaving an honest review on your favourite digital storefront. Hopefully, if enough people are made aware, and get excited, about wellbeing, we can make a positive vision for the future come true!

NOTES

MAKING THE MOST OUT OF THIS BOOK

1. Duhigg, Charles. *The Power of Habit: Why We Do What We Do, and How to Change.* s.l. : Random House, 2013.

1. COURSE CORRECTION

1. Goleman, Daniel. Daniel Goleman. *Daniel Goleman Emotional Intelligence.* [Online] http://www.danielgoleman.info/topics/emotional-intelligence/.
2. Dan Chisholm PhD, Kim Sweeny PhD, Prof Peter Sheehan PhD, Prof Bruce Rasmussen PhD, Prof Filip Smit PhD, Prof Pim Cuijpers PhD, Shekhar Saxena MD. *Scaling-up treatment of depression and anxiety: a global return on investment analysis.* s.l. : The Lancet, Pyschiatry, April 12, 2016. Vols. VOLUME 3, ISSUE 5, P415-424, MAY 01, 2016.
3. United Nations. United Nations. *United Nations Sustainability.* [Online] 2016. https://sustainabledevelopment.un.org/.
4. *The benefits of frequent positive affect: Does happiness lead to success?* Lyubomirsky, S., King, L., & Diener, E. No. 6, 803– 855, s.l. : American Psychological Association, 2005, Psychological Bulletin, Vols. 131, pp. 131, 803-855.
5. "*Earth Overshoot Day – #MoveTheDate of Overshoot!.*" https://www.overshootday.org/. Accessed 30 Apr. 2019.
6. "Universal Declaration of Human Rights | United Nations." https://www.un.org/en/universal-declaration-human-rights/. Accessed 30 Apr. 2019.
7. Office for National Statistics. The National Archives. *ONS - National Wellbeing, Measuring What Matters.* [Online] ; www.ons.gov.uk/ons/guide-method/user-guidance/well-being/index.html
8. "Global Warming of 1.5 oC — - IPCC." https://www.ipcc.ch/sr15/. Accessed 30 Apr. 2019.
9. The Intergovernmental Science-Policy Platform on Biodiver! sity and Ecosystem Services (IPBES) Report 'Nature's Dangerous Decline Unprecedented; Species Extinction Rates Accelerating' May 2019; https://www.un.org/sustainabledevelopment/blog/2019/05/nature-decline-unprecedented-report/
10. The Intergovernmental Science-Policy Platform on Biodiver! sity and Ecosystem Services (IPBES) Report 'Nature's Dangerous Decline Unprecedented; Species Extinction Rates Accelerating' May 2019; https://www.un.org/sustainabledevelopment/blog/2019/05/nature-decline-unprecedented-report/

2. SUFFER, SURVIVE, OR THRIVE?

1. *The benefits of frequent positive affect: Does happiness lead to success?* Lyubomirsky, S., King, L., & Diener, E. No. 6, 803– 855, s.l. : American Psychological Association, 2005, Psychological Bulletin, Vols. 131,, pp. 131, 803-855.
2. United Nations. United Nations. *United Nations Sustainability.* [Online] 2016. https://sustainabledevelopment.un.org/.
3. OFFIce for National Statistics. The National Archives. *ONS - National Wellbeing, Measuring What Matters.* [Online] http:// webarchive.nationalarchives.gov.uk/20160105160709/http:/www.ons.gov.uk/ons/guide-method/user-guidance/well-being/index.html.
4. OECD. OECD Statistics. *OECD Guidelines on measuring subjective wellbeing.* [Online] http://www.oecd.org/statistics/oecd-guidelines-on-measuring-subjective-well-being-9789264191655-en.htm

3. THE AGE OF WELLBEING

1. https://en.wikipedia.org/wiki/Six-factor_Model_of_Psychological_Well-being

BUILDING RESILIENCE

1. Chartered Institute for Professional Development. *ANNUAL SURVEY REPORT: Absence Management.* s.l. : CIPD in partnership with Simply Health, 2016.

5. IMPROVING MENTAL WELLBEING

1. Business in the Community. *Mental Health at Work Report 2016. National Employee Mental Wellbeing.* s.l. : Business in the Community, 2016.
2. BUPA. Health information. *bupa.co.uk.* [Online] BUPA. http://www.bupa.co.uk/health-information/directory/s/stress- workplace.
3. Crum, Salovey and Achor; "Rethinking Stress: The Role of Mind-sets in Determining the Stress Response".

THINKING

1. Megan Reitz, Michael Chaskalson. How to Bring Mindful! ness to Your Company's Leadership. *Harvard Business Review.* 01 DECEMBER 2016.
2. Kahneman, Daniel. *Thinking, Fast and Slow.* s.l. : Penguin, 2012.
3. Blalock, Kadiyali, & Simon; "The Impact of 9/11 on Road Fatalities: The Other Lives Lost to Terrorism"

4. Carver, C. S., & Scheier, M. F. (2005) Optimism. In Snyder, C. R., & Lopez, S. J. Handbook of Positive psychology (pp. 632-645) New York. Oxford University press; Scheier, M. F., Weintraub, J. K., & Carver, C. S. (1986). Coping with stress. Divergent strategies of optimists and pessimists. Journal of personality and social psychology, 51, 1257-1264.
5. Anticipation and the Valuation of Delayed Consumption Author(s): George Loewenstein Source: The Economic Journal, Vol. 97, No. 387 (Sep., 1987), pp. 666-684 Published by: Blackwell Publishing for the Royal Economic Society Stable URL: http://www.jstor.org/stable/2232929
6. Duhigg, Charles. *The Power of Habit: Why We Do What We Do, and How to Change.* s.l. : Random House, 2013

FOCUS

1. Parkinson, Cyril Northcote. *Parkinson's Law.* London : The Economist, 1955.
2. Koch, Richard. *The 80/20 Principle - The Secret of Achieving More with Less.* London : Nicholas Brealey Publishing, 1997. ISBN 1-85788-167-2.
3. Hardy, Ian. Losing focus: Why tech is getting in the way of work. *BBC News.* [Online] BBC, 8 May 2015. http://www.bbc.co.uk/news/business-32628753
4. Aarstol, Stephan. What Happened When I Moved My Company To A 5-Hour Workday. *Huffington Post.* [Online] 10 April (Updated in October) 2016. [Cited: 11 November 2016.] http:// www.huffingtonpost.com/entry/what-happened-when-i-moved-my-company-to-a-5-hour-work-day_us_57f4086fe4b0ab1116a54ab1?platform=hootsuite.
5. The Guardian. Small business Showcase. *Guardian.* [Online] 2015. https://www.theguardian.com/small-business-network/2015/apr/02/remote-working-talent-edinburgh-agency#img-1.
6. Hardy, Ian. Losing focus: Why tech is getting in the way of work. *BBC News.* [Online] BBC, 8 May 2015. http://www.bbc.co.uk/news/business-32628753.

REGARD

1. Covey, Dr Stephen R. *The 7 Habits of Highly Effective People: Powerful Lessons in Personal Change.* s.l. : Simon & Schuster UK Ltd., 2005.

FLEXIBILITY

1. Dweck, Carol. *Mindset: The New Psychology of Success.* New York : Ballantine Books, 2007.

IMAGINATION

1. Silvia, P. J., Beaty, R. E., Nusbaum, E. C., Eddington, K. M., Levin-Aspenson, H., & Kwapil, T. R. (2014). Everyday creativity in daily life: An experience-sampling study of "little c" creativity. *Psychology of Aesthetics, Creativity, and the Arts, 8*(2), 183-188. http://dx.doi.org/10.1037/a0035722
2. *Decisions for Others Are More Creative Than Decisions for the Self.* Evan Polman, Kyle J. Emich. no. 4 , 11 February 2011, Personality and Social Psychology Bulletin April 2011 , Vol. vol. 37, pp. 492-501.
3. Darya L. Zabelina & Michael D. Robinson (2010) Don't Be So Hard on Yourself: Self-Compassion Facilitates Creative Originality Among Self-Judgmental Individuals, Creativity Research Journal, 22:3, 288-293, DOI: 10.1080/10400419.2010.503538
4. Sugiura, Y. & Sugiura, T. J Happiness Stud (2019).Relation Between Daydreaming and Well-Being: Moderating Effects of Otaku Contents and Mindfulness

6. IMPROVING EMOTIONAL WELLBEING

1. *Dynamic spread of happiness in a large social network: longitudinal analysis over 20 years.* Christakis, J.H. Fowler and N.A. s.l. : British Medical Journal, December 2008.

CONTROL

1. Goleman, Daniel. Daniel Goleman. *Daniel Goleman Emotional Intelligence.* [Online] http://www.danielgoleman.info/topics/emotional-intelligence/.

BEHAVIOUR

1. Achor, Shawn. *The Happiness Advantage: The Seven Principles of Positive Psychology that Fuel Success and Performance at Work.* s.l. : Crown Publishing Group, 2010.
2. Duhigg, Charles. *The Power of Habit: Why We Do What We Do, and How to Change.* s.l. : Random House, 2013.
3. *How are habits formed: Modelling habit formation in the real world.* Lally, P., van Jaarsveld, C. H. M., Potts, H. W. W. and Wardle, J. 6, pages 998–1009, s.l. : Eur. J. Soc. Psychol, 2010, European Journal of Social Psychology, Vol. 40.
4. *Ibid.*
5. Eisenberg, Richard. Personal Finance. *Forbes.* [Online] 7 June 2016. http://www.forbes.com/sites/nextavenue/2016/06/07/swedens-intriguing-6-hour-workday-experiment/#6c4a1f1a16 .

6. Aarstol, Stephan. What Happened When I Moved My Company To A 5-Hour Workday. *Huffington Post.* [Online] 10 April (Updated in October) 2016. [Cited: 11 November 2016.] http://www.huffingtonpost.com/entry/what-happened-when-i-moved-my-company-to-a-5-hour-work-day_us_57f4086fe4b0ab1116a54ab1?platform=hootsuite.
7. The Guardian. Small business Showcase. *Guardian.* [Online] 2015. https://www.theguardian.com/small-business-network/2015/apr/02/remote-working-talent-edinburgh-agency#img-1.

INTERACTION

1. Covey, Dr Stephen R. *The 7 Habits of Highly Effective People: Powerful Lessons in Personal Change.* s.l. : Simon & Schuster UK Ltd., 2005.
2. *The Ideal Praise-to-Criticism Ratio.* Folkman, Jack Zenger and Joseph. s.l. : Harvard Business review, March 2013.
3. *Influence: The Psychology of Persuasion.* Cialdini, Robert. s.l. : Harper Collins.
4. Kahneman, Daniel. *Thinking, Fast and Slow.* s.l. : Penguin, 2012.
5. Keltner, D. *The power paradox: how we gain and lose influence.* s.l. : Penguin, 2016.
6. Cuddy, Amy; *Your body language shapes who you are.* TEDGlobal, 2012.
7. Whitmore, Sir John. *Coaching for Performance* . Second. s.l. : Nicholas Brealey Publishing, 1996. ISBN 1-85788-170-2.
8. Glaser, Judith E. *Conversation Intelligence How Great Leaders Build Trust & Get Extraordinary Results,* . s.l. : Bibliomotion, 2013. ISBN-10: 1937134679.

HEALTH

1. Silverberg, David. BBC Business. *bbc.co.uk.* [Online] BBC, 13 June 2016. http://www.bbc.co.uk/news/business-36641119.
2. British Heart Foundation. British Heart Foundation Health at Work. *Eating well: ideas and inspiration.* [Online] British Heart Foundation, 2016.

IDENTITY

1. Bartels, M. Genetics of Wellbeing and Its Components Satisfaction with Life, Happiness, and Quality of Life: A Review and Meta-analysis of Heritability Studies. Behav Genet 45, 137–156 (2015). https://doi.org/10.1007/s10519-015-9713-y
2. Dolcos, S., Moore, M., & Katsumi, Y. (2018). Neuroscience and well-being. In E. Diener, S. Oishi, & L. Tay (Eds.), Handbook of well-being. Salt Lake City, UT: DEF Publishers. DOI: nobascholar.com
3. Gallup. *GLOBAL GREAT JOBS REPORT.* s.l. : Gallup, 2016 .

4. Niemiec, R. M. *VIA character strengths: Research and practice (The first 10 years).* . New York : Springer, 2013. pp. In H. H. Knoop & A. Delle Fave (Eds.), Well-being and cultures: Perspectives on positive psychology (pp. 11-30).
5. Business in the Community. *Mental Health at Work Report 2016. National Employee Mental Wellbeing.* s.l. : Business in the Community, 2016.
6. Megan Reitz, Michael Chaskalson. How to Bring Mindfulness to Your Company's Leadership. *Harvard Business Review.* 01 DECEMBER 2016.

MOTIVATION

1. Sinek, Simon. *How great leaders inspire action.* [Video] Washington : TED - Ideas worth spreading, Sep 2009.
2. Council, C.L. *Driving Performance and Retention Through Employee Engagement.* s.l. : Corporate Executive Board, 2004.
3. Deci, Edward L.; Ryan, Richard M. (1985). *Intrinsic Motivation and Self-Determination in Human Behavior.* Springer US. doi:10.1007/978-1-4899-2271-7. ISBN 978-1-4899-2273-1.
4. *High income improves evaluation of life but not emotional well-being.* Deaton, Daniel Kahneman and Angus. no. 38, s.l. : PNAS, 2010, Proceedings of the National Academy of Sciences USA, Vol. vol. 107 .
5. $75,000 taken from research conducted in 2010. Conversions as at 8th August 2016. $1 = £0.77

STORIES

1. Why inspiring stories make us react. *The DANA Foundation.* [Online] http://www.dana.org/Cerebrum/2015/Why_Inspiring_Stories_Make_Us_React__The_Neuroscience_of_Narrative/.

PURPOSE

1. Pink, D. *Drive: The Surprising Truth About What Motivates Us.* 2009.
2. Collins, Jim. *Good to Great.* 1st. s.l. : Random House Business, 2001. ISBN-10: 0712676090.

FRIENDSHIP

1. *Social Baseline Theory: The Social Regulation of Risk and Effort.* Coan, J. A., & Sbarra, D. A. (2015). Social Baseline Theory: The Social Regulation of Risk and Effort. Current Opinion in Psychology, 1, 87–91. February 2015, Pages 87–91, s.l. : Current Opinion in Psychology, 2015 , Vol. 1.

2. CIPD. *Getting under the skin of conflict: Tracing the experiences of employees.* s.l. : CIPD, April 2015.
3. Ury, Roger Fisher and William L. *Getting to Yes.* s.l. : Penguin, 1981.

SUPPORT

1. Achor, Shawn. *The Happiness Advantage: The Seven Principles of Positive Psychology that Fuel Success and Performance at Work.* s.l. : Crown Publishing Group, 2010.
2. Collins, Jim. *Good to Great.* 1st. s.l. : Random House Business, 2001. ISBN-10: 0712676090.
3. *Is it ok to care? How compassion falters and is courageously accomplished in the midst of uncertainty.* Jason Kanov, Edward H Powley, Neil D Walshe. s.l. : Sage Publications, 2016, Human Relations, pp. 1-27.

EMPOWERMENT

1. *Job strain, job demands, decision latitude, and risk of coronary heart disease within the Whitehall II study.* Kuper H1, Marmot M. 57(2):147-53, s.l. : Journal of Epidemiol & Community Health., 2003 , Vol. Feb.

10. IMPROVING CULTURAL WELLBEING

1. https://ec.europa.eu/jrc/sites/jrcsh/files/20150611ImpactCultureIndividual-Wellbeing.pdf
2. 'Enculturation', not 'acculturation': Conceptualising and assessing identity processes in migrant communities. Peter Weinreich, School of Psychology, University of Ulster, UK. International Journal of Intercultural Relations 33 (2009) 124–139 doi:10.1016/j.ijintrel.2008.12.006
3. Acculturation and Enculturation: Ethnic Identity Socialisation Processes. Julie Hakim-Larson, Rosanne Menna University of Windsor Psychology Publications Department of Psychology
4. Social Indicators Research, November 2010, Volume 99, Issue 2, pp 315–332| Culture and Wellbeing: The Case of Indigenous Australians Alfred Michael Dockery
5. Diener, E., & Diener, M. (1995). Cross-cultural correlates of life satisfaction and self-esteem. Journal of Personality and Social Psychology, 68, 653-663.

WAY OF LIFE

1. Cultural Influences on Mental Health & Wellbeing in Scotland Phil Hanlon & Sandra Carlisle Public Health & Health Policy Section University of Glasgow

2. Medawar, E., Huhn, S., Villringer, A. et al. The effects of plant-based diets on the body and the brain: a systematic review. Transl Psychiatry 9, 226 (2019) doi:10.1038/s41398-019-0552-0

GOVERNANCE

1. Beauregard, T. A. (2011) Direct and indirect links between organizational work-home culture and employee well-being. British journal of management, 22 (2). pp. 218-237. ISSN 1045-3172 DOI:10.1111/j.1467-8551.2010.00723.x

DIVERSITY

1. McKinsey & Company Insights. *McKinsey.com.* [Online] Jan 2015. http://www.mckinsey.com/business-functions/organization/our-insights/why-diversity-matters.

11. IMPROVING ENVIRONMENTAL WELLBEING

1. "The Global Liveability Index 2019: The free overview report." https://www.eiu.com/public/topical_report.aspx?campaignid=liveability2019. Accessed 29 Jan. 2020.

AFFINITY

1. Annerstedt van den Bosch and Depledge BMC Public Health (2015) Healthy People With Nature in Mind 15:1232 DOI 10.1186/s12889-015-2574-8
2. "Thriving Places Index"; https://thrivingplacesindex.org; Accessed 29 Jan. 2020.
3. "OECD Better Life Index." oecdbetterlifeindex.org/. Accessed 29 Jan. 2020.
4. Bhutan, Kingdom of. Gross National Happiness. [Online] http://www.grossnationalhappiness.com/home/.
5. "Well-being - Office for National Statistics." Accessed 29 Jan. 2020.
6. "The Wellbeing Budget 2019 - Treasury NZ." 30 May. 2019, https://treasury.govt.nz/sites/default/%les/2019-05/b19-wellbeing-budget.pdf. Accessed 29 Jan. 2020.
7. "Home | Canadian Index of Wellbeing | University of Waterloo." https://uwaterloo.ca/canadian-index-wellbeing/. Accessed 29 Jan. 2020.

CULTIVATION

1. World Health Organisation http://www.who.int/mediacentre/news/releases/2014/air-pollution/en/. Published 2014

2. https://airqualitynews.com/2020/06/04/lung-conditions-improve-for-millions-during-lockdown/
3. California Energy Commission. Windows and Offices: A Study of Work Performance and the Indoor Environment. 2003. doi:10.1175/1520-0450(1998)037<0414:TDFBIM>2.0.CO;2.
4. Lee IM, Shiroma EJ, Lobelo F, et al. Eect of physical inactivity on major non-communicable diseases worldwide: An analysis of burden of disease and life expectancy. Lancet. 2012;380(9838):219-229. doi:10.1016/S0140-6736(12)61031-9.
5. Seppanen O, Fisk WJ, Faulkner D. Control of Temperature for Health and Productivity in Offices. 2004. https://escholarship.org/content/qt39s1m92c/qt39s1m92c.pdf
6. "Toxicity of building materials - Smart Cities Information System." Link. Accessed 29 Jan. 202

COHESION

1. https://reports.weforum.org/global-risks-report-2020/survey-results/global-risks-of-highest-concern-for-doing-business-2020/
2. Laurence, J. (2017). Wider-community Segregation and the Effect of Neighbourhood Ethnic Diversity on Social Capital: An Investigation into Intra-Neighbourhood Trust in Great Britain and London. Sociology, 51(5), 1011–1033. https://doi.org/10.1177/0038038516641867
3. https://www.rics.org/uk/wbef/megatrends/urbanisation/fostering-social-cohesion-in-the-built-environment/#_ftn1

ADAPTATION

1. Household actions can provide a behavioral wedge to rapidly reduce US carbon emissions; Thomas Dietz, Gerald T. Gardner, Jonathan Gilligan, Paul C. Stern, Michael P. Vandenbergh; Proceedings of the National Academy of Sciences Nov 2009, 106 (44) 18452-18456; DOI: 10.1073/pnas.0908738106
2. "The Emissions Implications of Modern Retailing: Omnichannel vs. Stores and Online Pure-Plays"; https://cdn.corporate.walmart.com/00/5a/3c20743a4f0db2d00c452aebea95/omni-channel-emissions-modeling-whitepaperfinal04182017.pdf

RENEWAL

1. MAO Gen Xiang, LAN Xiao Guang, CAO Yong Bao, CHEN Zhuo Mei, HE Zhi Hua, LV Yuan Dong, WANG Ya Zhen, HU Xi Lian, WANG Guo Fu, YAN Jing. Eects of Short-Term Forest Bathing on Human Health in a Broad-Leaved Evergreen Forest in Zhejiang Province, China[J]. Biomedical and Environ! mental Sciences, 2012, 25(3): 317-324. doi: 10.3967/0895- 3988.2012.03.010

2. https://eatforum.org/eat-lancet-commission/
3. Wanger, T.C., DeClerck, F., Garibaldi, L.A. et al. Inte! grating agroecological production in a robust post-2020 Global Biodiversity Framework. Nat Ecol Evol (2020). https://doi.org/10.1038/s41559-020-1262-y
4. http://www.fao.org/3/CA2227EN/ca2227en.pdf
5. https://www.pmi.com/media-center/news/transforming-our-business-the-sustainable-way
6. https://www.hopkinsmedicine.org/health/wellness-and-prevention/5-truths-you-need-to-know-about-vaping
7. Roberts, Peter, K. C. Shyam, and C. Rastogi 2006. Rural Access Index: A Key Development Indicator. Transport Papers TP- 10. Washington, DC: World Bank.
8. https://sum4all.org/
9. https://www.un.org/sustainabledevelopment/blog/2017/06/sustainable-development-goal-9-investing-in-ict-access-and-quality-education-to-promote-lasting-peace/
10. https://www.un.org/en/pdfs/DigitalCooperation-report-for%20web.pdf
11. https://kenoteq.com/
12. https://www.wildlifetrusts.org/sites/default/files/2018-05/homes_for_people_and_wildlife_lr_-_spreads.pdf
13. https://www.seasteading.org/startup-seasteading-business/
14. https://www.forbes.com/sites/scottsnowden/2020/07/29/solar-glass-windows/#24862a1b3382
15. https://ec.europa.eu/energy/sites/ener/files/hydrogen_strategy.pdf
16. https://www.forbes.com/sites/davidrvetter/2020/07/23/european-renewables-just-crushed-fossil-fuels-heres-how-it-happened/#2c09706c15df
17. https://ec.europa.eu/energy/sites/ener/files/hydrogen_strategy.pdf

12. IMPROVING ECONOMIC WELLBEING

1. Collins, Jim. *Good to Great.* 1st. s.l. : Random House Business, 2001. ISBN-10: 0712676090.

IMPACT

1. United Nations. UN Human Development Index. *United Nations Development Programme.* [Online] http://hdr.undp.org/en/humandev.
2. Legatum Prosperity Index. *Legatum Institute.* [Online] http://www.li.com/programmes/prosperity-index.
3. "Gross National Happiness"; http://www.grossnationalhappiness.com; Accessed 29 Jan. 2020.
4. Linton M, Dieppe P, Medina-Lara A Review of 99 self- report measures for assessing well-being in adults: exploring dimensions of well-being and developments over timeBMJ Open 2016;6:e010641. doi: 10.1136/bmjopen-2015-010641
5. See "Commentary" at the back of the book.

6. Maggino F. Assessing the subjective wellbeing of nations. In: Glatzer W, Cam%eld L, Møller V, Rojas M, eds. Global handbook of quality of life. Springer, 2015:803–22.
7. Kaplan Financial Knowledge Bank. *Kaplan.* [Online] Kaplan Publishing. http://k&nowledgebank.kaplan.co.uk/KFKB/Wiki%20-Pages/The%20Balanced%20Scorecard.aspx?mode=none.

FAIRNESS

1. Prilleltensky, Isaac; University of Miami; "Wellness as Fairness"; 2011.
2. https://happiness-report.s3.amazonaws.com/2020/WHR20.pdf
3. https://worldjusticeproject.org/our-work/wjp-rule-law-index/wjp-open-government-index/global-scores-rankings
4. https://www.bertelsmann-stiftung.de/en/publications/publication/did/social-justice-in-the-eu-and-oecd
5. https://www.weforum.org/agenda/2019/06/an-economist-explains-how-to-create-a-fairer-society/
6. Isaac Prilleltensky; University of Miami; "Wellness as Fairness"; 2011.
7. Oxfam; "Time to Care"; Jan 2020; https://www.oxfam.org/en/research/time-care
8. Barry Swartz; TED; https://www.ted.com/talks/barry_schwartz_what_role_does_luck_play_in_your_life?language=en#t-95867.
9. https://en.wikipedia.org/wiki/Thomas_Piketty
10. https://www.fairtrade.net/
11. https://www.gov.scot/publications/2019-review-fair-trade-scotland/
12. https://www.cipd.co.uk/about/media/press/high-pay-day-2020
13. https://www.livingwage.org.uk/
14. https://employeeownership.co.uk/resources/facts-and-figures

INTEGRITY

1. O'Neill, D.W., Fanning, A.L., Lamb, W.F., and Steinberger, J.K. (2018). A good life for all within planetary boundaries. Nature Sustainability 1, 88-95. doi: 10.1038/s41893-018-0021-4.
2. OECD (2019) Global Material Resources Outlook to 2060: Economic Driver and Environmental Consequences, OECD Publishing, Paris https://doi.org/10.1787/9789263407452-en; https://read.oecd-ilibrary.org/environment/global-material-resources-outlook-to-2060_9789264307452-en#page4
3. https://eur-lex.europa.eu/legal-content/EN/TXT/PDF/?uri=CELEX:52020DC0474&from=EN
4. https://www.footprintnetwork.org/our-work/ecological-footprint/#:~:text=Today%20humanity%20uses%20the%20equivalent,we%20use%20in%20a%20year.
5. https://www.overshootday.org/
6. Campaign For Nature; https://www.campaignfornature.org/protecting-30-of-the-planet-for-nature-economic-analysis

7. https://reports.weforum.org/global-risks-report-2020/survey-results/global-risks-of-highest-concern-for-doing-business-2020/

FREEDOM

1. In rallying the American people to support war efforts, President Roosevelt imagined a better post war period based on four essential freedoms. These were freedom of speech, freedom of worship, freedom from want, and freedom from fear. After the war, these four freedoms played a large part in the development of the Charter of the United Nations.
2. https://happiness-report.s3.amazonaws.com/2020/WHR20.pdf – note page 162: are there trade-offs between the SDGs and human well-being?
3. http://www.oecd.org/economic-outlook/june-2020/

WELLBEING-FOCUSED EDUCATION

1. https://www.youthsporttrust.org/news/parents-say-wellbeing-school-more-important-academic-results

WELLBEING-FOCUSED COMMUNITIES

1. https://www.centreforthrivingplaces.org/

COMMENTARY

The domains used in Linton M, Dieppe P, Medina-Lara A Review of 99 self-report measures for assessing well-being in adults: exploring dimensions of well-being and developments over time BMJ Open 2016; 6:e010641. doi: 10.1136/bmjopen-2015-010641 are as follows:

- mental well-being
- social wellbeing
- physical well-being
- spiritual well-being
- activities and functioning
- personal circumstances

In respect to the CANBE Model I believe splitting out emotional and mental wellbeing is a positive step to differentiate thinking and feeling. Whilst I appreciate the researchers have only used the 'Activities and functioning' and 'Personal circumstances' themes to group measures these descriptions are too vague and broad and would likely lead to confusion if people were asked to discuss how their wellbeing related to these two concepts.

Within the personal circumstances domain they include the following measures: community, community wellbeing, environmental mastery, environmental quality of life, financial distress/wellbeing, financial situation, functional wellbeing, future security, home, housekeeping, interactive function, neighbourhood, personal safety, satisfaction of material needs, self-realisation, social & economics, stability and status.

Within the activities/functioning domain they includes the following measures: achievement, achievement at work, alcohol consumption, civic action, competence, control, creativity, eating, elimination, enjoyment, environmental mastery, fulfilment of needs, functional wellbeing, general health, goal congruence, independent living, interactive function, interest/hobbies, learning, leisure situation, life engagement, life purpose & satisfaction, objective factors, occupational functioning, personal fulfilment, physical activity, physical functioning, psychological wellbeing, realising life potential, recreation, role, role emotional, role physical, self care, self control, self-realisation, self satisfaction, sex life, sleep, social and economics, social function, speech, stability, usual activities, vacations and work.

The dimensions included within these two themes can also be split amongst the 8 domains of the CANBE Model. Further, I believe environmental, cultural and economic wellbeing are better understood terms with greater meaning across individuals, organisations, communities and even nations.

Printed in Great Britain
by Amazon

57610327R00281